CW00954306

Scientific Editor
Luca Molinari

Editing
Anna Albano

Layout
Paola Ranzini

First published in Italy in 2000 by
Skira editore S.p.A.
Palazzo Casati Stampa
via Torino 61
20123 Milano
Italy

© 2000 by Skira editore

All rights reserved under international
copyright conventions.
No part of this book may be reproduced
or utilized in any form or by any means,
electronic or mechanical, including
photocopying, recording, or any
information storage and retrieval system,
without permission in writing
from the publisher.

Printed and bound in Italy. First edition

ISBN 88-8118-741-8

Distributed in North America and Latin
America by Abbeville Publishing Group,
22 Cortlandt Street, New York, NY
10007, USA.
Distributed elsewhere in the world by
Thames and Hudson Ltd., 181a High
Holborn, London WC1V 7QX,
United Kingdom.

Acknowledgments

I have been fortunate to have received the support of many people without whom this book would not have been possible. I would like to begin by thanking the publisher, Skira editore. Luca Molinari has assisted me throughout the process and shown great patience. My editor, Anna Albano, sculpted the final book with attentive care and wodehousesque humor. I owe my fondest appreciation, and respect, to the guest editor and distinguished architectural historian who oversaw my project with intelligent guidance and critical support, Marco De Michelis.

I thank each and every office whose work is included in this book. Many people have provided assistance and support in innumerable ways. In particular I would like to thank:
Anna Alvarez
Joseph Barnes
Chris Bennett
Karen Cooper
Jaime Correa
Luis Van Cotthem
Robert Davis
Michael Dennis
Andres Duany
Phil Enquist
Raymond Gastil
Vince Graham
Ken Greenberg
Xavier Iglesias
Nicola Jancso
Michael Jasper
John Kaliski
Ken Kay
Robert Lane
Frank Martinez
Denis McGlade
William Morrish
Paul Mortensen
Elizabeth Plater-Zyberk
Shelly Poticha and the CNU
Warren Price
Michael Pyatok
Janet Sager
Matthew Sloan
Howard Smith
Daniel Solomon
Jeff Speck
Robert Steuteville
Matt Taecker
Dawn Thomas
John Torti
Henry Turley
Sergio Vasquez
Mike Watkins

There are two architects whose illustrations stand out for their compelling means of communicating urban space, and who are amply represented in the following pages. They are Xiaojian He and the late Charles Burnett.
I appreciate invitations to present my ideas at various institutions, seminars, and conferences. In particular I would like to thank Wallis J. Miller, Sandy Eisenstadt, and Dean David Mohney at the University of Kentucky, Sverker Sörlin of the Department of the History of Ideas and Science at Umeå, and all the participants of Studio E in Malmo, Sweden.
Particular appreciation goes to Stefanos Polyzoides and Elizabeth Moule for sharing their passion and wisdom about cities and towns, as well as for their friendship and support.
Moshe Sluhovsky and Jeffrey Sherman edited parts of the manuscript and made insightful suggestions for which I am most grateful. Gwendolyn Wright provided invaluable intellectual inspiration and guidance, as well as perceptive and challenging readings of my manuscript.
My partners in architecture and urban design, Susan Budd and William Nicholas at Nicholas/Budd/Dutton, have shown tremendous patience and support. Their talent and passion for design

is an inspiration to me.
The incomparable Vinayak "Bobby" Bharne
has assisted me throughout this project,
providing long hours, intelligent criticism,
and invaluable enthusiasm.
Thanks to Jennifer Levin for use of her
garden cottage, and my Dutton, Hollenberg,
and Morton families. To my parents, Carol
and John, I owe particular appreciation
for their unfailing love and support. My
extended siblings, Lauren, Lissa, Beth, Clark,
Danny, Glen, Eric, and Ramzi, have blessed
me with distraction and encouragement.
Finally, I extend my love and gratitude to
Patricia Morton. This project benefited
greatly from years of conversation and travel
we have shared, from her incisive readings
of my manuscript, and her patience
and compassion.
I would like to dedicate this book to John W.
Dutton, and the late Virginia Jeffers.

*Research supported by a grant
from the Graham Foundation
for Advanced Studies in the Fine Arts*

Contents

Preface

Most of us, intentionally or inadvertently, shape the built environment. Only a few have the mixed privilege of being the urban designers, developers, bankers, architects, traffic engineers, or public officials who make direct decisions about the scope and form of a project, while the rest of us will all make more oblique yet no less consequential decisions regarding the shape of the world. We vote on bond issues for a new school or transit system; we move to a new location where we can get more housing for less money; we vote, perhaps, for the candidate who promises to prompt new development, or for his/her opponent who promises to stop it. For the most part, we will make these choices with very parochial interests in mind, with at best a loose value system about "community" or "the environment." Architects, urban designers, and planners, too, are often at a loss to explain why they choose one design or another, more of this and less of that, and find themselves even more hapless at explicating the scale and character of contemporary urbanization.

They look at an American life that is generating a vast, undistinguished urban condition, one where we are all in the same matrix of highways, telephone lines, and satellite dishes, whether we call it city or suburb, town or country. We still call it sprawl, a word first coined in the 1950s, but it is really beyond that, and conceptually has been since the beginning of the industrial revolution—by the late eighteenth century, Jean-Jacques Rousseau, coming upon a factory in the Swiss hills, had declared that nature was vanquished, the city was everywhere. More than two hundred years later, looking at, say, the 130-mile wide expanse of greater Atlanta, or at the hole in the ozone layer over Antarctica, who can doubt Rousseau's prescience?

While hardly unique to the United States, our current urban form came earliest to America, and it is no surprise that American architects have been the first to respond by initiating a new urban movement, drawing on a range of early twentieth-century town and regional planning in the United States, and the European urbanism movement of the late 1970s and 1980s. For reasons of ecology, economy, and social equity, a multi-disciplinary group of urbanists finds itself dissatisfied with this urban condition, both the way it is now and the way it threatens to become. John Dutton's *New American Urbanism: Re-forming the Suburban Metropolis* addresses this situation, demonstrating that the promise of American life is alive in the theories and practices of urbanists—an emerging, in part self-defined discipline—who are working to build and rebuild the physical infrastructure of "the good life" that most of us seek, consciously or unknowingly.

Dutton makes clear that this urbanist approach is not a monolithic movement, despite the rise of "New Urbanism" and the "Congress for New Urbanism." No one group has the franchise on the goals of finding a balance between the automobile and the pedestrian, private needs and public functions, and the need for architectural expression that will have meaning and resonance for more than half a decade. "New Urbanism" is often accused of being nostalgic, and certainly in the marketing approach of much reported places such as Celebration, Florida, there is an explicit invocation of the good old days. Yet as Dutton shows in his explanation of codes, guidelines, and typology, many new developments, even those marketed as "New Urbanist," do not, in fact, demand forms driven by historic precedent. American critic Lewis Mumford would have found much to praise in these projects, matching his call for "biotechnic" balance, even as he might question their stylistic expression and financing.

Dutton's overview does show that for the most part American urbanism, unlike much new European work, resists the urge to glamorize the North American banal: after a half-century of strip malls and subdivisions, it is difficult to embrace them as expressions of a valid pattern of growth. By contrast, this volume shows infill projects in traditional cities, pedestrian-oriented patches of suburbia, ambitious new metropolitan districts, even projects that try to go beyond the "small-town" values that drive much new urban work and try to achieve a "metropolitan" dynamic, one usually found in only a handful of North American cities. For the most part, these projects are done with a researched sense of what will last over time, what will be a sustainable structure. They show a determination to give form to life, no matter how difficult the prospect or how many times the average American moves in his/her lifetime. Dutton's book paints a full picture of the housing, public spaces, and commercial developments undertaken with a long-term civic notion of "return" on investment, as opposed to the short-term demands of most development.

New American Urbanism makes clear that urban design can and should meet community needs in a way that respects the environment, urban context, and acknowledges the most successful examples of the past. This is a message that policy-makers can understand, perhaps the first fully comprehensible message from the design and planning community in fifty years. It has had a powerful and positive influence on politics and policy at the highest level, changing the Department of Housing and Urban Development's building practices, as well as the 2000 presidential campaign, and, one hopes, the next administration's policies. It would be a great mistake for the academic design leadership of America to reject this message, and its power, because of ideological differences with the particular "New Urbanist" agenda, given the much broader base of activity. Every alternative is urban, there is no escape from our current matrix, but some matrices are better than others—by laying the groundwork of urban form we can insure a more sustainable, equitable, visually and culturally rich "Suburban Metropolis."

In approaching the work in this volume, the chief recommendation is to have an open mind.

1. Recognize that the way things look is part of the way things work. You may not agree with the stylistic requirements of a particular design or planning code, but shaping physical form is part of a profound functionalism.

2. Acknowledge the possible value of popular taste. It can be learning from Las Vegas, it can be learning from Scarsdale, but the people have a right to be consulted on what they like, and their aspirations can be part of making meaningful places. Be open to different perspectives on what constitutes sentimental or retrograde urban form or architectural style.

3. Be open to the inevitable gap between rhetoric about reforming society and the realities of prototypical projects, especially regarding site selection, when most projects in the American suburban metropolis are done in locations that will not work, at least for now, without a car, nor will they achieve an urban density immediately. They may, however, through density and street pattern, lay the groundwork for a different future.

4. Recognize that most newer urban projects, like most older urban projects before them, are done for citizens with strong incomes, and that it is, ultimately, far more socially advanced to experiment with living patterns for the affluent, as opposed to an earlier planning and architecture practice of imposing experiments on the poor.

Raymond Gastil
Van Alen Institute
New York, 2000

Introduction

Over the past few decades, many American architects have reclaimed land development patterns as an important, even central, *architectural* issue. This renewed interest in "town planning" emphasizes the relationships between buildings and open spaces that form urban patterns. A range of appropriate urban patterns organized into neighborhoods, these architects argue, can best meet the physical and social needs of increasingly diverse residents, and restore a sense of community. Architecture and urbanism, in this view, become agents of social change and reform.

The projects in this book represent this attempt to restructure urban growth into cohesive designs that balance buildings, open space, infrastructure, landscape, and transportation. In place of what the designers see as the piecemeal advance of placeless, car-dominated suburban sprawl, they envision dense, mixed-use neighborhoods with walkable streets, civic amenities, defined open spaces, and, if possible, connections to transit. Regional preservation of open land is enabled by concentration of dense, compact development. Much of the architectural designs are based on local building types and attempt to respect the local ecological conditions. The work ranges from entire new towns to urban infill. Many of the architects practicing these ideas have formed a movement called the Congress for New Urbanism (CNU), which most clearly and effectively has articulated this alternative vision.

The impetus for this renewed emphasis on town planning has been a rampant suburbanization of unparalleled magnitude throughout America, and indeed much of the western world. Particularly over the past half-century, the suburbs have exploded at a pace which has decimated many cities and consumed open land at an unsustainable rate. Towns and neighborhoods, the critics of sprawl argue, have been supplanted by subdivisions, malls, and office parks connected by an ever-expanding system of roadways. The mobility and freedom promised by the automobile have not been delivered by its dominance. Rather, a growing frustration has emerged, both popularly and with some architects and planners, that the forms of development geared solely to the automobile cannot produce livable places that serve a larger range of community interests. New Urbanists in particular have carefully crafted a critique of this sprawl that serves as the rationale for their urban interventions and new towns.

Much of the recent urbanism, especially that of the New Urbanists, focuses on rebuilding "community." As the historian Thomas Bender makes clear, "modern Americans fear that urbanization and modernization have destroyed the community that earlier shaped the lives of men and women, particularly in the small towns of the American past."[1] Interestingly, if Americans historically feared urbanization as destructive of community, the New Urbanists see rampant *suburbanization*, in the form of sprawl, as the destructive agent. Reestablishing urban priorities in architecture, whether in a small town, vacation resort, or dense urban infill, is central to the movement.

The contradictions found in this movement make it a fascinating case study of architectural ideology at this particular point in time. It is a small movement, whose members have designed only a fraction of contemporary development, yet has a large impact. It is primarily an architectural movement, yet depends on the alliance and cooperation of other professions (particularly engineers, planners, and developers). It is critical of current development as the simplistic translation of suburban conventions, yet promotes its own standards in the hope of enabling new conventions. It is an inherently conservative movement, yet is radically challenging and changing the way America builds. It is anti-heroic, yet produces leaders with vision and followings. Finally, it presents itself as antimodern, yet is fundamentally part of the larger modern project of reform.

It is important to understand that this book is about particular tendencies, not ownership of ideas. Although the movement of the Congress for New Urbanism presents its position in the proprietary form of a charter, its ideas are representative of much broader strains of architectural ideology, and, indeed, are part of a larger search to find ways to address the problems of the modern city. New Urbanism is merely the latest movement to seek alternative forms to reshape society. In this way, it can be seen as a continuation of modernism, not its antithesis.

The positioning of the city, and urban space, as the site of architectural investigation and practice has a long tradition in the twentieth century, including such diverse work as Otto Wagner, Raymond Unwin, Le Corbusier, Archigram, Robert Venturi, and Rem Koolhaas. It would be too simplistic to claim that the New Urbanists represent a reinvigoration of the suburbs as an antithesis to this urban condition. Rather, they have attempted to broaden the idea of "urban" to include all settlement patterns, regardless of density, and thereby claim the ubiquitous suburb as an urban form with its own particular characteristics. The implications of this recognition for an architectural profession that has principally ignored suburbs is immense. Although the ideas of the New Urbanists have met much resistance within the profession, and confront the overwhelming inertia of conventional development practices, they have reached a level of success that cannot be ignored. The directions indicated by the movement are no longer a footnote to the history of American urban development but part of it, and need to be reassessed in that context.

The purpose of this book is to explain and demonstrate this work, not through projects, but through a critical narrative of themes. The first four chapters outline the theoretical position of the work. Chapter One describes the critique of sprawl that has been so effectively developed and used as a foil to New Urbanist work. What is sprawl, and is it a uniquely contemporary occurrence? How have the construction of the critique and its response been formulated? Chapter Two explores methodologies and practices, that is, how the practices of urban design and architecture have been affected and how the idea of the "project" has been reframed. Chapter

Three investigates the renewed emphasis on building "typology" as the mediation between architecture and urban design. The fourth chapter focuses on the restructuring of built environments through new codes and conventions.

The last two chapters explore the incarnation of these ideas in two kinds of broad applications. The projects in Chapter Five illustrate how urban and suburban transformation can occur through interventions in existing urbanized areas. Chapter Six focuses on new towns and neighborhoods, where a more unadulterated realization of New Urbanist ideas can occur. Finally, although this book is not a monograph and is based around a narrative of specific themes, six case studies are presented in a more complete representation. These are intended to help the reader understand the different incarnations and applications of the ideas discussed in previous chapters.

I have tried to distill this recent American urbanism into constituent parts, or themes, that are central to the work. In doing so, I hope to give the reader the ability to understand the work in a more complete context, so he/she can judge the success of the ideas and their applications. Although much has been written recently about the American revival of town planning in general, and the New Urbanism in particular, most of the writing consists of either partisan declarations of New Urbanism's ability to rebuild American community or facile dismissals of the movement as nostalgia-peddling suburbanism. The truth, of course, is somewhere in-between. There is undoubtedly, as one sympathetic critic has claimed, "an odd disconnect between what is exciting about the ambitious New Urbanist agenda and the places New Urbanists claim as success."[2] This book will hopefully present readers with their own chance to judge the ideas and work, and to participate in the ongoing search for alternative forms of the contemporary city.

[1] Thomas Bender, *Community and Social Change in America* (Baltimore: The Johns Hopkins Press, 1978), 3–4.

[2] Ellen Dunham-Jones, "New Urbanism as a Counter-Project to Post-Industrialism," in *Places* 13, no. 2 (spring 2000), 28.

View of Watercolor,
Florida, Cooper Robertson
and Partners, 1996.
This new town is
conceived as an extension
to Seaside. (see fig. 2.6)

Chapter One

Critique and Response

In the 1980s, a group of architects and planners began to perceive that the way we build suburbs directly affects our existing cities and regions. Land development patterns at all scales—region, town, neighborhood, and building—are interconnected, they argued, and need to be reassessed in terms of one another. Only a coordinated approach to regional planning, town planning, and architecture could redress the recent deterioration of our built environment by the onslaught of "sprawl."

This critique focused on the rapid growth of low-density suburbia, and the associated social, environmental, and economic costs. Despite its sometimes simplistic hyperbole, it is an important product of recent architectural thought, for it has spawned alternative tendencies in practice. Much of the critique was later canonized in a Charter by the self-proclaimed movement of New Urbanism, which has had a growing influence on policies of urban and suburban development. One of the more far-reaching effects has been the recuperation of land development patterns and building conventions as viable architectural subjects once again.

Although the focus of the critique is the recent sprawl of post-World War II suburbs, and in particular the explosive development of the past two decades, sprawl can be seen as a symptom of larger transformations of the modern city. For over a century architects have tried to contain and shape the form of the modern city, largely through the discipline of town planning. The idea of town planning in the modern age, according to architectural historian Leonardo Benevolo, emerged in England during the industrial revolution as a "corrective intervention" to the seeming chaos of burgeoning industrial cities. Town planning, therefore, by its very nature "retains a strictly remedial character."[1] The recent critique of sprawl sets the stage for a similar act of contemporary "corrective intervention."

New Urbanism continues the paradoxical stance of previous modern movements, from the Garden City Movement to CIAM (Congrès Internationaux d'Architecture Moderne), by combining remedial intervention with a utopian agenda. In both cases, urban and architectural form becomes the agent for societal reform. Cognizant of the pattern of failure of previous purely architectural movements, however, New Urbanists have encouraged the inclusion of a broad coalition of non-architects. Planners, environmentalists, developers, politicians, and engineers have forged an alliance to reform current building and development practices. Yet the sources of the modern city's problems for the New Urbanists are still, at the core, the physical symptoms—patterns of conventional suburban development labeled "sprawl." This chapter will describe how a critique of sprawl and post-war planning has been constructed and used as a foundation for a renewed emphasis on town planning principles.

From Suburbia to Sprawl

Since the critique of sprawl centers on suburbia and in particular its pervasive, prevailing patterns of development, it is important to understand some of its history. How did the forms of sprawl emerge and so dramatically alter our built environments? The history and patterns of suburbia are actively cited by New Urbanists—both as model and foil—for their projects.

The growth of the suburbs is perhaps the most significant change in the American postwar physical and cultural landscape. The phenomenon has been well documented for the Anglo-American model, with an awareness of parallels to the rest of the world.[2] Suburbia, originally situated as a distinct middle landscape between city and country, has now become the armature and model of growth everywhere. Its original dependence on the commercial, social, and civic life of the city has dissipated. Today suburbia has become autonomous and pervasive, invading both traditionally urban and rural areas.

The original forms of suburban development as created by John Nash in England, or Frederick Law Olmsted and later John

Subdivisions in Gaithersburg, Maryland, within the larger Washington, D.C., metropolitan area, showing conventional suburban development of single-family houses on cul-de-sacs, 1995. (Photo: Alex MacLean)

Nolen in the States, were distinct places with their own particular urban characteristics and identities. No one could mistake Olmsted's Riverside with George Merrick's Coral Gables or Nolen's Mariemont, for example. Today, suburbia is created by national developers who construct nearly identical housing subdivisions, shopping centers, and office parks across America. But it is not merely the architecture that is homogeneous; it is the pattern of development. The ubiquitous, contemporary suburban landscape of highways, shopping centers, parking lots, housing subdivisions, streets lined with strip malls, or repetitive three-car garages along cul-de-sacs is a far cry from the bucolic promise of early suburbia.

The origins of suburbia represented a transformation of the notion of urban life, of work and family, and of the relative value of city center and periphery, notions still relevant in the unfolding history of contemporary suburbia. The earliest suburban houses, outside of London, were presented as "ideal villas in nature." These houses were, in accordance with contemporary evangelicalism, places to nurture family life and protect children from urban vice.[3] This moralistic tone was evident in the writings of early American proselytizers of suburban life too, such as Calvert Vaux, Andrew Jackson Downing, and Catharine Beecher. These nineteenth-century reformers promoted the suburban detached dwelling as a place of isolated domesticity within a moral community.

The earliest planned suburbs, although still financially dependent on the city, especially for jobs, did possess a mix of uses other than housing that contributed to a larger autonomous community. The pre-World War II suburban developments in America, particularly in the 1920s in places like Mariemont, Ohio or Country Club District in Kansas City, were more than just bedroom communities for commuters. They were neighborhoods with diverse housing, civic buildings, town centers, and dedicated open spaces such as parks and squares. Like much of suburbia, they were relatively exclusive communities, segregated by race and class from the nearby urban neighborhoods. These towns are important formal precedents for many New Urbanists, who have strived to accommodate their planning principles in a more inclusive form of suburbia.

The suburbs expanded at an enormous pace after World War II. By 1980, two thirds of America's 86.4 million dwelling units consisted of single-family houses surrounded by a private yard.[4] Metropolitan areas were "suburbanized" as their residents moved to new single family houses on the periphery. By 1990, 60 percent of the metropolitan population lived in suburbs. Open land was being consumed at an enormous rate that far outpaced population growth. From 1960 to 1990 the population of metropolitan areas grew by less than 50 percent, while the amount of developed land doubled. Perhaps most striking, the amount of land developed between 1982 and 1992 equaled one sixth of the total land developed in the history of the United States.[5] (see opening image)

The reasons for such growth, amply covered in contemporary literature on the subject, are cultural and social, sustained by specific policies of the federal government. Those who marketed suburbia tapped into American ideals of individualism, domesticity, and upward mobility as represented by the image of the detached house. Anti-urban sentiment, as well as blatant racism, helped propel people from cities to suburbs. Affordable car ownership made the suburbs accessible for many Americans. Two federal policies in particular promoted and enabled the outskirts of long-settled metropolitan areas to be developed at rapacious speed: the Federal Highway Act of 1954, which began the creation of the largest highway system in the world, and Federal Housing Authority mortgage programs, which subsidized and guaranteed mortgages for much of middle-class America.

That more people suddenly had access to these suburbs certainly created some of their problems. No longer exclusive enclaves for the wealthy, vast tracts of land were opened up to the middle classes. Developers streamlined procedures for building the new houses as efficiently as possible to keep up with demand. With the lack of support for good housing options in the inner cities, it is not surprising that a wholesale relocation of the middle and sometimes working classes occurred. Many of the critiques of suburbia in the past decades, not surprisingly, have, therefore, an air of class snobbery. Since many of the valued historical suburbs are low-density enclaves for professionals who commute to the city, a challenge for New Urbanists, to live up to their own claims, is to successfully adapt these earlier conventions of suburbia for the diversity and size of the contemporary suburban population.

For the most part, the growth and form of suburbia occurred with the tacit acquiescence of the planning and architectural professions. At first, after the widespread introduction of the automobile, there was experimentation with suburban forms, such as Wright and Stein's Radburn, New Jersey, or Greenbelt, Maryland. These developments focused on separating cars from pedestrians by creating superblocks of development ringed by access roads. Yet most of suburban expansion has occurred beyond the purview of the architectural profession. By contrast, by making their critique of sprawl an architectural one, New Urbanists are able to make the claim for the renewed relevance of architecture and planning professionals in redressing the problems of contemporary development.

A Theory of Sprawl

Despite the popular appeal of the recent critique of sprawl, it is a difficult term to define precisely. Like the cliche regarding jazz ("I can't describe it, but I know it when I hear it"), sprawl is amorphous and eludes easy description, but everyone seems to recognize his/her own version of it. Although not inherently bad in itself, sprawl is a symptom of problems with the modern city that have existed for over a century. It is also a sign, a rhetorical construct, representing frustration and dissatisfaction toward the seemingly chaotic condition of the late modern city and suburb. Originally employed to describe the peripheral expansion of cities, sprawl is applied today more commonly to suburbia. Yet, despite the ambiguity of sprawl and its often histrionic invocation, post-war suburbs do represent the largest land development changes and growth in American history. Recent critics of suburbia have pointed out that these settlement patterns of post-war America are a radical disjunction from previous urban tendencies, and can be identified through shared characteristics. The New Urbanists, in particular, have freed the idea of sprawl from its geographical moorings. For them, sprawl no longer implies merely the centrifugal development at the periphery, but rather a form of development pervasive everywhere. This form of development certainly has its most unadulterated incarnations at the periphery, but it has also become the convention for new development anywhere, including within existing metropolitan areas.

Today, sprawl most commonly refers to the low-density, amorphous, aggregate development of single-use "pods" (e.g., housing subdivisions, office parks, shopping malls) connected by few and large roadways. It is diffuse, de-centered, without clear boundaries, and car-dominated. It is typically a patchwork of privatized spaces, with little figural public space such as squares, greens, or plazas. Open space is therefore merely residual. The dispersed development of sprawl forces residents to depend on cars for mobility: rarely are daily activities such as shopping and working accessible to pedestrians, and densities are too low to support mass transit. Consequently, sprawl is marked by excessive space for roadways and parking lots, and building access is typically oriented toward the car, rather than the pedestrian as in a traditional town or city. Street networks in sprawl suburbs are based on a sparse hierarchy, meaning that individual developments with local cul-de-sacs or long loopy roads feed large collector streets. All car trips feed into a decreasing number of roadways, from local streets to collectors to arterials, which become increasingly overburdened and congested with new development. Widening these streets usually results in streets inhospitable to pedestrian life and does little to reduce traffic (in fact some argue that adding lanes actually increases traffic).[6]

Are such patterns and methods of building merely a reality of post-industrial capitalism, the inevitable form of market-driven development? What has caused, according to architectural and social critic Mike Davis, "the downward spiral from garden city to crabgrass slum?"[7] New Urbanists, in formulating a general theory of sprawl, have identified five primary reasons for its emergence.

Lack of Regional Planning

The lack of coordination and planning at a regional scale results in great ecological and economic costs, which impact metropolitan areas as well as surrounding suburbs and open land. It also abets the coalescence of cities, countryside, first ring and new suburbs, and even edge cities, into a single, sprawling, suburban metropolis. The separate and inequitable tax bases of suburbs and cities have also left many cities poorer cousins to their surrounding suburbs, exacerbating further flight to the suburbs. Without a regional plan, it is difficult to direct growth to preserve land and natural resources while encouraging urban and suburban infill. Transit, which many New Urbanists emphasize as an effective alternative to the automobile, requires certain population densities and compact development patterns that are best encouraged and coordinated at a regional level.

Lack of Neighborhood Design

New Urbanists also blame sprawl on the lack of design and planning which focus on the neighborhood as the primary pedestrian-oriented unit of design. As critics of sprawl, they point out that contemporary suburbia has all the elements of a traditional town or neighborhood, but dispersed in isolated, car-accessible pods. Piecemeal agglomerations of single-use projects, such as housing subdivisions and malls, do not add up to a sense of place or a coherent neighborhood. Andres Duany and Elizabeth Plater-Zyberk even postulate a simplistic but convincing hypothesis that there have only been two types of urbanism in America: a neighborhood pattern and a suburban pattern.[8] The richness and complexity of the traditional neighborhood pattern, they argue, can be found in urban areas like Georgetown or Greenwich Village, suburbs like Forest Hills or Coral Gables, or traditional New England villages. But after World War II the suburban pattern became dominant, leading to the isolated and dispersed forms of sprawl. The physical isolation of projects and the inevitable grouping of similar populations in suburban housing subdivisions prevent the serendipitous physical contact with different people they believe necessary for community.

Zoning and Government Policies

New Urbanists charge that zoning policies and other governmental programs have explicitly encouraged sprawl development. Zoning is a modern system of regulating building uses to separate human activities. Its original purpose, to separate noxious industries from residential areas, is mostly unnecessary in today's post-industrial cities. Now zoning is an instrument of separation and segregation, resulting in thousands of acres equally divided into identical lots, typically housing people of similar socio-economic status. While zoning is not necessarily the cause of the resulting racial segregation, it does reinforce certain tendencies in American culture through its parallel segregation of forms of development. The multiple and layered uses that once coexisted in cities and towns are now separated and isolated from each other, connected by vast roadways. Zoning is a "one size fits all" policy; that is, its regulations are established for universal application across a municipality. A zoning designation of multifamily residential, for example, applies the same regulations in any loca-tion where such a use is allowed. New Urbanists contend that such zoning guidelines are, therefore, unable to accommodate different urban situations or densities and contribute to a homogeneous built landscape. Zoning also results in temporal segregation, producing places that are used only for certain times of day or night. Business districts and office parks are active in the day and stand empty in evenings. Conversely, entertainment districts are oriented to evening activity, often remaining desolate during the days.

Specialization and Standardization

An increased specialization and standardization of the building, development, design, and engineering industries has also contributed to sprawl, according to its critics. In the early twentieth century, specialties emerged to address the seemingly chaotic qualities of the modern city. Cities and suburbs began to be built by associations of specialists each working to resolve problems in a particular realm of expertise. New Urbanists see this as a significant departure from the tradition of building places by generalists, whether architects or developers, up to the 1920s, when the ideas of the Modernist functionalist city began to develop. In their view, the generalist can provide an overview for development missing in current, overspecialized processes.

The separation of uses, as prescribed by zoning, has corresponded to specialization within professions. Builders, developers, and architects specialize in components of suburban development, whether single-family housing, multifamily housing, office parks, or retail (malls and shopping centers). Banks typically lend money only for single-use projects (mixed-use projects don't conform to their pro-formas). The consequences of this specialization and separation are buildings developed in isolation from each other. The relationships between buildings and a larger urban context are subsumed by the splintered focus of specialization. Traffic engineers connect these islands of unique development. Resolving access and parking for each building becomes paramount. Ironically the mall, that great icon of suburbia, is in many ways an exemplary demonstration of the inherent urban relationship of parts to the whole. Its success in incorporating mixed uses and shared parking in the service of a well-maintained pedestrian environment has influenced the New Urbanist design of new towns and neighborhoods.

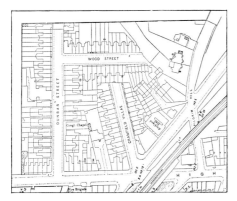

1. Plan of West Norwood, London, showing what Raymond Unwin calls the "futile arrangement resulting from lack of town planning powers." (From Unwin's *Town Planning in Practice*, 1909. Reprinted by Princeton Architectural Press)

Role of Automobile and Highways

The invention and widespread ownership of the automobile gave the middle class a new mobility that enabled the rapid development and dispersion of suburbs. Unlike the railroad suburbs, such as those west of Philadelphia which emerged along fixed rail lines, the car suburbs were able to spread wherever the seemingly cheap roadways could be constructed. With the federal government building an ever-expanding national network of highways and local municipalities absorbing the costs for local roadways to new developments, roads seem plentiful and free. The single-minded goal of efficient car movement has altered the forms of new and existing development to consist of large curb radii at intersections, multilane roadways with accelerator and left-turn lanes, three car garages facing the street, large setbacks of parking, vast network of wide uncrossable arterials and highways.

Sprawl and the Modern Metropolis

Sprawl, for all its impact on late twentieth-century urban landscape, is not a uniquely contemporary phenomenon. One can find similar complaints about uncontrollable development patterns in previous eras, particularly in cities at the onset of industrialism. Paradigmatic transformations in the economy at that time resulted in explosive, new patterns of urban growth. If cities, according to one historian, reached their apotheosis with the industrial age,[9] is suburban sprawl the built legacy of the post-industrial, service economy?

The similarities between the criticism of late twentieth-century suburban sprawl and contemporary criticisms of late nineteenth-century urban expansion highlight the extent to which the modern city continues to challenge, and resist, its critics. For example, the work of Raymond Unwin, one of the founding theorists and practitioners of the early twentieth-century Garden City Movement, was a reaction to the haphazard urban development accompanying rapid industrialization. Today, the New Urbanists and other suburban critics react against the physical results of an equally powerful transformation into a post-industrial, service-oriented economy. England first experienced the urban impact of industrialism at a scale which made it the laboratory for the rest of the soon-to-be-industrialized world. America, similarly, has created the world's first and largest post-industrial economy. Its forms of sprawl are now being replicated across the globe. How

America addresses its sprawling suburban metropolis will no doubt influence other countries confronting similar predicaments.

The struggle against uncontrolled development pervades modernism's approach to the city and, later, the suburbs. Unwin's description of urban development in late nineteenth-century England could have almost been written by today's critics of sprawl:

"Miles and miles of ground, which people not yet elderly can remember as open green fields, are now covered with dense masses of buildings packed together in rows along streets which have arisen in a completely haphazard manner, without any consideration for the common interest of the people."[10] (fig. 1)

Similarly, the Athens Charter of CIAM (1933), written by Le Corbusier, proclaimed:

"It is the uncontrolled and disorderly development of the Machine Age which has produced the chaos of our cities.

"Modern suburbs have developed rapidly, without planning and without control... Their process of growth and decay often escaping all control, frequently these suburbs take on the shape of shack-towns—disorderly groups of hovels constructed of all imaginable kinds of discarded materials."[11]

Although this view of an uncontrolled chaos pervades much of the recent criticism of today's suburban sprawl, there has also been, significantly, a shift to an almost contradictory position. Rather than unformed chaos, some critics of sprawl, like Andres Duany and Elizabeth Plater-Zyberk, contend that suburban sprawl is a ruthlessly rational product:

"Unlike the traditional neighborhood model, which evolved organically as a response to human needs, suburban sprawl is an idealized artificial system. It is not without a certain beauty: it is rational, consistent, and comprehensive. Its performance is largely predictable. It is an outgrowth of modern problem solving: a system for living."[12]

These present-day critics value the "traditional," or pre-modern town, for its "organic" forms, and consider systematic and orderly suburbs problematic. Their valorization of the organic town echoes the work of Camille Sitte in the nineteenth century, who favored picturesque urban form based on medieval precedent.

There is already concern that American settlement patterns will soon be transformed into a new type of "digital sprawl." These even-lower density settlement patterns would result from the ability to work from one's home via

2. Urban sprawl in the form of big box retail encroaches into farmland in Clay, New York, 1997. (Photo: Alex MacLean)

computer. As the mobility promised by the car has proven unattainable, the networked computer is being claimed by some as the next decentralizing technology. Such a vision is, perhaps, the logical extension of media hype (particularly computer laptop commercials) claiming that we will soon all lead dispersed and isolated lives in unspoiled nature, connected only by broadband data pipes and satellite transmissions.[13]

The Costs of Sprawl

Is sprawl as bad as its critics suggest, or is their criticism merely nostalgia for the small-town America of yesteryear? Is it simply an aesthetic reaction to the mass culture detritus of strip malls and spec housing subdivisions? While sentimentalism plays a role in much of the criticism of sprawl, even Duany and Plater-Zyberk, designers of some of the most traditionally "beautiful" new towns, realize "the problem with suburbia is not that it is ugly." They continue: "The problem with suburbia is that, in spite of all its regulatory controls, it is not functional. It simply does not efficiently serve society or preserve the environment."[14] A number of organizations, researchers, and journalists have studied sprawl,[15] and many conclude that there are serious social, financial and environmental implications to the current pattern of development.

Recent studies have found an inverse correlation between density and municipal capital cost. For example, one study calculated the costs of providing infrastructure and services for low-density, non-contiguous development at $69,000 (1998 dollars) per dwelling, compared to $34,500 per dwelling for contiguous, compact development.[16] Much of the difference is caused by reliance on the automobile and its associated infrastructure, comprehensively described in Jane Holz Kay's *Asphalt Nation*.[17] Many of those costs are hidden, since they are paid from general taxes and not levied specifically on the user. The federal government, for example, subsidizes highway infrastructure and fuel.

The direct costs, in time and money, for the average family is enormous. A typical suburban household owns 2.3 cars, and takes 12 automobile trips a day while driving 31,000 annual miles. Except for housing costs, suburbanites spend more on cars than any other category of expenses, including food. Car ownership costs the average American $6,000 annually per car. Commuting time continues to increase, especially as the suburbs sprawl outward and traffic worsens. Vehicle miles traveled increased by

40 percent between 1983 and 1990.[18] In Atlanta, a resident drives an average of 34 miles each day. American newspapers are filled with anecdotal evidence about the erosion of family time spent together under such circumstances.

A particularly compelling argument against the current suburban patterns of development is that the environment costs have been considerable and irreversible. The Natural Resources Defense Council reports that in the 1980s America lost 400,000 acres per year of prime farmland. (fig. 2) In California's Central Valley, containing some of the nation's most productive farmland, the population is expected to triple in the next four decades, resulting in a loss of an estimated one million acres of farmland. Energy costs are high: Americans use more than one third of the world's transportation energy, although they constitute only 4.7 percent of the world's population. A large percentage of air pollution results from cars emanating carbon monoxide, benzene, formaldehyde, and volatile organic compounds (VOCs). The health damage from car-related ozone pollution causes economic losses estimated between one and two billion dollars annually. Wildlife habitat and ecosystems, which depend on large uninterrupted areas, are also threatened. California alone has lost more than 91 percent of its original wetlands. Runoff pollution "is now the nation's leading threat to water quality, affecting about 40 percent of our nation's surveyed rivers, lakes, and estuaries."[19] Such pollution and general watershed degradation results from the increasing imperviousness of the ground, since the concentrations of pollutants on the transportation-related pavement which supports sprawl development (parking lots, roadways, sidewalks, etc.) are particularly high in pollutants.

There are also many criticisms of suburbia as a place that spawns social isolation. The disconnected, piecemeal patterns of suburbia which eschew complexity and diversity, and discourage walking, has exacerbated segregation by race and class. Its dispersed, auto-oriented patterns have left many people, particularly those who cannot drive or own a car (the very young, the very old, and the poor), socially isolated and dependent on the service of others. The serendipitous encounters of many types of peoples so necessary to urban culture is less likely to occur, it is argued, in the isolation of sprawl suburbs where most human contact is planned and controlled.[20]

The flight to suburbs has created severe disinvestment in the central cities, an imbalance difficult to rectify because of unequal tax rolls. Metropolitan areas find themselves with costly and increasing demands for their services (schools, utilities, garbage collection, etc.) over an ever-widening suburban periphery. While the government has subsidized much of the middle class flight to suburbia, there has not been a corresponding investment in affordable housing in the inner cities, further exacerbating the race and class divisions between suburbs and cities. Nor have the effects on first ring suburbs and urban neighborhoods been only financial: many have been decimated by the highway infrastructure built to accommodate commuters from the expanding suburbs.

Response to Sprawl

The current attempt to reform contemporary cities and suburbs continues a century-long response to the problems of the modern city through architectural and urban intervention. The origin of modernism's critique of the city, however, was a simplistic history that reified the city as inherently chaotic, violent, and unforgiving. Le Corbusier declared this assessment as a matter of fact:

"…we may admit at once that in the last hundred years a sudden, chaotic and sweeping invasion, unforeseen and overwhelming, has descended upon the great city; … The resultant chaos has brought it about that the Great City, which should be a phenomenon of power and energy, is to-day a menacing disaster, since it is no longer governed by the principles of geometry."[21]

Urban reformation, therefore, required a wholesale introduction of new solutions and forms. Ebenezer Howard, in *Garden Cities of To-morrow* (1898), justifies the adoption of a new type of settlement pattern because of the social consequences of the previous urban form:

"These crowded cities have done their work; they were the best which a society largely based on selfishness and rapacity could construct, but they are in the nature of things entirely unadapted for a society in which the social side of our nature is demanding a larger share of recognition."[22]

New Urbanist theories have emerged as a hybrid between this modernist view negating the existing city and the belief in pragmatic adaptation.

The creation of a critique of sprawl is the first step in this process of redeeming cities and suburbs. By presenting their history of the form of sprawl as a crisis in modern planning, the New Urbanists are able to architecturalize the problem. In this way, particular responses that redress the situation seem logical if not inevitable. By focusing on the physical ramifications of sprawl, they are able to offer specific design solutions at scales ranging from regional planning to architecture. They present building type and design, open space and landscape, street networks and block configuration, transportation design, regional planning, and sustainability as interdependent design issues.

Ironically for a movement steeped in modernist tendencies, much of the architectural response to sprawl is inspired by the study of pre-modern urbanism and town design. Undaunted by a century of failed movements intended to reform cities, New Urbanists press ahead by looking to the past. Speaking about this seemingly contradictory stance, historian Robert Fishman remarked:

"At a time when the global economy really threatens to submerge all differences, when the avant-garde is indeed paralyzed by the multiple possibilities and dangers of change, that it's precisely in this context that the past paradoxically becomes our best source of innovation and difference that we so desperately need."[23]

The distinction between inspiration and simulation, however, is not always understood. As Unwin, a prime influence on the New Urbanists, proclaimed in his *Town Planning in Practice* in 1909:

"Though the study of old towns and their buildings is most useful, nay, is almost essential to any due appreciation of the subject, we must not forget that we cannot, even if we would, reproduce the conditions under which they were created … . While, therefore, we study and admire, it does not follow that we can copy; for we must consider what is likely to lead to the best results under modern conditions, what is and what is not attainable with the means at our disposal."[24]

New Urbanist design of new settlement patterns is oriented toward minimizing, but not eliminating, the need for automobile travel, and containing the low-density sprawl of the past decades. Compactness is therefore an important goal as an efficient form of building, but also to generate densities that permit such urban advantages as transit, pedestrian activity, and shared public space. A number of models have been postulated in opposition to the conventional model of suburban planning. One of them is the "traditional neighborhood unit" of Duany Plater-Zyberk (DPZ), a re-

- **Neighborhood:** the fundamental human habitat; a community sustaining a full range of ordinary human needs. In its ideal form, the neighborhood is a compact urban pattern with a balanced range of living, working, shopping, recreational, and educational accommodation. There exists a variety of models, some old, and some of relatively recent derivation that incorporate the attributes of the neighborhood.

NEIGHBORHOOD UNIT 1927

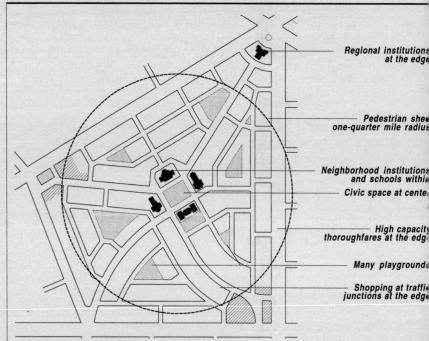

Regional institutions at the edge

Pedestrian shed one-quarter mile radius

Neighborhood institutions and schools within

Civic space at center

High capacity thoroughfares at the edge

Many playgrounds

Shopping at traffic junctions at the edge

Neighborhood Unit: A diagram and description from the First Regional Plan of New York (1927) which conceptualizes the neighborhood as the fundamental element of planning.

Size is determined by the walking distance of five minutes from center to edge, rather than by number of residents. Density is determined by the market. A community coalescing within a walkable area is the invariant.

An elementary school is at the center, within walking distance of most children. This is the most useful civic building, providing a meeting place for the adult population as well.

Local institutions are located within the neighborhood. Regional institutions are placed at the edges so that their traffic does not enter the neighborhood.

There is a civic open space at the center of the neighborhood, and several smaller playgrounds, one in close proximity to every household.

A network of small thoroughfares within the neighborhood disperses local traffic.

Larger thoroughfares channel traffic at the edges.

Retail is confined to the junction having the most traffic, accepting the realities of the automobile.

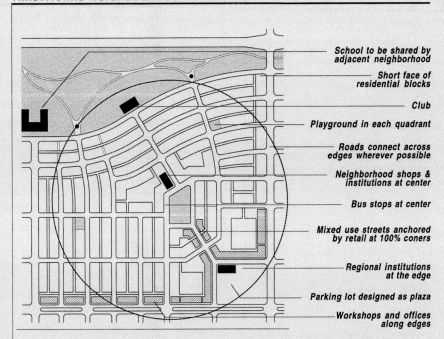

School to be shared by
adjacent neighborhood

Short face of
residential blocks

Club

Playground in each quadrant

Roads connect across
edges wherever possible

Neighborhood shops &
institutions at center

Bus stops at center

Mixed use streets anchored
by retail at 100% coners

Regional institutions
at the edge

Parking lot designed as plaza

Workshops and offices
along edges

3. These diagrams
compare the
Neighborhood Unit
of the first Regional Plan
of New York (1929)
with the Traditional
Neighborhood
Development
of the New Urbanism.
(From Duany Plater-
Zyberk's *Lexicon*, 1999)

Neighborhood Development: A diagram that updates the Neighborhood Unit and reconciles current models.

The school is not at the center but at an edge, as the playing fields would hinder pedestrian access to the center. The school at the edge can be shared by several neighborhoods, mitigating the problem created by the tendency of neighborhoods to age in cohorts generating large student age populations that then drop off sharply.

There are few sites reserved for local institutions at the center and more for regional institutions at the edge. Ease of transportation has made membership in institutions a matter of proclivity rather than proximity.

The shops at the busiest intersections have been modified to accommodate larger parking plazas for convenience retail and extended by an attached main street for destination and live-work retail.

More service alleys and lanes have been added to accommodate the increased parking requirements.

The minor thoroughfares are connected with those outside the neighborhood in order to increase permeability and disperse traffic. This modification, however, increases the possibility of shortcuts.

The thoroughfare types support a transect from rectilinear streets at the urban center to curvilinear roads toward the rural edge.

The traffic along the boulevards at the edges is more unpleasant than originally envisioned. Three mitigating strategies are proposed: the provision of an end-grain of blocks at all edges, a green buffer shown along the bottom edge, and the location of resilient building types, such as office buildings, shown along the bottom edge.

The traffic along the highway shown at the top is assumed to be hostile and therefore buffered within a parkway.

4 a, b, c. Demonstrating the importance of regional coordination of urban development, these diagrams by The Regional Planning Association (RPA) illustrate scenarios showing a: the existing conditions of a region, b: the sprawl pattern after conventional suburban development and c: the pattern of clustered development that preserves open space and natural ecosystems, as recommended by RPA.

a

b

c

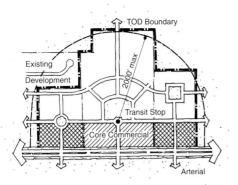

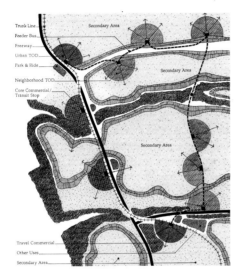

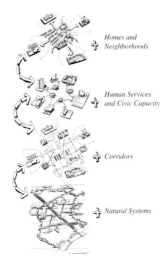

5. Diagram showing
the concept of Transit
Oriented Development
(TOD). The TOD, centered
on a transit stop and
adjacent to an arterial,
mixes residential, retail,
office space and public
uses. The size of the
development is limited by
the distance pedestrians
will walk. (Calthorpe
Associates)

6. Diagram showing
a proposed regional
relationship of
transportation to urban
development. Transit
Oriented Developments
are located on trunk
transit lines or feeder bus
route within ten minutes
transit travel time from
a stop on a trunk line.
(Calthorpe Associates)

7. Analytic diagram
of the "Metropolitan
Town" model proposed by
William Morrish illustrates
his concept of the layered
ecologies of housing,
infrastructure, corridors
and natural systems.

sponse also to the neighborhood unit proposed by the Regional Plan Association of New York in 1929. (fig. 3) In powerful but essentializing rhetoric, DPZ describes the neighborhood as a "fundamental human habitat, a community sustaining a full range of ordinary human needs."[25] Collections of neighborhoods create districts, villages, or towns. The size of neighborhoods is limited by the distance one can walk within five minutes, usually about 1/4 mile in radius for a moderate climate. The ideal Traditional Neighborhood Development contains a range of housing types, a discernible center (often a square or plaza), places to work, places for everyday shopping, an elementary school, and civic or community buildings.

Streets and blocks are the infrastructure of the new neighborhood pattern. The connected street network, commonly found in developments before the 1940s, is once again employed in place of the dendritic, cul-de-sac patterns of sprawl. The prominent transportation engineer Walter Kulash declares that such a connected network is advantageous because: 1) it reduces congestion by keeping local traffic, which comprises the majority of vehicle trips, on local roads instead of major arterial roadways; 2) travel is more direct and flexible; 3) a town center, accessible by traffic from all directions, can be concentrated in the center rather than dispersed in thin strips along highways; and 4) non-vehicle travel including walking, biking, and public transit, becomes possible, safe and more enjoyable than similar travel on arterial and collector roadways.[26]

The building of new neighborhoods and towns, and the reworking of existing suburbs and cities require planning at a regional scale. (fig. 4 a, b, c) Ideally, the region is comprised of collections of neighborhoods focused on transit lines in what Peter Calthorpe calls "Transit Oriented Districts." (figs. 5, 6) Limiting metropolitan sprawl, whether through Urban Service Boundaries (USB), or Urban Growth Boundaries (UGB), such as in Portland, is a regional issue of balancing urban and rural areas. A regional plan helps direct growth in appropriate areas in order to preserve environmental assets such as watersheds, farmlands, wildlife, vegetation, and natural terrain features. Regional planning can also ensure minimum densities necessary for shared services, including utilities, stores, places of work, and other services. Such agglomerations of people can, if sufficiently sizable, support transit and other alternatives to the automobile.

8. Master plan for Potomac Yard illustrates large urban infill development utilizing New Urbanist principles. (Cooper, Robertson & Partners, 1999)

9. Master plan for Winter Springs Mall in Florida illustrates the application of New Urbanist principles in making a new "town center" in a suburban setting. (Dover Kohl and Partners, 1998)

The diagram of Transit Oriented Districts dispersed discretely throughout otherwise un-spoiled nature is, of course, an ideal that hard-ly seems attainable in areas that have already felt the impact of sprawl development. First ring suburbs, for example, were once the pastoral suburban surrounds of a city. Now they suffer from traditionally urban problems of crime and drugs, decaying infrastructure, traffic conges-tion, and aging housing stock. The architect William Morrish believes such a place should "reposition itself within the evolving regional environment" as "metropolitan towns." (fig. 7)

These models propose principles for structuring settlement patterns that can be ap-plied to cities and suburbs equally, as well as applied outside the States. (figs. 8, 9, 10) The flexibility of these models, their popular appeal, and their ability to accommodate different scales and densities of development, set them apart from previous urban strategies this cen-tury. Yet despite the cogent, self-assured cri-tique of sprawl developed by the New Urban-ists, it does not necessarily follow yet that they alone possess the solutions to the problems of the modern city. Any civic community based on New Urbanist ideals of place will take gener-ations to evolve, and undoubtedly in ways not predicted by the designers. As these models are considered by a wider range of architects, and for a wider range of places, the true potential of these models will be best tested.

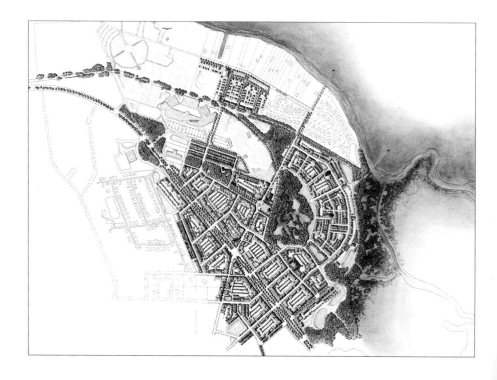

[1] Leonardo Benevolo, *The Birth of Modern Town Planning*, 4th ed., trans. Judith Landry (Cambridge, Mass.: The MIT Press, 1980), ix.

[2] See for example: Robert Fishman, *Bourgeois Utopias: The Rise and Fall of Suburbia* (New York: Basic Book Inc., 1987); Kenneth T. Jackson, *Crabgrass Frontier* (New York: Oxford University Press, 1987); John R. Stilgoe, *Borderland* (New Haven: Yale University Press, 1988); and Andres Duany, Elizabeth Plater-Zyberk, and Jeff Speck, *Suburban Nation: The Rise and the Decline of the American Dream* (New York: North Point Press, 2000).

[3] Fishman, *Bourgeois Utopias*, 119.

[4] Jackson, *Crabgrass Frontier*, 7.

[5] F. Kaid Benfield, Matthew D. Raimi, and Donald D. T. Chen, *Once There Were Greenfields* (The Natural Resources Defence Council, 1999), 4–6.

[6] Duany, Plater-Zyberk, and Speck, *Suburban Nation*, presents a comprehensive argument about the nature of sprawl in Chapter 3, "The Devil is in the Details."

[7] Mike Davis, "Ozzie and Harriet in Hell," *Harvard Design Magazine* (winter–spring 1997), 4.

[8] The illustrated argument can be found in *Design Quarterly* 164.

[9] Robert Fishman, "Cities after the End of Cities," *Harvard Design Magazine* (winter–spring 1997), 14–15.

[10] Raymond Unwin, *Town Planning in Practice* (1909; reprint, New York: Princeton Architectural Press, 1994), 2.

[11] "The Town Planning Chart, Fourth C.I.A.M. Congress, Athens, 1933," in José Luís Sert, *Can Our Cities Survive?: An ABC of Urban Problems, Their Analysis, Their Solutions* (Cambridge, Mass.: Harvard University Press, 1942), 247.

[12] Duany, Plater-Zyberk, Speck, *Suburban Nation*, 4.

[13] For discussions on the unlikeliness of such a scenario see William J. Mitchell, *E-topia: "Urban life, Jim, but not as we know it"* (Cambridge, Mass.: The MIT Press, 1999).

[14] Duany, Plater-Zyberk, and Speck, *Suburban Nation*, 14.

[15] Many of the negative conclusions regarding the impact of sprawl can be found in Benfield, Raimi, and Chen, *Once There Were Greenfields*; James Howard Kunstler, *Home from Nowhere* (New York: Simon & Schuster, 1996); *New Urban News*; Duany, Plater-Zyberk, and Speck, *Suburban Nation*.

[16] James Frank, "The Costs of Alternative Development Patterns: A Review of the Literature," as reported in Benfield, Raimi, and Chen, *Once There Were Greenfields*, 97–98.

[17] Jane Holtz Kay, *Asphalt Nation* (Berkeley: University of California Press, 1997)

[18] Benfield, Raimi, and Chen, *Once There Were Greenfields*, 31.

[19] The studies and statistics referred to in this paragraph are from Benfield, Raimi, Chen, *Once There Were Greenfields*, Chap. 2, "Sprawl and the Environment," 29–88.

[20] This critique, however, has been challenged lately by revisionist historians who argue that suburbs have become more complex, more urban, and more diverse over the recent decades.

[21] Le Corbusier, *The City of Tomorrow*, trans. 8th French ed. (Cambridge, Mass.: The MIT Press, 1986), 31.

[22] Ebenezer Howard, *Garden Cities of To-morrow* (Cambridge, Mass.: The MIT Press, 1965), 145–146.

[23] Robert Fishman, Proceedings from "Exploring (New) Urbanism," Harvard University Graduate School of Design, March 4–6, 1999.

[24] Unwin, *Town Planning in Practice*, 13.

[25] *The Lexicon of the New Urbanism* (Duany Plater-Zyberk & Company, 1999) C-2.1

[26] See essay by Walter Kulash in Michael Leccese and Kathleen McCormick, eds., *Charter of the New Urbanism* (New York: McGraw Hill, 2000), 84–85.

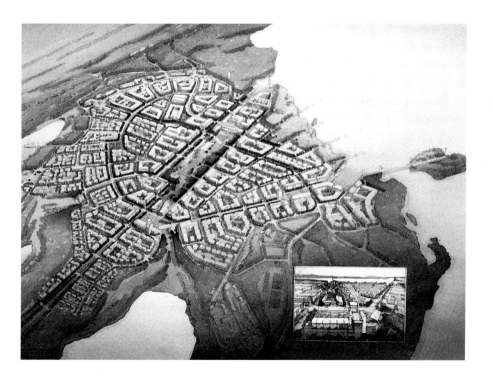

10. Proposal for Fornebu, Norway, on Oslo's old airport site, illustrates one of a number of increasing examples of the application of New Urbanist principles outside the United States. (Duany Plater-Zyberk, Div. A architects, Sundt & Thomassen landscape architects, and Berdal Stromme, 1997)

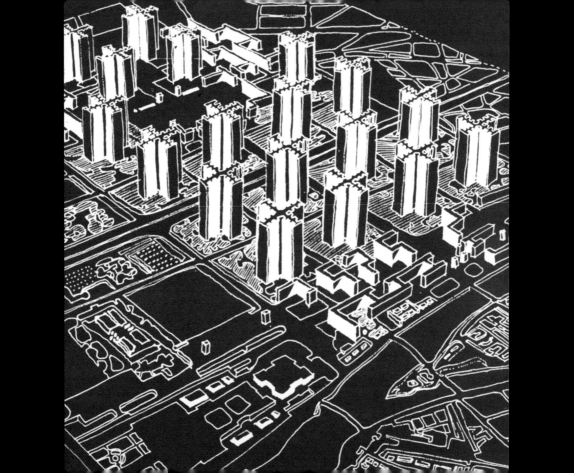

Chapter Two

Methodologies and Practices

The reformation of cities and suburbs in recent American urbanism, particularly by the New Urbanists, might seem to be simply the replacement of one set of design principles (conventional suburban design) with another (New Urbanism). In fact the goals and strategies are much more complex. The generally conservative aesthetics of New Urbanist design mask unconventional, even subversive, approaches to reforming cities and suburbs. The New Urbanists have attempted, with increasing success, to transform the framework of architecture at two levels: that of the profession, and that of the project. Specifically, they have attempted to redefine the architectural profession and its responsibilities and means of engagement with society while simultaneously redefining conventional notions of the architectural and urban "project."

This chapter will first briefly examine the formation of a movement of "experts"—the Congress for New Urbanism (CNU)—to develop and disseminate ideas and practices at the professional level. Secondly, the chapter will examine a redefinition of the urban "project" that de-emphasizes the singular act of design and favors, instead, a more nuanced and complex series of related practices that affect urban structure.

The Formation of a Movement

The Congress for New Urbanism has an ambivalent, sometimes paradoxical, relationship with modernism. It is a movement searching for alternative solutions for the future city, a goal shared by earlier twentieth-century avant-garde and modernist movements. It is also a self-proclaimed movement of experts, the latest in a series of movements that demonstrate both the promise and the hubris of modernism. CNU's focus on reforming building industries, its faith in standards and conventions, and its fervent belief in the role of design to reform society, are all staunchly held beliefs of twentieth-century modernists, particularly as represented by the CIAM (Congrès Internationaux d'Architecture Moderne).

The structure of CNU, as admitted by its founders, is based on that of CIAM. There are, for example, annual congresses to discuss particular themes. "Working groups" are formed to study particular issues and report to the general congress. Both organizations are based on a Charter of Principles to which its members must subscribe. Leveraging its collective power as a movement, CNU, like CIAM before it, attempts to lobby organizations of authority to disseminate its ideas and construct its visions.

Both CIAM and CNU have had considerable success with governmental agencies and development organizations, although the impact of CNU is just beginning to be felt on a national scale. CIAM's architectural influence on governmental agencies was often "top down," deriving from large municipal and state-sponsored projects. By contrast, CNU's influence is more "bottom up." They are primarily concerned with restructuring codes and regulations with an impact at the local level. Its processes involve interaction with local residents and developers. CNU's ambitions are national, to be sure, but their foothold on development practices was gained primarily through numerous small-scale projects with a localized impact. In recent years, their effectiveness at a national level can be evidenced by the adoption of many of their principles by the Environmental Protection Agency and the Department of Housing and Urban Development. Unlike CNU, CIAM had great influence amongst professional architects as well as with educational institutions. Many prominent members, such as José Lluís Sert, held positions at the most prestigious schools and universities. Their teachings have influenced generations of students. New Urbanism, on the other hand, has more popular support outside the profession.

The topics of CNU's congresses are remarkably similar to those of CIAM. Both organizations' first meetings, CIAM in 1928 and CNU in 1993, established a declaration of principles. The following congresses for CIAM focused on "rational lot division," zoning "the functional city," housing and leisure, the ur-

Plan Voisin for Paris,
Le Corbusier, 1922.

1, 2. Bunker Hill urban
renewal, Los Angeles,
1950s. The plan,
a version of which was
built, cleared acres
of historic urban fabric
and proposed superblocks
zoned for isolated uses.
(From *Los Angeles
1900-1961* published
by the Los Angeles
County Museum, 1961)

banism of rural areas, community, and city cores. CNU's congresses have focused on scales of design (region; neighborhood and corridor; street, block and building), environmental issues, urban infill, and social, political, and physical aspects of cities.

The charters of both organizations address similar topics, such as reforming the inherited chaos of existing cities, and linking physical, economic, environmental, and social elements in the design of cities and suburbs. (See Appendix for the CNU Charter). Both charters explicitly seek social community through urban reform. Their principles outline broad guidelines for what each organization envisions as healthy human settlement patterns. CIAM's focus, at least as envisioned by the Charter of Athens, was on the functional city as the source of solving contemporary urban problems. CNU's focus is on promoting compact neighborhood design and ameliorating the impact of the automobile.

The CNU assumes the structure and method of modernist reform—the movement. In a sense, the strategy of New Urbanism is quite subversive; CNU uses its power as a movement to selectively undermine and control various institutions which disseminate architectural knowledge. Andres Duany, in reference to his own Cuban-American background, has remarked "instead of exhausting ourselves with endless frontal attacks, we capture the radio stations and the revolution is won. No bloodshed, exactly what Fidel Castro did."[1] The CNU has analogously attempted to "capture" what they see as four powerful bureaucracies which affect the built environment: the Urban Land Institute (ULI), Graphic Standards, the Department of Housing and Urban Development (HUD), and Harvard's Graduate School of Design (GSD). Although with different levels of responsiveness, the CNU has been able to engage these representatives of four spheres of architectural influence—developers, architectural standards, federal building policy, and education.

Unlike CIAM, which eschewed planners and other non-architectural professionals, the CNU has sought to broaden their coalition by including non-architectural professionals to help implement and market New Urbanist principles in their respective professions. The CNU also engages building professionals—developers, builders, financial lenders—and much of the built success of New Urbanism can be attributed to this professional collaboration. The collective power of an organization gives

the New Urbanists leverage with industries that they would otherwise lack as individual architects and planners. The Urban Land Institute, for example, probably the most powerful developers' organization in the States, had for many years resisted inroads by "neotraditional" planners. After the formation and rapid growth of the CNU, there are now sanctioned ULI analyses of New Urbanist projects, professional partnerships between the two organizations, and joint conferences.

Reframing the "Project"

The architectural "project" has been reframed over the past decade, particularly in relation to urban and suburban design. This is partly a deliberate strategy of New Urbanists, and partly the inevitable results of architects and planners searching for new ways to engage cities and suburbs in the 1980s and 1990s. The result of this experimentation has been an expanded architectural practice relinked to urban design. Although the New Urbanists cannot claim authorship of many of these ideas, they have been largely responsible for codifying them into conventions that are increasingly accepted by the building and development industries. This broader conception of the architectural project includes, for example, analytical research, feasibility studies, strategic plans, municipal ordinances, development codes, and implementation strategies. The design of objects, such as buildings and landscaped spaces, is still central to the work, but understood in a larger, cumulative urban context governed by specific processes.

These methodologies and practices follow urban renewal, the massive federal program to reform urban "slums" in the 1950s and 1960s. The relationship between architecture and the city in contemporary America must be seen in light of this program, the apotheosis of modernist architectural intervention in the city. Although urban renewal was a debased form of early Le Corbusien urbanism conceived by municipal functionaries, and not representative of contemporaneous modernist thought in the 1950s and 1960s, it nonetheless became the convention of urban planning in America. The dire results of American urban renewal was the death knell of modernist planning in the popular imagination, particularly after Jane Jacobs' attack in *The Death and Life of Great American Cities* in 1961.

The irony is that New Urbanism is in many ways a resurrection of modernism, but cloaked in the dress of the pre-modern era. Its success in distinguishing itself from modernism is in part due to a deliberately simplistic reading of modernism. By focusing on the monumental urban follies of early modern urbanism, in particular those of Le Corbusier, rather than the vast range of explorations of community, tradition, and urban fabric by later modernist figures, New Urbanism presents a reductive and mythic modernism as a foil to its own reformist agenda.[2] For example, CIAM had, since the 1940s, been interested in creating community through town centers, a central aim of New Urbanists. Although CIAM's belief that community was best represented by monumental civic gestures contrasts dramatically with the forms of community that New Urbanism proposes, there is nonetheless a shared search for a relationship between built form and community life that has long preoccupied modernism.

In the past couple of decades, some American architects have reacted against the scorched-earth policy of urban renewal and its reliance on the singular masterplanned project. Like the early work of Le Corbusier, the urban renewal project was typically envisioned by one "master" architect, and presented as a singular, sanitized project, distinct from the messy, fine-grained context of the surrounding older city. Typically there was little connection to the surrounding street grid or scale of adjacent buildings. Massive, isolated buildings "floated" in superblocks, set back from the street and surrounded by diffuse space. Existing buildings were obliterated for these new developments, erasing any architectural connection to the past.

The redevelopment of urban centers (figs. 1, 2) through wholesale clearance and rebuilding did not deliver the invigorated civic urban life that was promised. New Urbanists do not believe that this failure was the result of architecture's incapability to reform society; rather they believe that the particular forms of the architecture and planning employed were antithetical to real community. Furthermore, they criticize the way that urban renewal, and much of modernism, conceived of urban design through monolithic projects. New Urbanists present premodern urban form as deriving from the collective presence of numerous and diverse projects developed over time. This slow, organic growth had been disrupted by the singular vision of grand intervention after the 1950s. In contrast, New Urbanists have attempted to return to a model of subtle and fine-grained strategies, but applied to the large-scale urban and suburban interventions of today.

The critical reaction to urban renewal had the effect of renewing appreciation of the ordinary neighborhoods and "Main Streets" that are so valued by New Urbanists today. New Urbanist projects are presented in contradistinction to previous urban design intentions this century, and as a considered appeal to common and everyday urbanism. Yet by the late 1940s there was already criticism within the modern movement by the English branch of CIAM, the MARS Group, that CIAM's ideals failed to address "the man in the street." CIAM's building aesthetics, they claimed, contained no "symbolic or emotional significance for ordinary people."[3] The critical reaction in the States that emerged in the 1960s, and continues to New Urbanism today, is therefore not new, but part of a longer debate within modernism itself. Jane Jacob's influential *The Death and Life of Great American Cities* criticized the profession of modern planning and architecture as an elitist institution that was out of touch with the "real" needs of citizens. Modern planning, she claimed, was responsible for the destruction of thriving traditional urban neighborhoods. Architects Robert Venturi, Denise Scott-Brown, and Charles Moore were also important forces of post-urban renewal design who set the stage for ideas that later coalesced into New Urbanism. Their focus on main streets and vernacular commercial architecture helped deflate the self-important visions of urban renewal in favor of an increased acceptance of popular taste and culture. Venturi and Scott-Brown proclaimed "Main Street is almost OK" and Moore, long before Disneyland became *de rigueur* for a postmodern understanding of the city, trumpeted the relevance and elegance of the theme park's "Main Street."

The New Urbanist concept of the master planned project accepts both the aggrandizing and homogenizing tendencies of large capital and the postmodern reading of the city as a fractured, decentered place of heterogeneity and complexity. The reality is that increasingly wealthy and powerful corporate developers are building new communities for an increasingly diverse population. New Urbanism may seem a denial of big development today, a situation celebrated by Dutch architect Rem Koolhaas' emphasis on "bigness." Yet one could also see in New Urbanism an attempt to mediate this paradoxical situation by creating large projects for national developers that allow for flexibility and diversity at local levels.

I. Framing the Project

None of these architectural practices is truly revolutionary, but, taken together, they indicate a new and expanded means of engagement by a coordinated group of professionals. They encompass not just design, but research, analysis, coding, feasibility studies, strategic plans, and implementation strategies. They combine the analytic surveys that CIAM performed on the city with a savvy understanding and manipulation of the processes of implementation and building.

The range of projects also opens up the field of practice. Whereas only a large architectural firm possessed the resources and expertise to manage the grand and singular architectural project of urban renewal, many firms of varying sizes can be involved in a New Urbanist plan. For the same project, separate firms might be responsible for creating the master plan, writing the code, developing a pattern book, and designing the buildings, open spaces, and landscape. Young architects can be hired to design smaller civic elements or houses, thus giving them entrée into a world of large-scale development from which they would otherwise be excluded.

In contrast to the seemingly amorphous scale of contemporary suburbia, New Urbanist projects are typically contextualized within one of three scales: 1) the Region (metropolis, city, town); 2) the Neighborhood, District, and Corridor; and 3) the Street, Block, and Building.[4] The Charter of the New Urbanism itself is structured on these three scales. Analyzing the relationship of neighborhood to city to region has been part of coming to terms with the modern metropolis. Although the New Urbanist focus on scale is presented as the antithesis of modern planning (which it is if compared to the early emphasis on functional zoning as prescribed by the 1933 Athens Charter), the conception of the region as comprised of concentric spatial "zones" is actually quite modern. Such preoccupation began with Ebenezer Howard and continued in America with Benton McKaye, Lewis Mumford, and the Regional Plan Association of America. Even in CIAM, the shortcomings of the "functionalist city" were already apparent by 1951 when the Congress at Hoddesdon examined community at different scales, from the village to the town to the metropolis.

New Urbanism renews the importance, and relevance, of a regional approach to planning. "An architecture of the region," according to architect Peter Calthorpe, "creates the

3. Regional plan for San Diego, Calthorpe & Associates, 1991. The plan diagrams the transit oriented development potential of San Diego's 330 square miles.

4. Greater Lake Okeechobee, Dover Kohl and Partners, 1996. The purpose of this plan was to advance a vision which balances tourism development with the desire to protect the features that make its communities livable and unique.

GREATER LAKE OKEECHOBEE

REGIONAL PLAN
for
TOURISM
in Towns, Countryside, & Fresh Water Frontiers

GREATER LAKE OKEECHOBEE TOURISM ALLIANCE
DOVER, KOHL & PARTNERS

context for a healthy urbanism in neighborhoods, districts and at the city center. The two forms of urbanism work together."[5] The Charter for the New Urbanism describes the physical geography of regions as bounded by "topography, watersheds, coastlines, farmlands, regional parks, and river basins,"[6] and the social geography comprised of "multiple centers that are cities, towns, and villages, each with its own identifiable center and edge." The Charter calls for development patterns that do not "blur or eradicate" the edges but rather are "organized as neighborhoods and districts, and ... integrated with the existing urban pattern." Regions are also called "the fundamental economic unit of the contemporary world." Such a "new reality" should be reflected in "governmental cooperation, public policy, physical planning, and economic strategies." Controlling growth at a regional level is the only way of engaging such issues as open space and habitat conservation as well as mobility, in particular transit. Without a regional and environmental strategy, even the best-designed New Urbanist projects run the danger of cumulatively creating "New Urbanist sprawl."[7] (figs. 3, 4)

Neighborhoods, districts, and corridors represent the middle scale in the regional diagram. They are, according to the Charter, "the essential elements of development."[8] The neighborhood, in New Urbanist parlance,

should be "compact, pedestrian-friendly, and mixed-use," and contain a "broad range of housing types and price levels" as well as a "range of parks." In contrast to the car-dependent contemporary form of suburbia, New Urbanist neighborhoods should have "many activities of daily living ... within walking distance, allowing independence to those who do not drive." The neighborhood, district, and corridor are also the units of design that New Urbanists believe most affect social behavior, since they "form identifiable areas that encourage citizens to take responsibility for their maintenance and evolution." The inclusion of a variety of housing types and prices "can bring people of diverse ages, races, and incomes into daily interaction, strengthening the personal and civic bonds essential to an authentic community." This latter claim is perhaps the most important goal of New Urbanists and one that so far has been relatively difficult to attain.

The neighborhood of New Urbanists is similar to that proposed by the Regional Plan Association in 1929: a compact, mixed-use, pedestrian-oriented area of about 1/4 mile in radius (the distance a person can comfortably walk) with a clear sense of center and edge. Seaside, for example, at 80 acres, is an isolated neighborhood which presently exists as a self-contained resort town. (fig. 5) Isolation and autonomy are not prerequisites, however. Neigh-

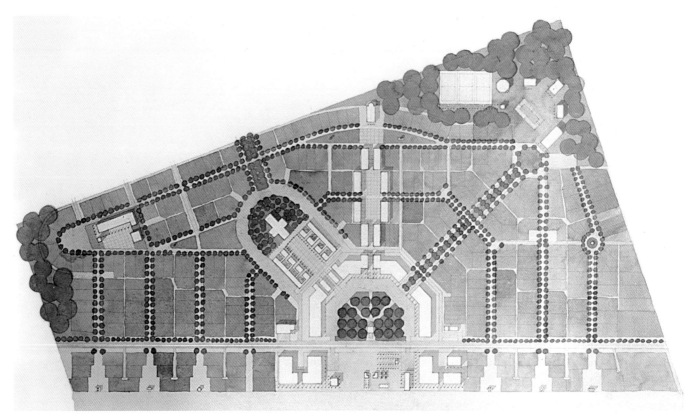

5. Plan of Seaside,
Florida, by Duany Plater-
Zyberk and Company,
1980. Although primarily
a resort community,
Seaside is probably
the first and most
influential of New
Urbanist new towns.

6. Plan of Watercolor,
Florida, by Cooper
Robertson & Partners,
1996.
The development
is conceived as
an extension of Seaside.

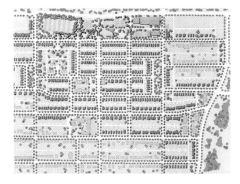

7. Master plan for Randolph Neighborhood, Richmond, Virginia, by Urban Design Associates, 1979. The plan establishes the pattern of streets, setbacks for houses and the design of public open space including three parks. Its urban pattern connects to the surrounding context.

8. Cornell New Town, Canada, by Duany Plater-Zyberk and Company, 1991. The diagram shows how multiple neighborhoods, each based on a quarter mile radii (five minute walk) together form a larger town.

CORNELL
FIVE MINUTE WALK
ILLUSTRATION

9, 10. Milwaukee Riverfront plan, Ken Kay & Associates, 1996. The master plan reestablishes the river's downtown presence by creating multiple access points between city and river's edge. The river serves as a linear urban hub, connecting different parts of the city together. A promenade gives pedestrians direct access to both sides of the river and to various newly created public spaces. (Courtesy: Ken Kay & Associates)

borhoods can be created as well for large urban infill projects (fig. 7), and additions or extensions to a city or town. (fig. 6) Multiple neighborhoods together form towns or cities. (fig. 8)

The third, and smallest, scale of urban design consists of the block, street, and building. Despite recent post-modern theories of fractured urban space, and the increased heterogeneity of urban cultures and institutions, New Urbanists assert a renewed faith in the traditional urban assemblage of buildings, streets, and blocks as the essential elements of our cities and suburbs. "A primary task of all urban architecture," states the Charter, "is the physical definition of streets and public spaces as places of shared use."[9] In this way, neighborhoods can transform over time, building by building. By contrast, large single-use suburban projects are difficult to transform except in their aggregate form.

The focus on the street continues a modernist preoccupation. First Le Corbusier declared its death in 1929, and thirty years later the mutinous CIAM members Team X, particularly Peter and Alison Smithson, resurrected it. The Smithsons declared the importance of the street for neighborhood cohesion and identity, realizing that "the short narrow street of the slum succeeds where spacious redevelopment frequently fails."[10] Similarly, the New Urbanists claim that the street permits an "attitude of expression that values the cultural variety inherent in climactic, social, economic and technical difference."[11] But the street of the Smithsons was an isolated megastructure, hovering independently over the ground plane. By contrast, the New Urbanists emphasize a finer-grained urban infrastructure of integrated streets and blocks.

Landscape design has a renewed importance in New Urbanist design because it spans all three scales of development, helping

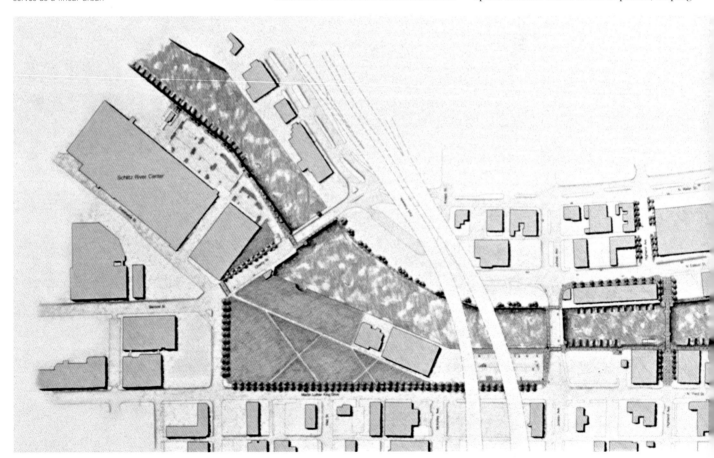

11. Photograph
of architect Andres Duany
presenting material
at a charrette for a new
town in Texas, 1999.
(Photo: author)

to knit them together. Landscape creates a public structure of open space; either squares and other bordered open spaces, or a more diffuse system that is transformed throughout the city. Abandoned and underutilized areas such as former rail tracks and yards, or obsolete industrial sites, have been resuscitated as parkland. In Milwaukee, landscape architect Ken Kay redesigned the riverfront spaces throughout downtown, ingeniously transforming a previously ignored infrastructure into a celebrated urban feature that reappears in different forms (a promenade, a small park, an amphitheatrical space, etc.) throughout the city. (figs. 9, 10)

II. Designing and Executing the Project

Frequently New Urbanists create a master plan through an integrated design process known as a "charrette," an intensive, collaborative workshop, often held on the project site. Over a short period of time, usually no more than one week, the design team, consultants, clients, and any group with an interest in the project (neighbors, city staff, elected officials) work continuously together to produce a draft master plan. The charrette is an open elicitation of ideas, but it is also a carefully packaged "event," often covered by local newspapers and television stations. In this way, according to a New Urbanist handbook of practices, it is also a "good marketing tool" with "news value."[12] The process is usually tightly controlled, and its procedures, although not its products, are carefully choreographed. (fig. 11)

The presence of multiple constituencies and consultants at the charrette produces plans that are inevitably, to some measure, the result of consensus and compromise. This approach differs from that of the Master Architect, who

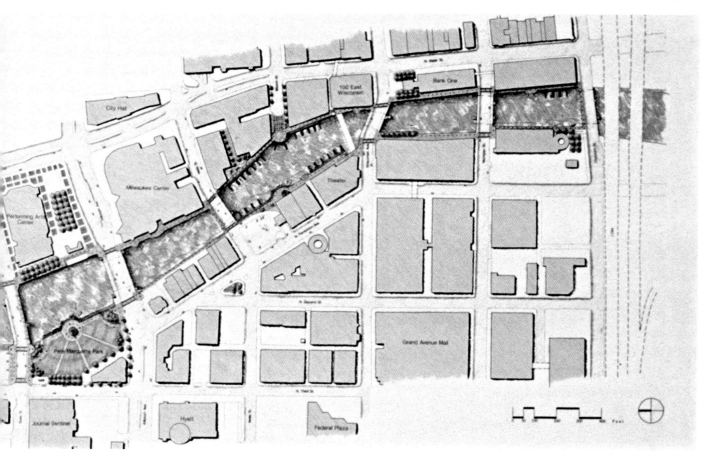

is the sole author of a master plan. It is also a departure from the conventional means of building contemporary suburbia, a legacy of the modern planning practice of segregating the components of city design into specialties. The charrette, as generator of the New Urbanist master plan, can therefore be seen as a forthright attempt to reaffirm the importance of the architect as both generalist and leader. The charrette is also a campaign of ideas on behalf of the architect planner, and includes public lectures, project presentations, and meetings with various constituencies and municipal authorities. The charrette is therefore a crucial instrument of communication and edification and not merely a means of embodying popular consensus. As one seasoned charrette New Urbanist handbook reminds the reader, "If a number of persons are not in some way angry at the planner, then no principles have been presented; the planner has been merely a secretary to the mob, and the plan will be weak to the point of being useless."[13]

Groups of designers working together produce a master plan that is a synthesis of four related urban frameworks: open space/void; transportation/parking; buildings; and landscape. Specific attention is paid to the void of the city as an important site for design and not merely the residual space between buildings. Indeed, this network of open spaces is presented as a separate design armature that includes streets and public spaces such as parks, squares, parkways and transition zones between street and private lots. (fig. 12) Their forms are shaped by building mass and placement. Technical and design considerations are often resolved simultaneously and in balance. Parkland, for instance, may serve as water retention basins or preserved wetlands. Swales along streets can serve as drainage culverts and planting strips.

Similarly, the design of streets is not relegated to a transportation department which is typically interested solely in moving cars efficiently, regardless of the quality of urban spaces such functional goals produce. New Urbanist designers and engineers actually promote some "stickiness," or slow moving traffic, for pedestrian-intensive shopping streets. Residential streets are also designed to slow traffic down, mainly through narrow widths and on-street parking, to produce safer, more intimate streets. Vehicle speed becomes something to be modulated through design as part of an overall urban plan. To this effect, the design team

12. Open Space plan, Glendale Town Center, Glendale, California, by Moule & Polyzoides Architects and Urbanists with the Olin Partnership, 1995. Streets and dedicated open spaces establish the urban armature of this downtown revitalization plan.

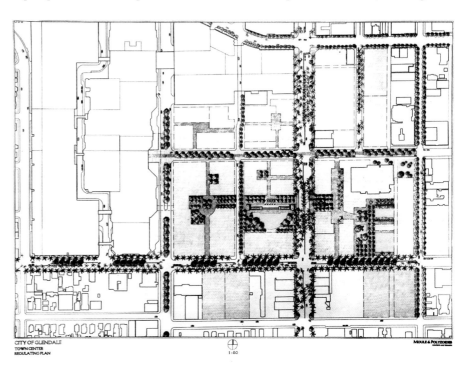

CITY OF GLENDALE
TOWN CENTER
REGULATING PLAN

1:60

MOULE & POLYZOIDES

38

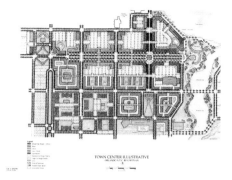

13. Plan, Orlando Naval Training Center conversion, Calthorpe & Associates, 1998. Parking is strategically placed within the blocks behind buildings as well as along the street.

considers not only the technical requirements for traffic flow and patterns (street grid layout, lane configurations, right-of-way width, etc.), but all design issues within the right-of-way including sidewalk width and materials, planter design, on-street parking configuration, medians, street trees, surfacing materials, crosswalk configuration, street lights, pedestrian lights, and furniture. (fig. 14)

In New Urbanist master plans, traffic engineering and parking policy balance the requirement of the car with that of the pedestrian. The requirements of the automobile translate into vast areas of pavement devoted to accommodating traffic capacity and parking. Parking in many of America's town and suburban centers, for instance, has been distributed in a haphazard manner on empty lots or in 180' deep parking lots along the street. The typical suburban zoning requirement that each building provide for its own parking demand, as if it were an isolated use, creates vast and redundant parking areas. The physical results are increased road capacity and traffic, with a sea of pavement in front of buildings, making pedestrian movement impossible, and sometimes deadly, in much of suburbia.

In place of individual parking lots for each building, particularly in more urbanized areas, New Urbanist traffic engineers like Walter Kulash advocate "park-once" districts. Such a concept places shared garages throughout an area, so that visitors can park once and walk to multiple destinations. On-street parking, another type of "shared parking," is commonly encouraged in New Urbanist design. On-street parking also slows traffic speed and buffers pedestrians on sidewalks from adjacent traffic. This is, of course, not a new concept, as most cities in the world have on-street parking. Employed in the suburbs, however, it is almost revolutionary. Where large parking lots are required in New Urbanist plans, they are located in the center of the block behind buildings instead of fronting the street. (fig. 13) Parking structures in New Urbanist neighborhoods are often "wrapped" with ground floor commercial space to present livelier street frontage to the pedestrian. "Park-once" lots are strategically placed so that any part of a neighborhood is accessible by foot from at least one lot. (fig. 15)

New Urbanism advocates the goal of building sympathetically within existing "context." Such a term is complex and ambiguous;

14. Street intersection plan for Playa Vista new town, Hanna Olin Ltd., 1989. Street design standards include roadways, sidewalks, crosswalks, curbs, lighting, planter strips, and street trees.

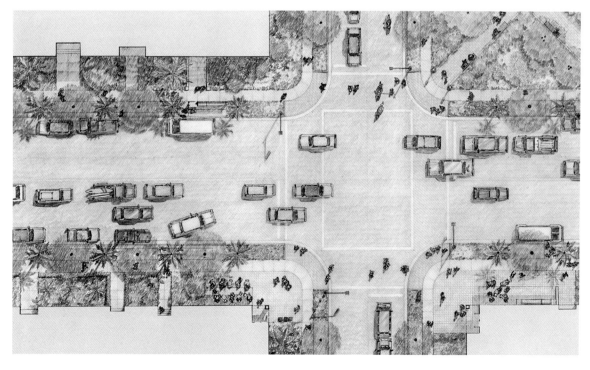

15. Diagram for parking garage catchment areas, Baton Rouge, Duany Plater-Zyberk and Company. The diagram indicates quarter mile radii (five minute walk) around key parking garages strategically located to generate a park-once pedestrian experience.

when used in the Charter it refers to the cultural and architectural precedents of a place, in particular patterns of historic urban development. More often than not, however, history is invoked literally through facile quotations. In many projects, a simplistic pretense to context in the form of style is a way of invoking history and tradition as a marketing device. There are serious explorations of the relationship of architecture to regional context and climate in projects like Seaside, which began with an exploration of local precedents of Florida "cracker houses," and Moule and Polyzoides' University of Arizona master plan and dormitory, which use desert building form and construction technique to mitigate climate. On the other hand, many new towns and neighborhoods, particularly those that rely on master builders' products, never achieve this level of sophistication. The notion of precedent can also be applied to streets and

open spaces. Many firms often catalog the best local street morphologies in order to use them as models for their master plan.

In the final phase of executing a project, most New Urbanist master plans make implementation recommendations. For example, blocks are typically divided into multiple smaller parcels with limits placed on the number of contiguous parcels any one builder can develop. Therefore, unlike the typical urban renewal master plan as well as much of contemporary suburbia, one developer does not have control over the entire site, and monolithic repetition of similar houses is minimized. Project phasing often allocates greater upfront costs to public open spaces and important community buildings. New towns like Seaside in Florida, and Civano in Tucson, have built a neighborhood center first as a means of attracting homebuyers. By contrast with conventional suburban

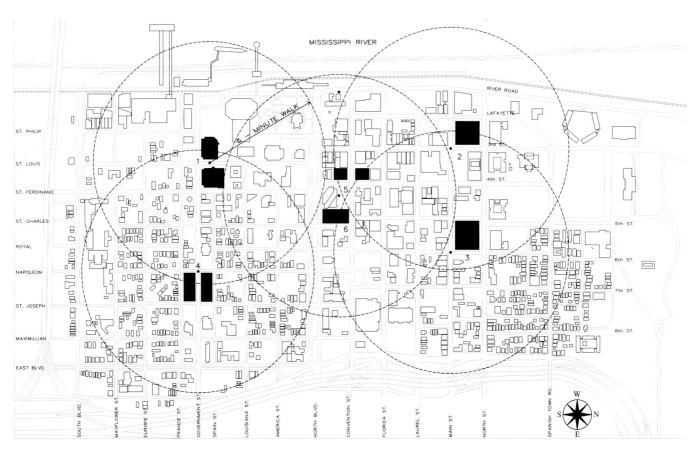

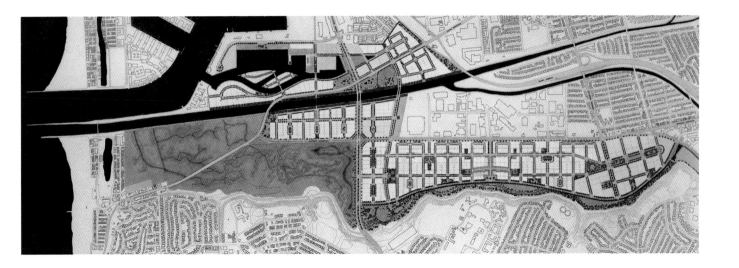

16. Regulating plan for
Playa Vista, Moule
& Polyzoides Architects
and Urbanists, Duany
Plater-Zyberk and
Company, Moore Ruble
Yudell, Legorreta
Arquitectos, Hanna/Olin.
The regulating plan
establishes the street
and block structure, open
space network, location
of civic buildings, and
platting of individual lots
to accommodate a range
of development types
and densities.
Original master plan
(unrealized) 1989.

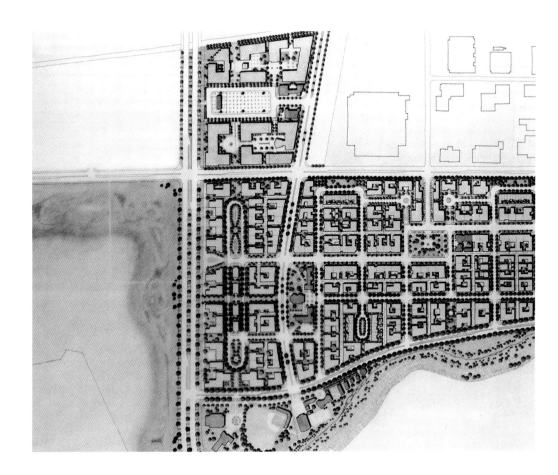

17. Illustrative plan
for Playa Vista, Moule
& Polyzoides Architects
and Urbanists, Duany
Plater-Zyberk and
Company, Moore Ruble
Yudell, Legorreta
Arquitectos, Hanna/Olin.
The drawing illustrates the
possible development
of the regulating plan.

41

development, which is constructed block by block, development in New Urbanist towns emphasizes the street. By building the two halves of blocks facing each other, the public space of the street is also created.

III. Representing the Project

New Urbanists are acutely aware of the relationship between ideas and representation. As architects of reform, they need to be able to powerfully communicate their ideas in a persuasive way. The forms of representation they employ range from dry diagrams and charts to lush renderings of plans and vignettes. This range of tools of communication allows them to address a wide range of people involved in the development process, including developers, bankers, engineers, residents, the media and, perhaps, other architects. The method of presenting ideas is, of course, linked to ideology; New Urbanist principles are clearly manifested in the way they document their work. An articulate and expansive investigation of representational techniques is laid out in the *Lexicon* which attempts to establish new conventions.

The master plan is typically represented in two kinds of plans: the regulating plan and the illustrative plan. (figs. 16, 17) The regulating plan defines the design of fixed elements in the public realm: road network, blocks divided into parcels (platting), dedicated open spaces, landscape features, and location of lots reserved for public buildings. Some regulating plans also govern building orientation by indicating building frontages. The lot parcels are keyed to a development code that governs the build-out of the various types of lots. (This will be discussed further in Chapters Three and Four) The illustrative plan is a roof plan that portrays a hypothetical example of the built regulating plan. Unlike the modernist master plan drawings of a typical urban or architectural "project," the illustrative plan is not intended to be a de facto design product. Rather it gives a sense of urban density, building type distribution, and the relationship between buildings and open space. The illustrative plan represents one possible manifestation of the master plan. The various parties involved in its realization—designers, builders, planning authorities, and clients—will inevitably shape the plan through their decisions during implementation. Much of the role of the Illustrative Plan is therefore representational, and helps the public visualize an otherwise ambiguous design process and product.

Aerial perspectives are another important means of representing urban space for New Urbanists. Utilizing a high horizon line, the drawings combine a bird's eye view from above with a sense of the ground plane in the foreground. Such drawings indicate the general urban layout and character, as well as the setting of the project in a larger context. Buildings are abstracted as generic masses, with minimal architectural detail, that define streets and open spaces. These drawings derive from the conventions of pre-CIAM modern architects like Eliel Saarinen, Daniel Burnham, Otto Wagner, and Hendrik Berlage, whose notion of urban space is so influential to that of the New Urbanists. (figs. 18–19, 20–21, 22–23) The drawings also illustrate the somewhat ambivalent attitude about urban edges that has long been a preoccupation with the modern city. Whereas the early nineteenth-century drawings indicate an expanding metropolis without limits, the later drawings represent the New Urbanist emphasis on clearer boundaries and contiguous, not continuous, development.

Vignettes are presented to give the viewer a sense of the project from particular vantage points. These drawings demonstrate the emphasis in recent American urbanism on small-scale interventions and the quality of "ordinary" places. A New Urbanist vignette is typically a perspective from eye level that portrays a view along a residential street, or within a park, or of a bustling town center with an active sidewalk life. Such colorful scenes of imagined daily life are, of course, as much marketing devices as architectural exposition. Many of these vignettes depict an image of the "good life," filled with children playing in yards, couples strolling, people shopping, and diners eating at sidewalk cafes. The subject matter of New Urbanist vignettes inevitably references lifestyle as much as urbanism, as well as a sense of instant tradition. This is difficult ideological territory to tread, for it is easy to default to a conception of "bourgeois utopia," as Robert Fishman calls the suburb, that does not reflect the complexity and diversity of today's suburban population.

Another representative tool used to illustrate the physical effects of policy and codes are comparative scenarios. Like the before and after diptychs often used by architects, these drawings show a place, usually in an aerial perspective, as it exists, as it would develop under current regulations and codes, and how it would develop under the proposed code changes.

These drawings, because of their clarity of extremes, are an effective tool of communication and persuasion. They are intended for a public audience to demonstrate how dry, technical codes are relevant to the quality of their built environment. (figs. 24, 25)

Codes, discussed in more detail in Chapter Four, have become a convention for new types of urban representation. While codes are the vehicle for translating the intentions of the master plan into built form,

they are also a form of representation in themselves, and reveal biases for how urban structure is created. By coupling a code, often an abstract document, with the lush drawings of plans and vignettes, a comprehensive package of urban representation is created. The manipulation of these tools can be quite sophisticated, especially as documents of particular methodological intent. They may serve, ultimately, as a transformative apparatus for architects addressing the modern city.

18. Urban plan for South
Amsterdam, 1914–17,
by Hendrik Berlage.

19. Aerial perspective
for Highland District,
University of Arizona,
Tucson, by Moule
& Polyzoides Architects
and Urbanists, 1990.

20. Aerial perspective of plan for Greater Helsinki by Eliel Saarinen, 1917.

21. Aerial perspective for a new neighborhood in West Sacramento, California, by Duany Plater-Zyberk and Company, 1992.

[1] From *ANY 1*, as quoted in Andrew Ross, *The Celebration Chronicles: Life, Liberty, and the Pursuit of Property Value in Disney's New Town* (New York: Ballantine Books, 1999), 77–78.

[2] Daniel Solomon is one of the few New Urbanists who acknowledges the influence of late modernists like Aldo Van Eyck, Herman Hertzberger, and Giancarlo De Carlo on his own work.

[3] J.M. Richards, editor of the *Architectural Review*, as quoted in Eric Mumford, "CIAM urbanism after the Athens Charter," *Planning Perspectives* 7 (1992), 403–404. Richards was a key member of the Modern Architecture Research Group (MARS).

[4] Introductory essays in Peter Katz, ed., *The New Urbanism: Toward and Architecture of Community* (New York: McGraw Hill, 1994). Those that discuss these topics are: "The Region" by Peter Calthorpe, "The Neighborhood and the District" by Andres Duany and Elizabeth Plater-Zyberk, and "The Street, the Block and the Building" by Elizabeth Moule and Stefanos Polyzoides.

[5] Calthorpe in Katz, *The New Urbanism*, xii.

[6] All quotations in this paragraph, unless otherwise noted, are from *The Charter of the New Urbanism*.

[7] Robert Yaro of the Regional Plan Association of New York, landscape architect Harry L. Dodson, and Armando Carbonell of the Cape Cod Commission expressed this concern in a letter to the Congress for New Urbanism. Cited in "The Urbanist's Reward," *Progressive Architecture* (August 1995), 84.

[8] All quotations in this paragraph, unless otherwise noted, are from *The Charter of the New Urbanism*.

[9] All quotations in this paragraph, unless otherwise noted, are from *The Charter of the New Urbanism*.

[10] Team X as quoted in Kenneth Frampton, *Modern Architecture: A Critical History*, 3rd ed. (London: Thames and Hudson, 1992), 271.

[11] Moule and Polyzoides, "The Street, the Block and the Building," in Katz, *The New Urbanism*, xxii.

[12] Andres Duany, "Notes on the Conduct of Charrettes," in *New Urbanism and Traditional Neighborhood Development: Comprehensive Report and Best Practices Guide*, eds. Staff of *New Urban News* (2000), 10–17.

[13] *Ibid.*

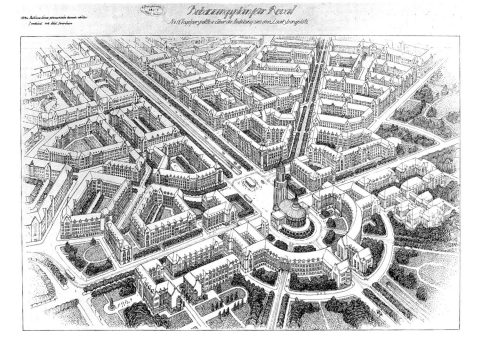

22. Aerial perspective for urban plan of Tallinn by Eliel Saarinen, 1913.

23. Aerial perspective for the new town of Wellington, Florida, by Duany Plater-Zyberk and Company, 1989.

24. Beltway Interchange, Regional Planning Association (RPA), New York, 1990.
The diagrams illustrate the three scenarios for development along a beltway interchange to support the RPA's planning recommendation. The first represents the existing conditions of an interchange providing access to an old town center located along a major metropolitan rail line. The second represents a scenario after typical car-oriented development showing how the existing municipal zoning encourages scattered and isolated commercial and industrial development. The third diagram illustrates the recommended development showing how new land use regulations as well as siting and design guidelines can encourage compact, pedestrian-oriented development.

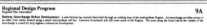

25. Florida Keys, Correa Valle Valle, 1996. These diagrams are meant to illustrate the different ways the same development can be accommodated in the environmentally sensitive Florida Keys. They indicate, from bottom to top, the existing conditions of the site, a worst case scenario following the existing zoning code, and a preferred scenario following a proposed zoning code by Correa Valle Valle. Their project strives to achieve a village scale redevelopment that best preserves the natural environment.

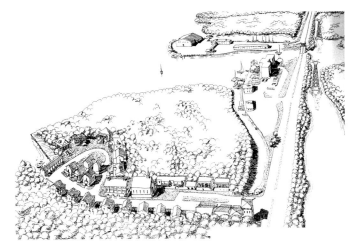

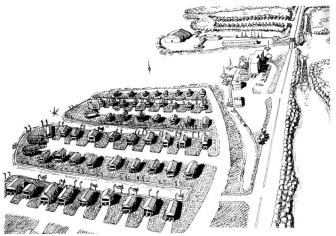

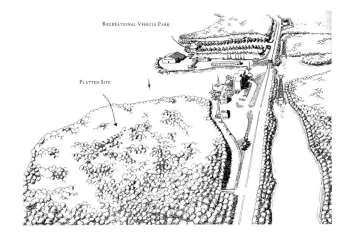

RECREATIONAL VEHICLE PARK

PLATTED SITE

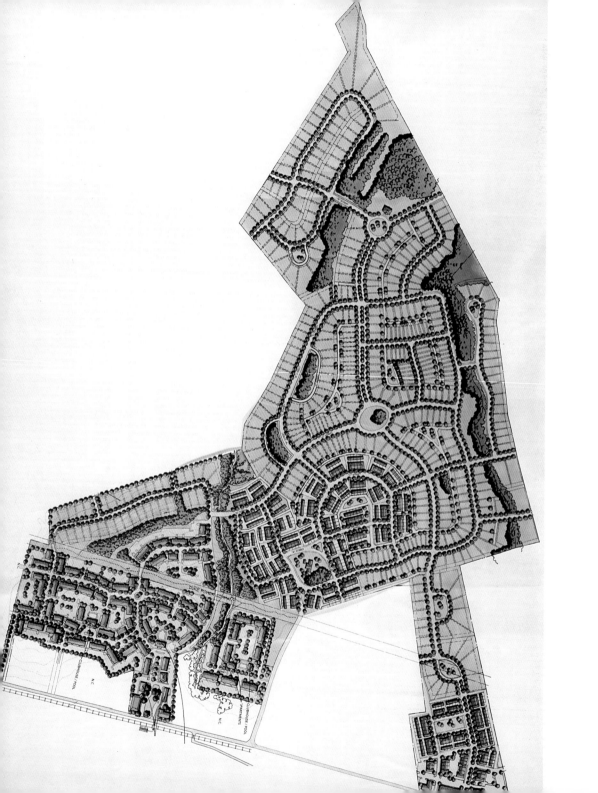

Chapter Three

Typology and Urban Design

Plan for the Village
of Caldwell Station,
North Carolina, Looney
Ricks Kiss Architects,
1998.
This 208 acre
development locates
the highest density types
of housing at the
neighborhood center
adjacent to the transit
station. Generally,
the density diminishes
toward the periphery
where the larger
single-family houses are
situated, but occasional
pockets of density help
define streets and small
parks and squares
throughout the plan.

During the last two decades, the *architectural type* has assumed a renewed importance as a critical instrument in urban design. New Urbanists in particular see type as the mediation between architecture and the city. Their master plans establish an inventory of select types that are then coordinated with platting. In this way, the contemporary suburban plan, including its buildings, becomes less a mechanistic exercise by civil engineers and developers, and more a deliberate act of design by an architect.

Although the idea of "type" has a long and complex history in architectural theory, it is generally assumed today to mean the formal configuration of a particular kind of building, often independent of use. Certainly there are traditional civic and culturally-oriented types, such as opera houses or train stations, which have particular programmatic requirements, and whose histories can be compared with other, similar types. But type also has a self-referential signification, one that responds to the history of a building's form and its relationship to the surrounding city. Some architects today are mining this history to revive traditional types, while others are transforming them into new amalgams appropriate for today's cities and suburbs. In particular, the hegemony of the archetypal single-family house is being challenged. Its proliferation at the expense of other housing options for suburbs has served to limit the suburbs from a wide range of residents. The exploration and employment of multiple housing types in New Urbanist projects can, in this way, be seen as a search for alternatives to the ubiquitous single-family house.

The focus on type by New Urbanists should be understood as only the latest incarnation of a continuous dialogue in the modern era about the relationship of buildings to the city. New Urbanists have been particularly influenced by the work of architects practicing at the turn of the twentieth century such as Saarinen, Berlage, Unwin and Parker. Type was used to create a density of urban fabric that could be sculpted and molded to design urban form as well as define figural open spaces like plazas, parks, circuses, etc. Except for deliberately monumental and prominent buildings, often civic or cultural institutions, buildings distributed by type often formed the background of the city. The subtle modulation of building type created a richness and variety for a city, and helped distinguish different places and neighborhoods. In other words, although there are obviously architectural implications in types, there are also, just as importantly for the New Urbanists, urban implications.

Most modernists, with their emphasis on functionalism and their dismissal of history as relevant to architecture, rejected the idea of type. By embracing industry and its efficient means of reproduction, "type had become prototype."[1] However, a few architects within CIAM (Congrès Internationaux d'Architecture Moderne) (e.g., Bruno Taut, Ernst May, Mart Stam, and Alexander Klein) did explore a new conception of type as an architecture of flexible structures that could be systematized, modified, and reassembled to meet modern requirements. This experimentation focused primarily on housing types. Early CIAM often focused on the question of dwelling, and its members explored multiple housing forms and their relationship to the city. However, soon after the formation of CIAM, a split emerged between those who favored neighborhood-based development, such as German and Czech architects who built continuous fabric of rowhouses (*Zeilenbau*), and those who followed Le Corbusier's vision of isolated slabs raised off the ground plane in large blocks.[2] With Le Corbusier's dominance in CIAM, his vision of the future city prevailed. The freestanding tall building became an essential unit of modern urbanism and, exported to the States, was the model for most post–World War II architectural interventions in the city, particularly in Urban Renewal programs. These modern architectural tendencies emphasized clearance and isolation. While the single-family detached house became the ubiquitous housing type of the suburbs, the singular

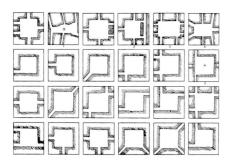

1. "Morphological series of urban spaces" by Rob Krier. (From *Urban Space* by Rob Krier, Rizzoli International Publications, 1979)

and isolate tall building became the ubiquitous urban building type, replacing the diverse and contiguous buildings of the historic city.

A renewed interest in the theory of type was stimulated in the 1970s through the writings of Aldo Rossi, Anthony Vidler, Alan Colquhoun, and the Krier brothers among others. The influence of post-structuralist thought, and in particular semiotics, created a new understanding of the language of urbanism, and typology was an important structure of such systems. Furthermore, the traditional city, often dismissively absent from modernist discourse, became the starting point for this renewed exploration of type.

Much of the New Urbanist interest in typology has evolved from a similar exploration of the city by French and Italian "New Rationalists" of the 1970s.[3] Their work centers on what Vidler calls the "third typology." He writes that this "new typology is explicitly critical of the Modern Movement; it utilizes the clarity of the eighteenth-century city to rebuke the fragmentation, de-centralization, and formal disintegration introduced into contemporary urban life by the zoning techniques and technological advances of the 1920s."[4] The Rationalists were interested in the city's form and spaces, "emptied of specific social content from any particular time and allowed to speak simply of its own *formal* condition."[5] Producing documents and analyses that were precursors to Duany Plater-Zyberk's *Lexicon*, the New Rationalists studied the traditional city in the belief that it "provides the material for classification, and the forms of its artifacts provide the basis for re-composition."[6] (fig. 1) It can be argued that social content has been injected back into the typology by New Urbanists, or at least a version of society envisioned by their often romanticized forms. Few rules, however, guided the recombination of abstract urban pieces with the New Rationalists, whereas a complex array of codes and regulations guide the compilation of New Urbanist typologies.

The American Experience of Housing Types

One of the challenges of New Urbanists and others concerned with changing the structure of the suburbs is countering America's dependence on the single-family house. There are many reasons why the single-family house became the suburban housing model to the exclusion of almost all others. Although an exhaustive study of these reasons is beyond the scope of this book, it is important to have some understanding in order to contextualize this recent suburban town design.[7]

As in the New Urbanist theory of sprawl, the reasons for the ubiquity of the single-family house are both ingrained in American culture and encouraged by federal policies. The house best represents the original Anglo-ideal of the suburb—the ideal villa in nature, a place dedicated to the moral protection of the family. In the second half of the nineteenth century, influential writers such as Catharine Beecher and Andrew Jackson Downing, and architects such as Calvert Vaux and Frederick Law Olmsted, as well as suburban developers, promoted the suburban single-family house as the bastion of American morality and character. Its pervasiveness was guaranteed by the invention of the automobile. The mobility promised by the automobile made the outlying regions of the city accessible and the relatively sparse density of single-family dwellings conceivable. The suburban dream was opened to all of middle-class America.

In seeking alternatives to the single-family house, today's architects are also struggling against the momentum of decades-long federal policy. Federal Housing Administration policies explicitly encouraged, through tax incentives and mortgage policies, the construction of new single-family homes rather than multifamily housing types. Similarly, federal fiscal policy rewarded new home construction over renovation of existing housing stock in support of the widely-held belief that civic responsibility was engendered in home ownership, not renting. Zoning made the single-family house the veritable architectural law in the suburbs, to the exclusion of all other types. Multifamily housing was viewed as "urban" and stigmatized as subsidized or working-class housing, reinforcing the perception of the single-family house as the sole domestic container of American middle class life.

Further resistance to multifamily housing comes from the architectural profession itself. The single-family house has long been the celebrated building type of architects in America. Residential buildings by high-design architects (even by non-American architects practicing in America, like Rudolph Schindler and Richard Neutra), have always focused on the house. Architects throughout the last century as diverse as Frank Lloyd Wright, Bernard Maybeck, Charles Moore, Richard Meier, and Frank Gehry gained much of their recognition through house designs. The media typically glamorize houses, even in urbanized neighborhoods, as isolated works of art independent of any built context. The celebrated Case Study houses in Los Angeles for example, built in the 1950s and 1960s, were an attempt to find solutions to urban living that typically belied the urban setting, or distanced and glorified it through panoramic views. This is distinct from Europe where there is a long, highly-valued tradition of social housing. There, urban, multifamily housing has always been an important focus of experimentation for high-minded architects of every generation, up to Renzo Piano and Rem Koolhaas today.

Alternatives to the Single-Family House

The reliance on low-density single-family house development has proven economically and environmentally costly, and no longer serves the increasing number of families who do not resemble the model two-parent nuclear family. The search for alternatives to the single-family house is also, then, a search for housing types for alternative forms of the family. Childless couples and "empty nestors," single parents, people who work at home, the elderly, and large families, for example, all have different needs. Since typical single-family house suburbia requires its residents to own an automobile, those who cannot drive, such as children, the elderly, or those unable to afford a car, are limited in mobility. Different types of housing assembled in a variety of settlement patterns give residents choices, including the possibility of not having to drive. Of course it is difficult to overcome suburbia's auto-dependency only through architecture, but types are used as part of a larger strategy of neighborhood planning that may limit excessive driving.

For architects interested in new housing alternatives in the mass market, collaboration with developers and builders is necessary. That some architects are willing to be involved in production housing is a departure for American architectural culture, which has tended to focus on custom houses. In engaging production housing, architects have had to learn to communicate with developers and builders, to understand ideas of density, economies of scale, phasing, financing, traffic engineering and parking policy, and, perhaps most anathema to the architectural profession, marketing and the housing "market." Armed with this knowledge, architects and organizations like the New Urbanism have attempted to harness the power, financial strength and organizational efficiency of suburban developers to alter their patterns of developments and diversify their housing products.

There is now a growing acceptance of multifamily housing as a viable alternative for middle-class America. Many established building and development institutions such as the Urban Land Institute, although initially skeptical, now promote these new types. The built results in many cases reflect an architectural compromise that architects who concentrate on custom single-family houses might find untenable. Even the architecturally-designed multifamily housing being produced today by American architects, especially in large developments, lacks the intelligent architectural exploration found in Europe or Scandinavia. Yet because developers and builders have recently become receptive to alternatives to the standard single-family house, there are great opportunities for the next generation of architects. Middle-class America has also been cautiously rediscovering multifamily housing. In many of the recent new neighborhood and town developments, such as Kentlands or Celebration, there are long waiting lists for apartments, row houses and other forms of attached housing.

What, then, are alternatives to the single-family house that can help build a more diverse and complex (sub)urban fabric? Of the various housing types enjoying a revival of interest, the rowhouse is the most prevalent. An enduring type that formed much of early eighteenth-century American cities like Boston, Manhattan, and Philadelphia, the rowhouse is extremely adaptable and efficient. Its narrow width (about 20') and its contiguous form when joined through party walls, creates human-scaled urban enclosure. It allows for densities of approximately 18–24 dwelling units per acre, at least five to ten times greater than that of single-family neighborhoods. It is a powerful type for designers, since its geometric flexibility through segmentation and its continuous street-wall make it eminently malleable to form urban spaces. They can have uniform facade treatments or be modulated to create a more dynamic and idiosyncratic street edge. Row-housing can be used judiciously as elegant background buildings to form streets and blocks, as in William Rawn's Mission Hill project or much of Daniel Solomon's buildings in San Francisco. It can also be employed to form grand figural spaces, such as in Celebration or parts of Kentlands, whose precedents are rooted in European examples of terraced housing like John Nash's Regent Street in London or John

Wood's crescents in Bath. Developers appreciate the rowhouse because it is efficient and cost-effective and, unlike other higher density housing types, can be sold in a fee-simple arrangement (where the owner owns everything from "the ground up.") Rowhousing has also become the principal type used in public housing, replacing the modernist slabs and towers so ubiquitous in American cities. (figs. 2–5)

Live/work units, combining living and working spaces, are similar to rowhouses. Typically the residence is above the place of work, with separate public entrances to each and sometimes an interior connection. In New Urbanist projects, live/work units are often located near the center of neighborhoods, as a transition between primarily commercial and primarily residential areas. Acceptable in already urbanized areas, live/work units are prohibited by zoning in most suburbs. Yet there is an increasing demand for such housing from two-income families, independent consultants, small retailers, and business "incubators" who may not be able to afford dedicated office space, or parents needing to stay home with their children. Unlike purely suburban residential areas, which tend to be deserted during the day, or suburban office districts, which tend to be deserted during the night, live/work units can provide activity and use day and evening. (fig. 6) As these kind of units are finally being built in New Urbanist neighborhoods such as Vermillion in Huntersville, North Carolina, Kentlands

outside Washington, D.C., or Middleton Hills in Madison, Wisconsin, the prototype is definitely geared toward the white-collar worker such as a small retailer or professional consultant. How this type can also accommodate the working class, whose work is often too unseemly for the well-manicured, picturesque New Urbanist towns, is a challenge that will have to be met if these new towns are truly able to accommodate a diverse citizenry.

Duplexes and triplexes, because they often look like single-family houses, are an effective means of introducing lower-density multifamily housing into suburban fabric. Developments such as Harbour Town in Memphis, Tennessee, or Park DuValle in Louisville, Kentucky, for example, intermix such units quite effectively. The small-scale clustering of dwelling units has precedent in early twentieth-century garden city housing of Europe. With duplexes and triplexes, densities of approximately eight dwelling units per acre can be obtained, at least twice that of standard suburban densities. (figs. 7, 8)

Courtyard and sideyard multifamily housing are used frequently in warm climates where a semipublic open space, the courtyard or sideyard, can be used during much of the year. Such housing can be single-family, like the traditional Charleston house, or multifamily, like that of the Spanish and Moorish inspired complexes of Los Angeles from the 1920s and 1930s. Single-family sideyard housing can be

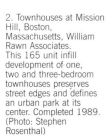

2. Townhouses at Mission Hill, Boston, Massachusetts, William Rawn Associates. This 165 unit infill development of one, two and three-bedroom townhouses preserves street edges and defines an urban park at its center. Completed 1989. (Photo: Stephen Rosenthal)

3, 4. Plan and
photograph of Fulton
Courts by Daniel
Solomon. The plan
illustrates the concept
of creating a new lane
on the old pattern
of San Francisco's
mid-block lanes. Sixteen
small three-story
townhouses, each with its
own entry, garage and
rear garden, face each
other along the new lane.
Completed 1992.
(Courtesy: Solomon
Architecture)

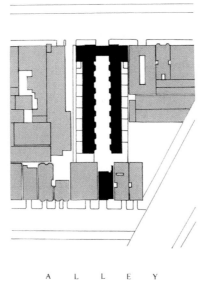

A L L E Y

5. Rowhouses at
Celebration, Florida.
(Photo: author)

53

6. Live/work townhouses,
Orenco Station, by
Fletcher Farr Ayotte.
A split entry goes up
to the main living area
and down to a home
office/commercial space.
Recessed tuck-under
parking is located behind
the live-work units.
(Courtesy: Fletcher Farr
Ayotte)

dense, yet provide considerable privacy. (fig. 9) By placing their "ends" along the street, side-yard housing requires narrower lots and can provide a more active and "urban" street wall than comparable single-family houses on wide lots. Courtyard housing creates a substantial presence on the street, yet often breaks down into more intimate semi-private courtyards within where unit entrances are located. (figs. 10, 11) With courtyard housing, densities of approximately thirty-six dwelling units per acre can be obtained. (fig. 12)

The aggregate collection of attached or unattached houses into compounds is another means of modulating densities and housing character. Compounds share a semi-public yard that is also used as a driveway. Typically the interior yard is unpaved and landscaped informally. (fig. 14) There are many precedents for compounds, from English and German garden city examples, to Santa Fe, New Mexico com-

pounds of the 1920s, to modernist examples like Jorn Utzon's 1962 elderly housing complex in Fredensberg, Denmark. The traditional Philippines compound was the inspiration for DPZ's Dos Rios project. (see Case Studies) Compounds have a density similar to small single-family housing lots, but, since they are clustered, more land is left open. By preserving more undeveloped open space, they can be a more environmentally sensitive form of suburban subdivision design. A similar strategy for clustering single-family house lots is made by Randall Arendt in his book *Rural By Design*. Instead of building houses sparsely at the typical suburban density of 4 du's per acre across an entire subdivision, they can be clustered at 8 du's per acre across half only the property, preserving the remainder as open space. The idea of compactness and aggregates of dwelling units is an important part of the town-planning strategies of the New Urbanists.

7. A single-family house, duplexes, and a triplex combined on one street. Park Du Valle, Louisville, Kentucky, Urban Design Associates. Completed 1999. (Courtesy: Urban Design Associates)

8. A quadruplex inserted into a street of primarily single-family houses. Harbortown, Memphis, Tennessee, Looney Ricks Kiss Architects. Completed 1997. (Photo: Jeffrey Jacobs/Mims Studios Looney Ricks Kiss Architects)

9. Sideyard houses at Windsor, Florida. Town plan by Duany Plater-Zyberk and Company. Master plan 1989. (Courtesy: Duany Plater-Zyberk)

10, 11. Harper Court, West Hollywood, California, Moule & Polyzoides Architects and Urbanists, 1999. Perspective from the street and one of the interior courtyards. The project was inspired by courtyard housing in Los Angeles of the 1920s and 1930s.

12. Esperanza Garden Apartments, San Diego, California, Rob Wellington Quigley Architect, 1994. Ten units of sideyard housing whose type reflects the classic California bungalow courts. (Photo: David Hewitt/Anne Garrison)

Accessory buildings such as garage apartment units or granny flats can be particularly useful to provide for a mix of residents in new developments. Such flats provide an inexpensive means of living for its occupant who may not otherwise be able to afford a single-family house, and can help the owner of the primary house pay the mortgage costs. DPZ's Kentlands includes many of these types, all of which are in high demand. They are also a way of providing semi-autonomous housing for elderly family members, and could prove to be a better alternative for America's aging baby boomers than isolated retirement communities and nursing homes. (fig. 13)

Mixed-use buildings that combine residential and commercial or civic uses have always been a part of the traditional city, and despite the tendency of current zoning policies to segregate uses, such hybrid types are once again being built. Although certainly not a radical concept for those familiar with Soho in Manhattan or Back Bay in Boston, mixed-use buildings can be created from the reuse of existing buildings (such as conversion of old warehouses into loft space) or created anew. This is an urban type that many architects, not just New Urbanists, are designing, but it is consistent with the New Urbanist strategy of dense mixed-use neighborhoods. (figs. 15–19)

The above are just a few of the main housing types that can be seen in their larger urban context in projects discussed in Chapters Five and Six. The exploration and development of other types is limited only by precedent and imagination. Now that the resurrection of traditional types is gaining acceptance, their combination into hybrid types as well as the search for new types could be a fruitful avenue of exploration for architects. If types are the building blocks of cities, what are the myriad ways of using and transforming them into complex new

13. Kentlands, Maryland. Master plan by Duany Plater-Zyberk and Company. An example of a garage apartment behind a single-family house. Such a juxtaposition of housing types is typical at Kentlands where affordable and smaller accessory buildings are in great demand. (Courtesy: Duany Plater-Zyberk)

14. Compound houses, Civano, Tucson, Arizona, Moule & Polyzoides Architects and Urbanists, 1997. An informal central open space provides both pedestrian and vehicular access to the units.

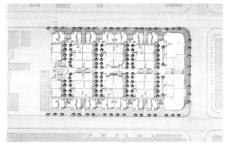

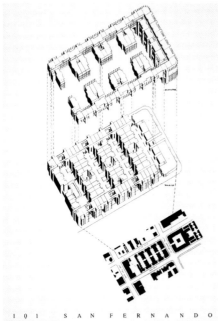

1 0 1   S A N   F E R N A N D O

FOREST CITY DEVELOPMENT   SAN JOSE REDEVELOPMENT AGENCY   SOLOMON ARCHITECTURE & URBAN DESIGN

15, 16. 101 San
Fernando, San Jose,
California, Solomon Inc.
The building consists
of 322 condominium
units and 10,000 square
feet of commercial space
organized around
pedestrian lanes that cut
through the block.
Completed 2000.

17. Birch Street Lofts,
Brea, California, Koning
Eizenberg. This mixed-use
building of 12,300
square feet ground floor
retail and 24 loft housing
units above is part of a
larger town center
revitalization plan.
Completed 2000. (Photo:
Greg Epstein)

urban pieces? Typology, through its emphasis on repetition and formal continuity, may deny the uniqueness of the architectural object, but it can also be, as architect Rafael Moneo states, "the frame within which change operates."[8]

Types Other than Housing

The renewed exploration of type is not limited to housing design. Another source of the idea of type, and one that has been very influential to the New Urbanists in particular, is the work of Werner Hegemann and Elbert Peets. Their 1922 book *American Vitruvius* presented a taxonomy of specific urban spaces and buildings as part of a larger agenda of town planning, or "civic art." *American Vitruvius* expands upon Unwin's history of urban elements (enclosed plazas, intersections, town gateways, and road arrangements) from his *Town Planning*, which in turn was greatly influenced by the work of nineteenth-century German architect Camille Sitte. More recently, Aldo Rossi and Rob Krier, amongst other New Rationalists, became interested in urban configurations of a distilled and abstracted urban space, one drained of overt references to history. The *Lexicon* by DPZ is perhaps the latest example of this ongoing search for urban types, representing a combination of Hegemann and Peets' categorical and historical examples with the abstracted permutations of the New Rationalists.

The emphasis on the range and variety of urban spatial types is intended to give developers and architects new possibilities beyond conventional suburban forms. For example, in a 400 acre project outside El Paso, Texas, DPZ and Moule and Polyzoides gridded the development into 300' x 300' square blocks and then illustrated fifteen examples of possible block configurations. (fig. 20) The block as a flexible and variable type contrasts with the typical blockless cul-de-sac development of modern suburbia. Indeed, the cul-de-sac was in-

vented by Unwin in 1909 at Hampstead as a means of relieving the relentless checkerboard of identical by-law streets. Unwin, however, used it sparingly, for urban effect. In his garden cities he created a variety of street types—wide and narrow, paved and unpaved, curvilinear and straight, with and without parking, or street trees—that together provided a rich infrastructure for varying urban character.

Similarly, the street is the primary public space for many of the projects in this book, and is treated as a type with numerous permutations and possibilities. The street has been a preoccupation of modernism, whether banished by Le Corbusier, used to create giant superblocks at Clarence Stein's Radburn, New Jersey, or elevated, literally, in monumentalizing gestures by the Smithsons in England in the 1950s. These were all attempts to understand the automobile's relationship to the pedestrian, to encourage standardization and efficiency, and to create urban space through a relationship, or not, of street to building.

While the open space of suburbia is mainly residual, a wide range of open space types can be designed as an integral part of town planning. If there is a growing and inevitable tendency, as many critics claim, toward homogenization and generic building, one means of architectural resistance might be through the design of public infrastructure—streets, blocks, platting, and open spaces—which house the generic buildings. Such spaces vary from small medians and courtyards to larger squares and parks. The plans for new towns in Chapter Six, for example, display a variety of such places which give individual neighborhoods their own urban character, as opposed to the often homogeneous places created from similar elements of modern suburbia. Even in projects with more uniform architectural aesthetics, a range of designed open spaces and streets give a richness and variety to the physical character of the place.

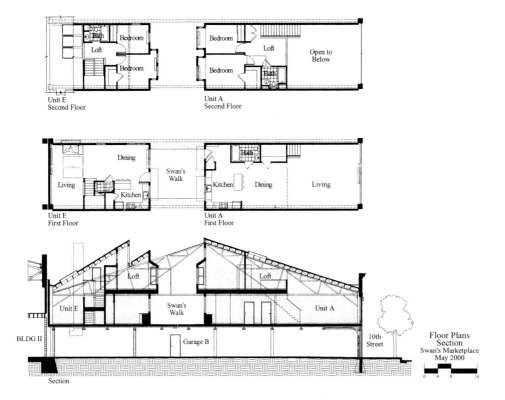

Unit E
Second Floor

Unit A
Second Floor

Open to Below

Unit E
First Floor

Unit A
First Floor

Dining

Swan's Walk

Living

Kitchen

Kitchen

Dining

Living

Bath

Loft

Bedroom

Bedroom

Loft

Bedroom

Bedroom

Bath

Loft

Loft

Unit E

Swan's Walk

Unit A

BLDG II

Garage B

10th Street

Section

Floor Plans
Section
Swan's Marketplace
May 2000

0   4   8   16

18, 19. Swan's Market, Oakland, California, Michael Pyatok Associates. The historic market building, encompassing an entire city block, was renovated into condominiums, rental apartments, live-work space, and over 50,000 square feet of commercial retail space. Portions of the existing roof are peeled away to let light into new interior courts. Completed 2000. (Courtesy: Pyatok Associates)

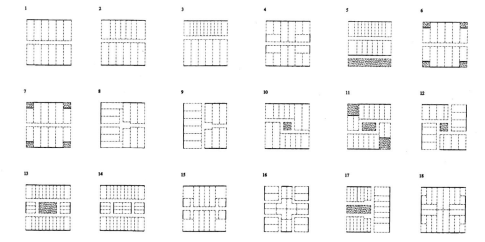

20. Block types, Hueco new town, Moule & Polyzoides Architects and Urbanists, Duany Plater-Zyberk and Company, 1999. The diagrams illustrate the various platting configurations of the typical 300 x 300 block used throughout the town.

Design by Typological Distribution

The recent resurgence of town and neighborhood design in America is based on a strategy of housing type distribution. This strategy is greatly influenced by Raymond Unwin and Barry Parker's methodologies, particularly for the towns of Letchworth and Hampstead. Unwin and Parker combined the modern twentieth-century concerns of standardization and technical progress with nineteenth-century picturesque design aesthetics. Their designs altered density through the careful relationship of platting to housing types, combined with the design of streets and open spaces. They explicitly linked the art of town planning with the arrangement of building types. (figs. 21, 22) Their book, *Town Planning in Practice*, studies different combinations of housing types and their effect on the perception of urban space. Vistas, terminuses, enclosures, open spaces, street edges, and intersections were carefully designed in terms of the perception of the resident moving along the street. The coupling of technical plans with pictorial perspectives is indicative of their attempt to bridge the technical and the aesthetic, and is a representative strategy borrowed by many New Urbanists today.

After the division of land into streets and blocks, a marking of the land which is the first act of town planning for New Urbanists, building types are ascribed to a system of platting. Because of the legacy of modern planning and zoning, the shaping of a town through subtle modulation of building types is an art rarely exercised in America since the time of renown town planner John Nolen and others in the 1920s, and some of Clarence Stein's new towns of the 1930s.

Type, in this method of town planning, acts as the mediation between urban design and architecture; it is through type that particular urban qualities are suggested. New Urbanists have shown again how type, independent of architectural style, can be used as a tool to affect density, architectural and urban character, street frontage, public spaces, open space, and the mixture of uses within an urban plan.

New Urbanist master plans are often accompanied by a code that stipulates possibilities for the distribution of particular types, as well as their architectural and urban characteristics. Such typological distribution occurred during conventional development of traditional towns and cities, and therefore architects today are studying these places to gain inspiration for present-day methodologies. How types intersect with platting, and the city in general, has been the focus of historical research that has informed design today. (figs. 23–26)

The convention, though with many exceptions, is for building types to be distributed in a progressive fashion from a dense center to a less dense edge. This linearity of distribution derives from an idealized reading of traditional cities and towns, and has been codified as the "transect" in DPZ's *Lexicon of the New Urbanism*. This gradual transition of densities is equally applicable to developments of all densities — whether towns or more rural neighborhoods. Often the center contains dense, contiguous housing types, such as mixed-use buildings of housing over retail, dedicated apartment buildings, work/live units or rowhousing. Less dense housing options, further away from the center, might include duplexes

21. Partial Plan, Hampstead Garden Suburb, Parker and Unwin. (From Raymond Unwin *Town Planning in Practice*, 1909, reprinted by Princeton Architectural Press).

22. Comparative diagrams by Raymond Unwin comparing detached housing with rowhousing, each configured at eight houses to the acre. (From Raymond Unwin *Town Planning in Practice*, 1909, reprinted by Princeton Architectural Press)

and triplexes, courtyard housing, as well as single-family houses on small lots. Larger single family houses would typically be reserved for the periphery. (figs. 27, 28)

Building types can also be employed to create varying localized densities outside of the center in order to define certain places, like avenues or squares. (fig. 29) Although both Kentlands and Celebration, for example, have a high density town center, there is quite a variety of densities and housing types beyond. Kentlands has blocks with row housing adjacent to single-family houses, and Celebration employs rowhouses to define small squares and greens throughout the town, reserving the larger mixed-use buildings of apartments over shops for the grander town center area. Similarly, Seaside uses rowhouses to define Ruskin Square in the middle of an otherwise single-family area.

Types, in New Urbanist plans, have a direct relationship to the street. Denser types at the neighborhood center, for example, typically have a small street setback or even a "zero lot line," typical of many traditional American town centers. Types that create a streetwall, such as continuous row housing, or large mixed-use buildings with commercial frontage, are often used in such places. The scale of these building types is sometimes complemented by a central square or public gathering space, as in Seaside. (figs. 30, 31) Less dense housing, such as sideyard housing, compounds, or smaller single-family houses, would then surround the neighborhood center, with detached houses on larger lots at the periphery.

The urban fabric created by private building types defines not only streets and open spaces but "public" or "civic" buildings. Unlike suburban planning and modern zoning practice in which public buildings are commonly grouped together in "civic centers," public buildings are distributed throughout New Urbanist neighborhoods in prominent sites. Diagrams showing the relationship of public buildings to private buildings, such as those of Seaside, reveal how the cumulative fabric formed by the distribution of housing types forms a backdrop for the insertion of more idiosyncratic public buildings. (figs. 32, 33)

Type vs. Style

The recent resuscitation of a traditional urbanism based on type has also seen a corresponding resurgence of traditional styles of architecture, particularly in New Urbanist projects. If type is the formal structure of architecture, style is the communication of sentiment. The debate about type and style, urbanism and architectural aesthetics, is a wholly modern one, and preoccupied CIAM too. It was Sigfried Giedion who moved CIAM toward a deliberately avant-garde style, despite numerous voices advocating an aesthetic that would appeal to more ordinary visions of the city. New Urbanism, involved in a similar debate a half century later, opts now for the opposite—ordinary over avant-garde.

Despite the claims of typological independence from style, there is nonetheless a revival of historical styles in New Urbanism. American architecture has, of course, a history of reanimating historical styles, such as the movements of Greek Revival, Queen Anne, Beaux-Arts classicism, and Arts and Crafts. American suburbia, following its English precedents, has

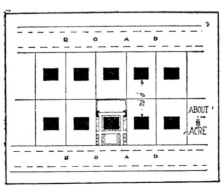

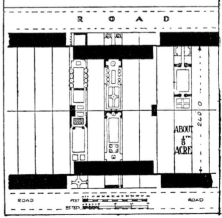

23. Illustration of housing types, Key West, Florida, from Erick Valle's *American Urban Typologies*, 1995.

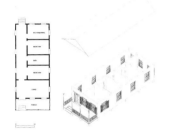

24, 25. Conch Shotgun Diagrams, Key West, Florida, from Erick Valle's *American Urban Typologies*, 1995. Sample diagrams from a typological analysis conducted throughout the town.

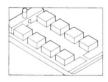
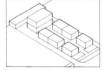

26. Diagrams of courtyard housing, from *Courtyard Housing in Los Angeles* by Stefanos Polyzoides, Roger Sherwood, and James Tice, Princeton Architectural Press, 1982.

KEY WEST BUILDING ANALYSIS — *CONCH SHOTGUN*

THE URBAN AND LANDSCAPE REGULATIONS WERE DERIVED FROM AN ANALYSIS OF SANDBORN MAPS, HISTORIC AMERICAN BUILDING SURVEYS, AERIALS, SITE VISITS, AND CONVERSATIONS WITH LOCAL RESIDENTS, HISTORIC PRESERVATION GROUPS, ARCHITECTS, LANDSCAPE ARCHITECTS, TRAFFIC ENGINEERS, SCHOOLS OF ARCHITECTURE AND PLANNING, AND ZONING DEPARTMENTS.

CIGAR-SHOTGUN

URBAN REGULATIONS

PLACEMENT
: 40 % MAXIMUM BUILDING LOT COVERAGE
: 65 % MINIMUM PERVIOUS AREA
: 60 % MINIMUM STREET FRONTAGE BUILD-OUT
: 8 FT MINIMUM FRONT YARD
: 2 FT MINIMUM SIDE STREET YARD
: 5 FT MINIMUM REAR YARD

ENCROACHMENT
: 4 FT MINIMUM DEPTH FRONT PORCH REQUIRED AND 100% MINIMUM WIDTH

PARKING / OUTBUILDING
: ONE CAR SPACE ALLOWED
: 2 FT MINIMUM SIDES SETBACK

HEIGHT & USE
: 12 FT MAXIMUM BUILDING EAVE
: FIRST FLOOR RESIDENTIAL

LANDSCAPE REGULATIONS

FRONT YARD
: MAY BE PLANTED WITH SHRUBS, HEDGES, FLOWERS AND/OR GRASS
: LAWN AREA MAY BE A MINIMUM OF 30 % OF THE TOTAL LOT AREA
: VINES MAY BE PLANTED TO GROW ON PORCHES

PERIMETER
: A CONTINUOUS HEDGE IS REQUIRED AT A MINIMUM OF 5 FT HEIGHT AT THE SIDES & REAR
: DEPENDING ON THE STREET TYPE, THE FRONT ELEVATION MAY BE SCREENED WITH TREES AND PALMS

DRIVEWAY
: MAY BE PLANTED WITH SHRUBS, HEDGES, FLOWERS AND/OR GRASS
: MAY BE A MAXIMUM OF 12 FT IN WIDTH
: SHALL BE A STRAIGHT, PERPENDICULAR PAVED AREA RUNNING FROM THE STREET TO PARKING

RIGHT-OF-WAY
: MAY BE PLANTED WITH PALMS AND TREES
: UNPAVED AREAS SHALL BE PLANTED WITH GRASS

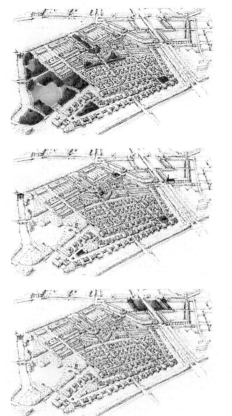

27. Building type distribution diagrams for the new town of Wellington, Duany Plater-Zyberk and Company, 1989.

28. Plan for Fairview Village, Washington, Lennertz Coyle and Associates, 1994. A commercial center contains the largest buildings, and housing densities are reduced further away from the center. The street and block structure also breaks down toward the periphery, responding to an existing creek.

often been cloaked in historical dress. The early proselytizers for suburbia, like Andrew Jackson Downing, saw historical style as a means of instantly producing a sense of history and character. In *Victorian Cottage Residences*, a popular pattern book and manifesto for suburbia published in 1842, Downing writes:

"Not a little of the delight of beautiful buildings to a cultivated mind grows out of the sentiment of architecture, or the associations connected with certain styles. Thus the sight of an old English villa will call up in the mind ... the times of the Tudors, or of 'Merry England,' in the days of Elizabeth. The mingled quaintness, beauty, and picturesqueness of the [house] ... seem to transport one back to a past age, the domestic habits, the hearty hospitality, the joyous old sports, and the romance and chivalry which invest it, in dim retrospect, with a kind of golden glow, in which the shadowy lines of poetry and reality seem strangely interwoven and blended."[9]

For Downing, as for the creators of the early Anglo suburb which influenced American suburbia, authenticity was irrelevant; what mattered was the provocation of sentiment through appearance. Since the inception of the Anglo-American suburb, historical styles have been mined for representative effect. The first weekend houses of the English aristocracy designed by Inigo Jones, Lord Burlington, and Alexander Pope, were adaptations of the ideal Renaissance Palladian villa (itself an interpretation of ancient Roman villas). Soon thereafter, the architect John Nash, in his early suburb of Park Village, used an eclectic array of styles that introduced a more studied picturesqueness rather than what he saw as the unnecessary formality of Palladian classicism. His "old English cottage," designed as an irregular cottage with the accidental charm of time and weather, was meant to stand for "stability, simplicity, domesticity, and retreat from worldly cares."[10] Style became inseparably linked to sentiments of fam-

N.E. HALSEY STREET

N.E. 207th CONNECTOR

223rd AVENUE

LISAN STREET

SIXTH STREET

FAIRVIEW VILLAGE

HOLT & HAUGH, INC.
DEVELOPER

LENNERTZ & COYLE
TOWN PLANNERS

SPENCER & KUPPER
CITY PLANNERS

ALPHA ENGINEERING
PROJECT ENGINEERS

KITTLESON & ASSOC.
TRAFFIC PLANNERS

WAYNE CHEN	BRAD HOSMAR	GARY REDDICK
STEVE COYLE	BILL LENNERTZ	BRUCE ROBINSON
BILL DENNIS	JERRY PALMER	MIKE STEFFEN
MIKE GATES	STEVE POLLARD	HEESUK STEFFEN
SARAH HOLT	ERIC SEIFER	SAM YODER
		CARY DASENBROCK

11 MAY 1994

0   5 MINUTE WALK   1300 FT

29. Row houses and single-family houses facing a small square at Kentlands. (Photo: author)

30. Central lawn in the town center of Seaside, Florida. (Photo: Stephen Brooke)

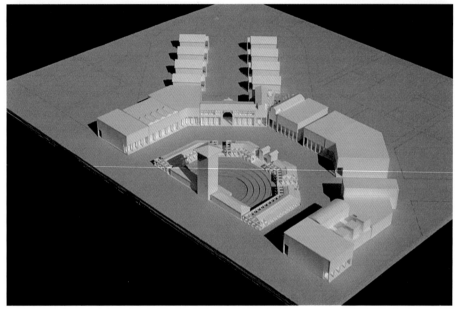

31. New commercial buildings proposed for the completion of the town center of Seaside, Florida, Daniel Solomon Architects, 1999–2000.

32. Diagram of public buildings, Seaside, Duany Plater-Zyberk and Company, 1982. Public buildings, such as town hall, tennis club, swim clubs, community centers, school, and post office, are dispersed throughout the neighborhood and correspond to public spaces like secondary squares and avenues.

33. Diagram of private buildings, Seaside, Duany Plater-Zyberk and Company, 1982. The form of the collective private buildings, such as houses, apartments, shops, offices, and hotels, generates the urban fabric. The urban behavior of these buildings is governed by a code.

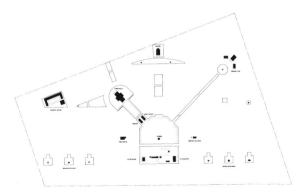

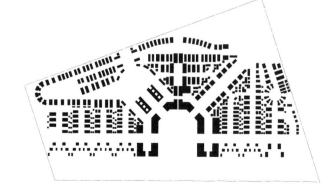

ily and community life. In the nascent American suburb, like its influential Anglo counterpart, "architects and clients turned inevitably to those historical styles which most forcibly suggested those emotions."[11]

Most architects today would appear naively sentimental to propose the same emotional associations of style as Downing did 150 years ago. Yet many New Urbanists walk a very delicate line between appealing to ordinary desires of suburban residents and pandering to potential consumers with sentimental visions of a mythic community. It is no surprise, therefore, that Disney, as the consummate packager of sentiment and thematic fantasy, evokes the mythic memory of small town America in its new town Celebration.

Style has always been the albatross of modern urbanism. The issue has been denied as central in the founding of both CIAM and CNU,[12] but the general conformance to international style by CIAM and a vague American historicism by many New Urbanists cannot be denied. And just as Giedion later moved CIAM toward the official adoption of modernist styles, there are powerful members of CNU advocating "traditional architecture."

Some New Urbanist architects justify the use of historical style on the basis of respecting urban or suburban context. Others believe in the cultural importance of a continuing architectural tradition, or at least representing a semblance of that tradition to the public. Employing a particular consistent style also creates the illusion of cohesion and unity, so important in most New Urbanist work, and indeed in most new town and utopian movements in the past two centuries. Andres Duany, for exam-

ple, claims that DPZ employs style as an essential tool to camouflage the dense, mixed-use developments which might otherwise be unpalatable to suburban America.[13] Stylistic consistency, in this view, softens resistance to typological difference and mix of use.

This begs the question of the future of architectural expression if such mixed-use neighborhoods become commonplace. Duany's stance can evoke indignant responses from an architectural profession steeped in modernism in which style and decoration were anathema. Yet traditional modernism is today a historical style. Indeed, the longing by many American architects for European modernism as the answer to current American social housing predicaments may be just as sentimental as the longing for pre-modern historical styles.

The design of cities through building types, and their evolution into hybrid types appropriate for today, may make the issue of style an open, flexible question. European cities, for example, have accommodated centuries of architectural evolution and experimentation within a broad typological consistency. A collage of styles can still maintain urban harmony through a common architectural attitude toward urban space, in particular the street. Style has become so commodified by suburban developers that it is difficult to see it any longer as a purely architectural question (and indeed, as Downing reminds us, perhaps never was). The independence of type and style is a promising, but so far rather unfulfilled, New Urbanist claim. If type can truly remain independent of style, the infrastructural challenges of the New Urbanists may indeed be able to evolve and gain wider acceptance.

[1] Rafael Moneo, *Oppositions* 13 (summer 1978), 33–35.
[2] John R. Gold, *The Experience of Modernism: Modern architects and the future city* (London: E & FN Spon, 1997), 61.
[3] For an excellent review and analysis of the influence of Italian theories of typology and urban architecture on 1970s France, see Jean Louis Cohen, "The Italophiles at Work," in K. Michael Hays, ed., *Architecture Theory Since 1968* (Cambridge, Mass.: The MIT Press, 1998), 506–20.
[4] Anthony Vidler, "The Third Typology," in Kate Nesbitt, ed., *Theorizing a New Agenda for Architecture: An Anthology of Architectural Theory 1965–1995* (New York: Princeton Architectural Press, 1996), 262–63.
[5] Vidler, "The Third Typology," 261.
[6] *Ibid.*, 260.
[7] See Robert Fishman, *Bourgeois Utopias: The Rise and Fall of Suburbia* (New York: Basic Book, 1987); Kenneth T. Jackson, *Crabgrass Frontier* (New York: Oxford University Press, 1987); and Gwendolyn Wright, *Building the American Dream* (Cambridge, Mass.: The MIT Press, 1995) who cover the subject of the single-family house and American suburbia.

[8] Moneo, 27.
[9] Andrew Jackson Downing, *Victorian Cottage Residences* (1842; reprinted, New York: Dover Publications, 1981), 24.
[10] Fishman, *Bourgeois Utopias*, 69.
[11] *Ibid.*, 70.
[12] The only official claim about building design in the CNU Charter states: "Individual architectural projects should be seamlessly linked to their surroundings. This issue transcends style." Similarly, "Though some of its members were deeply involved in the Bauhaus and other seminal developments in modern painting and sculpture, CIAM, in its early years, generally took the attitude that aesthetic questions were not part of its agenda." Eric Mumford, "CIAM urbanism after the Athens Charter," *Planning Perspectives* 7 (1992), 392.
[13] Andrew Ross, *The Celebration Chronicles: Life, Liberty, and the Pursuit of Property Value in Disney's New Town* (New York: Ballantine Books, 1999), 77.

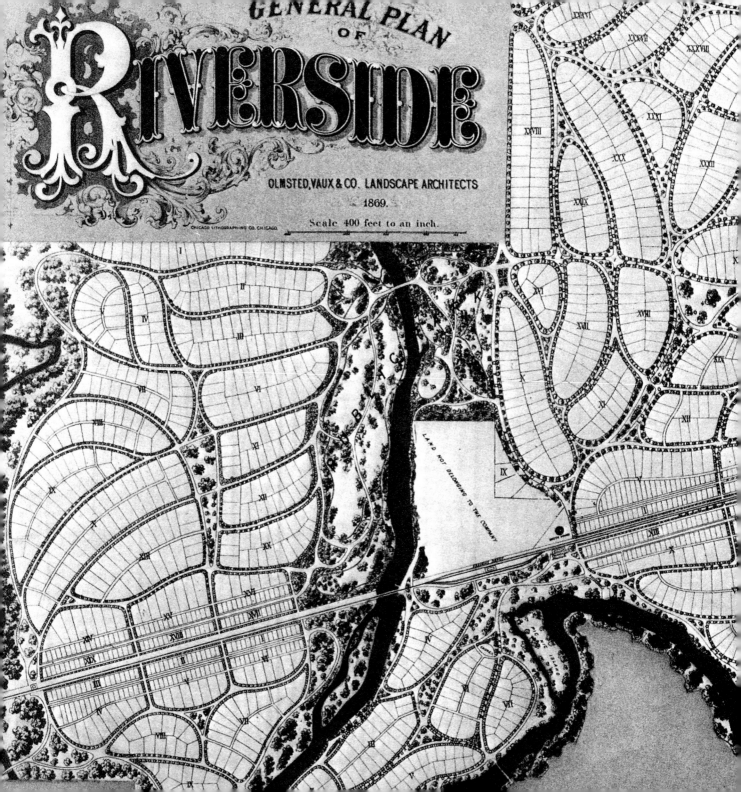

GENERAL PLAN OF RIVERSIDE

OLMSTED, VAUX & CO. LANDSCAPE ARCHITECTS

1869.

CHICAGO LITHOGRAPHING CO. CHICAGO.

Scale 400 feet to an inch.

LAND NOT BELONGING TO THE COMPANY

Chapter Four

Codes and Conventions

Much of the form and character of suburbia is the product of codes and conventions. The ubiquitous suburban development patterns of the last decades are the result of explosive growth governed by an almost slavish and unquestioning application of these codes and conventions. Specialists engaged in the production of suburbia (transportation engineers, civil engineers, planners, financial lending institutions, etc.) apply their profession's collection of codes, usually in isolation from any synthetic consideration of making a place. A standard albeit sentimental refrain of some critics of sprawl, such as writer James Kunstler, is that the historic American places commonly admired, like Nantucket, Alexandria, or a typical New England village, cannot legally be built anymore. The maze of regulations governing parking, traffic flow, separation of uses, etc. would not permit these dense, mixed-use, and pedestrian-serving places.

The vast and inexorable development of code-driven suburban form has occurred largely beyond the purview and interest of the architectural profession. Developers satisfying short-term mortgages, civil engineers solving utility infrastructural issues, traffic engineers imposing vast swaths of roadway, and planners drawing up municipal zoning maps all play more significant roles in creating our physical world and determining its character than do architects. Architects have been relatively impotent in affecting the larger built landscape, or even understanding how it is produced. Uncertain how to engage the processes of suburban development, they often have felt compelled to make a choice between complicity or self-exile.

In the past few decades, however, a growing number of architects and planners have studied the way suburbia is constructed, both physically and conceptually. They have identified and analyzed the codes, standards, and conventions which produce these common patterns of land development. Once understood, these codes then become important architectural

"sites" themselves, i.e., places to explore and create architecture and urbanism through the establishment of alternative norms. Collectively, these rewritten, restructured codes have the potential to promote new standards and practices for architects, engineers, and planning departments, as well as the building and development industries. New Urbanist architects have led much of this effort, and have incorporated these new methodologies and codes as an integral part of their work.

The goal of these endeavors is to "retool" the bureaucratic machinery of suburban production in order to produce better "products," i.e., places which are alternatives to sprawl. The means of retooling are located in the everyday realm of architectural production: housing, development standards, street standards, zoning ordinances, etc. The very mechanisms which have perpetuated suburban patterns are seen, in this view, as the tools for the patterns' subversion and alteration.

These efforts are part of a longer history of modernism's struggle to control urban growth. The standardization of building industry conventions was a strong component of early modernism, particularly with CIAM (Congrès Internationaux d'Architecture Moderne).[1] The Declaration from the first Congress at La Sarraz in 1928 read in part:

"The most efficacious production is derived from rationalization and standardization. Rationalization and standardization directly affect labor methods, as much in modern architecture (its conception) as in the building industry (its achievement)."[2]

The efforts today are comparable in intent and scope. Indeed, the collective efforts by the New Urbanists can be considered the most coordinated and systematic attempt, certainly by architects, to produce new building conventions in half a century.

Hand in hand with these attempts to control the physical conventions of urbanism have been recent attempts to control its language. The goal of these reforms is to disas-

Plan of Riverside, Chicago, 1868, by Olmsted, Vaux and Co. (From *Calvert Vaux: Architect and Planner*, Ink, Inc. Press)

1. The Plan of Sonoma, 1875, influenced by the Laws of the Indies. (From John W. Reps, *The Making of Urban America*, Princeton University Press)

semble urban concepts into their component parts and to distill and purify them into a common language. Such endeavors are part of a modern lineage concerned with naming and categorizing, from Durand's *Précis de Leçons d'Architecture* to Ebenezer Howard's Magnet Diagrams to CIAM's analytic diagrams and grids. Much of the New Urbanist discourse revolves around rediscovering urban "truths" and re-establishing a common language of urbanism. At its most effective, this control of language is a pragmatic attempt to enable communication amongst architects and to reassert the relevance of language in urban ideology. Yet New Urbanist discourse often wanders away from descriptive urban elements and lapse into a nostalgic conservatism that taps into myths of authenticity ("true community," "authentic civic character," etc.).

This chapter will first look at the history of coding, in particular that of suburbia, in order to situate the New Urbanist strategies into a larger historical context. Coding typically implies the abstraction of a series of principles into conventions and standards. Developer briefs, for example, assume certain rates of returns and marketing assumptions about housing types. Homeowner codes have emerged in recent decades, especially with the rise in condominium associations, as a powerful and legally recognizable form of local governance. The two most influential types of codes on urban form this century have been technical codes, which govern the form of urban infrastructure such as streets and blocks, and municipal codes, such as general plans and zoning codes. This chapter will examine ways that these existing codes have been reformed and altered.

The project code will be then be addressed as a new and powerful tool for architects. This design code stipulates urban and architectural rules and possibilities, in the most sophisticated cases, and specific architectural styles in the more prosaic examples. These codes have been refined over the years into instruments of control with varying degrees of flexibility. In contrast with the archetypal modernist master plans of the 1950s and 1960s that embodied the vision of a single architect, project codes can guide development to conform to general aims and urban design goals, yet be produced by a multitude of actors. This is also a dramatic divergence from the norms of post-war subdivision development in which a small number of housing prototypes are replicated and distributed evenly across a site.

Suburban Coding and its Antecedents

The New Urbanists recognize that much of America was built according to codes and standards, often to exemplary results. The use of codes and regulations to govern the building of towns and cities in the Americas has a long history. The Laws of the Indies, for example, codified by Philip II in 1573, governed the founding of civil settlements in the "New World." This code stipulated a physical urban structure—a standardized grid plan of square blocks around a large central plaza. The code guided building placement, orientation, and the arrangement of these elements relative to the sun and prevailing winds. Each town established under the general principles of the Laws of the Indies had certain similarities with the others, but was adapted to its own particular situation. The simple, abstract structure of Laws of the Indies' towns were flexible and thus enabled growth and evolution over time. Even today, one can read the underlying structure of the Laws of the Indies in towns such as Sonoma, California, or Pensacola, Florida. (fig. 1)

Some American cities, like Williamsburg, were governed by codes that dictated building lines, setbacks, architectural elements such as fences, and the location of public buildings. In Alexandria, Virginia, for example, private and public buildings were distinguished in part by their roof lines: private buildings presented their eave side to the street, while public buildings their gable end. Many cities reserved the most prominent locations, usually on squares or at the end of axes, for important public buildings such as churches and town halls. It could be argued that many of the early American codes such as these weren't so much arbitrary, as reflecting conventionally understood notions of urban form in their time.[3]

The architectural historian Leonardo Benevolo, in describing the birth of modern planning in nineteenth-century England, delineates two strands of planning—both of which depended to a large degree on coding.[4] One was a utopian description of a community in which the physical and social world were essentially linked. These codes, such as that of Robert Owen's ideal village (fig. 2) or Charles Fourier's Phalanstery, depicted ideal new communities. Their codes regulated all physical and social aspects of the town, including the layout of the buildings, the types of housing, the composition of its residents, and the jobs they would perform. Detailed guidelines for the architectural and urban spaces were intended to enable

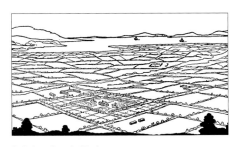

2. Robert Owen's ideal village, 1817. (From Leonardo Benevolo, *The Birth of Modern Town Planning*, The MIT Press)

3. Plan of Fulham, London, showing the arrangement of houses as stipulated by late nineteenth-century building bye-laws. (From Raymond Unwin, *Town Planning in Practice*, 1909, reprinted by Princeton Architectural Press).

political and social community. The codes could be precise in their aesthetic goals, and Fourier regulated everything from the overall division of the city into separate zones, to the ornamentation of facades, the horizontal spacing of buildings, the type of roofs (hip), and the desired vistas at the end of street axes.[5]

The other kind of codification, according to Benevolo, emerged as a corrective response to the highly insalubrious conditions of nineteenth-century English industrial cities. These were technical codes, passed as the Public Health Act of 1875, which attempted to remedy the overcrowding, lack of air and light, and streets filled with waste and sewage. Specific building regulations were intended as minimum standards governing height, detachment, and other physical properties, but instead were applied literally and absolutely by speculative builders. The results were endless rows of identical buildings with no variance for particular places or cumulative urban effect. There was no sense of a larger framework or plan, but rather a city evolved by piecemeal and expedient development of properties as they became available. (fig. 3)

The British architect Raymond Unwin, one of the first chroniclers of town planning and a seminal proponent of the Garden City Movement, lamented the haphazard and monotonous results of the application of these technical codes. Unwin's comments on the contemporary state of London urbanism at the end of the nineteenth century mirror those of many suburban critics one hundred years later:

"The truth is that we have neglected the amenities of life. We have forgotten that endless rows of brick boxes, looking out upon dreary streets and squalid backyards, are not really homes for people, and can never become such, however complete the drainage system, however pure the water supply ... . As important as all these provisions for man's material needs and sanitary existence are, they do not suffice."[6]

In the late nineteenth century, some American suburbs employed standards as a means of maintaining an aesthetic in keeping with the suburban models so recently imported from England, such as Park Village by John Nash. Detached house set back from a sidewalk, expansive lawns, curvilinear tree-shaded streets, and service from a back alley were all deliberately designed as a means of achieving a sense of isolated cohesion, a community in nature. In America, Frederick Law Olmsted, in his plans for Riverside outside of Chicago (opening illustration), first stipulated design guidelines that would enable this suburban ideal to be realized over time.

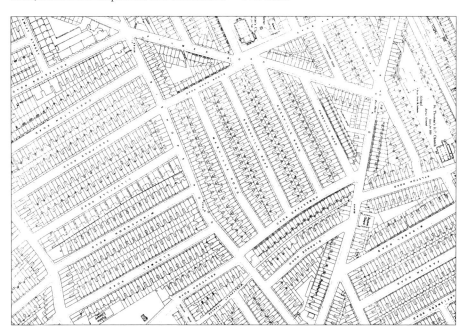

Olmsted realized that the suburb represented a delicate relationship between private and public. On one hand there was the "domiciliation of men by families..., the domestic indoor and outdoor private life," and on the other "the harmonious association and co-operation of men in a community,... and the inter-dependence between families." Olmsted assumed responsibility for the design of the public realm, but he realized "it can be no part of a general plan to provide for an interior arrangements of ground which is to be private." Therefore he placed special importance on "the arrangement of the means of division, and of passage between private and public ground." These in-between spaces "of division and passage" became a realm of design to be "enjoyed in themselves; they should on no account be imaginary lines, nor should they be obscured or concealed...."[7] Olmsted's plan required, for example, that houses to be set 30' back from the street and that a minimum number of trees be planted between the house and the street. The development of a code for these semipublic spaces allowed him to direct the intent of the private spaces and houses so that they would complement the overall design of the neighborhood. Private architecture, he realized, had a necessary and distinct public side which fostered the creation of a communal domestic setting.[8]

These ideas were further developed in the well-designed suburbs of the 1920s which have been so influential to New Urbanist design, such as Mariemont outside Cincinnati, and Coral Gables, Florida. One of the classic interwar suburbs was the Country Club District of Kansas City, designed in 1922. The ten square mile property was developed into 6,000 homes and 160 apartment buildings with lush landscape, streets rolling with the natural contours, an innovative shopping center, and schools. For the first time, codes were organized as self-perpetuating deed restrictions, and a homeowner association was created to supervise such community concerns as lawn care, street conditions, and garbage collection. Minimum setbacks and landscape standards were set, and a garage and driveway were required for all houses.[9]

The first decades of the twentieth century saw an increasing attempt to standardize modern living through a growing number of specialties. The emphasis was on efficiency, standards, and the progressive impulse to improve the domestic situation. A systematic approach to planning residential communities within regional contexts was fostered by the Regional Planning Association of America (RPAA), formed in 1923 by twenty planners and architects including Lewis Mumford, Clarence Perry, Clarence Stein and Henry Wright. Influenced by Raymond Unwin, Barry Parker and the English Garden City Movement, the RPAA tailored their standards to the realities of American suburban conditions, particularly the automobile. Clarence Perry proposed that new development be organized within a "neighborhood unit," which would govern sizes of developments, boundaries, open space allocation, street systems, and placement of institutional buildings.[10]

The form of suburban development was also the result of federal policy translated into codes and standards, particularly by the Federal Housing Authority (FHA) created in 1934–35. The FHA established technical standards for subdivisions as requirements for the issuance of federal insurance and mortgages. As the FHA's mortgages and insurance created the foundation for the postwar suburban explosion, its standards were typically followed precisely without deviation (much like the technical standards of industrial England.) The minimum standards stipulated, for example, street and sidewalk widths, block sizes and configurations, and typical lot and house sizes. It can be argued that the FHA was much more influential than planning agencies or architects in determining the emerging form of American suburbs. Their standards encouraged wide streets, cul-de-sacs, long blocks, and homogeneous residential developments. In short, these were standards which helped create the car-oriented sprawl model of subdivision development over the past half century.[11] (fig. 4)

The FHA also exacerbated the middle-class exodus from the central city to new, segregated residential subdivisions on the ever-expanding periphery. It did this by favoring new single-family housing over multifamily housing and by providing such favorable mortgage rates for new construction that it was often cheaper to build a new house than to rent and apartment or renovate existing houses.[12] The FHA also appraised subdivisions for creditworthiness, and minorities and low-income residents were deemed a liability: "If a neighborhood is to retain stability, it is necessary that properties shall continue to be occupied by the same social and racial classes," concluded the 1939 *Underwriting Manual* of the FHA.[13] Although not explicitly required, restrictive covenants were condoned by the FHA as a means of maintaining

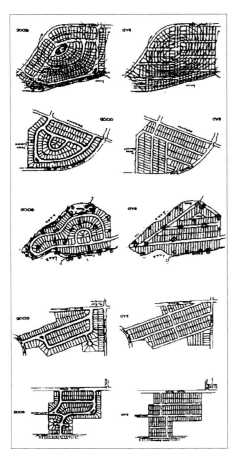

4. Recommendations for Street grids and subdivision layouts compositions by the Federal Housing Administration. (From Michael Housthworth and Eran Ben-Joseph, *Streets and the Shaping of Towns and Cities*, McGraw Hill Press)

property values. Subsequent zoning codes, which stipulated minimum lot and house sizes and excluded multifamily housing, helped perpetuate this growing segregation. The history of American suburbia cannot be separated from a long history of institutionalized racism.

Other national agencies, professional organizations, and municipal departments have impacted suburban form through their standards—policies which often aimed to maximize the goals of their respective constituencies. Streets, for example, became engineered as merely technical conduits for the most efficient distribution of water, sewage, utilities, and vehicles. The Urban Land Institute, an organization of builders and developers, published standards that helped reduce the costs of subdivisions for their members. Their standards strived to minimize the amount of roadway by emphasizing cul-de-sacs or long blocks to reduce the number of cross streets (making pedestrian connections quite difficult). The Institute of Transportation Engineers published manuals and standards aimed at the most efficient movement of vehicles.[14] The Civil Defense Committee of AASHTO (American Association of State Highway Transportation Officials) advocated street design criteria for the most efficient evacuation and subsequent cleanup of cities in the event of a nuclear strike. Fire departments still often require vast street widths, even in the most remote residential areas, to allow what some see as unnecessarily large fire trucks to be able to maneuver past improbable worst case scenarios. (Fire department standards also assume cul de sac subdivisions. The connected, gridded street network promoted by New Urbanists allows firetrucks to approach any destination from either direction.) Civil engineers impose their particular standards for right-of-way design to accommodate utility lines. Public Works departments often require run-off water to be collected in gutters and storm drains. This creates an ever expanding (and polluted) network of water collection, rather than retaining water on-site using swales and other natural retention measures.

Such stratification by specialization also informed the development process itself. Developers, architects and builders began to specialize in different types of construction—single-family homes, shopping centers, condominiums, or office parks, for example. Banks oriented their lending proforms to these various specialties. Banks were, and still are to some extent, unable to accommodate loans for projects

that do not meet generic criteria of conventional use, which they consider lower risk development. Introducing mixed-use buildings, such as apartments over commercial, is still a difficult proposition for most developers and banks. The financing of sprawl, in turn, has become as rigorously standardized as the forms it is promoting. "Form follows finance" is a slogan that is often heard from anti-sprawl advocates.

Typical municipal codes, in particular zoning ordinances, have been criticized as outmoded and destructive policies which systematically and inevitably create suburban sprawl. In many ways, zoning codes are a retrograde means of unnecessarily separating uses, a legacy of the industrial city's need to isolate noxious industries. Zoning by use is one legacy of functionalist modern planning as envisioned by CIAM.[15] Their 1933 Charter of Athens stipulated that cities were to be divided according to four functions: dwellings, workplaces, recreation, and transportation. This type of zoning valorizes use over form and creates a "one-size fits all" approach to planning. Use designations in current zoning, such as commercial, industrial, or different levels of residential, typically have the same regulations regardless of their location. Multiple uses are often prohibited, and abstract requirements such as parking requirements and Floor Area Ratios are emphasized. This is in contrast to recent projects which tend to stipulate formal conditions for how buildings form particular places—town centers, corridors, neighborhoods, for example—which can accommodate any number of uses. Zoning is also partly responsible for the extreme racial segregation of metropolitan areas in America. Although explicit segregation through covenants and zoning is now illegal, municipalities can use minimum requirements for lot and house sizes, for instance, to exclude anything but large, expensive single-family houses.

Over the past half-century, traffic engineering and parking policies have had a central role in the design of American cities and suburbs. Their sole goal of the fast movement of cars has become a sisyphian endeavor: the constant expansion of highways results in an environment intensely unfriendly to pedestrians, and ultimately still congested with automobiles. The designs of many of the projects in this book challenge the standards of right-of-way design that encourage the speeding automobile—multiple wide lanes, turn lanes, no on-street parking, one-way couplets, large corner radii at intersections, on and off-ramps. The suburban street network, based on a sparse hierarchy of arterials, collectors, and cul-de-sacs, rather than the traditional connected streetgrid, leads often to disorientation and bottlenecked traffic problems. Finally, the parking standards for suburban development, emphasizing abundant and "free" spaces, assume a worst case scenario, of an isolated use at peak-time.

Recently a new concept has emerged which looks at parking requirements not in isolation but as a part of a larger urban district. As illustrated in Chapter Two, "park-once" or "district parking" locates shared parking structures and lots within walking distance of particular neighborhoods, districts, or corridors, thereby reducing the overall parking demand. The driver will "park once" and walk to multiple destinations instead of being forced to drive to each destination no matter how proximate. This concept depends, however, on the creation of streets and sidewalks that are comfortable environments for the pedestrian.[16]

Even the relatively chaotic "edge cities" throughout America, often understood as a kind of spontaneous eruption of uncontrollable, mobile capital, have a set of rules and rational behind their forms. Joel Garreau, author of a book on the subject, abstracts a set of "laws" that have a general consensus amongst edge city developers. These include: how far people will walk; how fast they will walk past a shop window; how many residents should live in a certain circumference of a mall; how many stories an American will climb by stair; how much parking space is required for the average worker; what levels of density create traffic problems; and how to name subdivisions ("named after whatever species are first driven out by construction.")[17]

Changing Existing Codes and Conventions

Many municipalities have begun to claim that their municipal codes, which ostensibly govern abstract planning issues such as parking, FAR, height and setbacks, etc., are having adverse impacts on quality of life. The critique of sprawl by the New Urbanists clearly supports this position. Recently, a number of architects have been hired by municipalities, usually through progressive Planning Departments, to analyze existing codes and recommend revisions. In some municipalities, the entire zoning code is discarded and replaced with new types of ordinances.

Dan Solomon's Residential Design Guidelines for the City of San Jose, completed in 1986, was an early example of code rewriting. The population of San Jose had doubled between 1965 and 1985, and most of the housing built at the periphery consisted of isolated enclaves of walled subdivisions. Solomon's guidelines sought to not only govern the urban impact of specific buildings, especially in terms of garage placement, setbacks, orientation, and massing, but also to address "the public realm created by ... dwellings in aggregation." The guidelines were intended to improve the physical sense of neighborhoods and public open space by governing the "internal relationships between individual dwellings, groups of dwellings, common open space, streets, circulation, and parking."[18]

Similarly, the architectural firm Correa Valle Valle (CVV) recommended revisions to the municipal code for the City of Coral Gables, one of the finest examples of a planned suburb in the southeast United States. The City was concerned that the qualities of the neighborhood were being eroded by recent development. CVV analyzed the original intentions of the town "founder" George Merrick from 1925 and studied the evolution of the Coral Gables zoning code over the subsequent years. They began by noting that the zoning code of 1994 was eighteen times longer than that of the 1946 code, demonstrating that the quantity of regulations did not manifest a correlating accumulation of wisdom. Typological analyses of the original houses and the more recent suburban models were compared. Based on this comparison of such issues as setback, encroachment, ground coverage, garage location, height, etc., a series of recommendations were proposed for the modification of the existing building code.

Rather than modifying existing codes, dozens of municipalities have replaced or overlaid their zoning code with a version of a "Traditional Neighborhood Design" ordinance as developed by Duany Plater-Zyberk (DPZ).[19] This generic code is essentially a recapitulation of New Urbanist charter principles, emphasizing mixed-use neighborhoods of limited size, walkable, interconnected streets, a network of open spaces and parks, and civic buildings distributed on important sites throughout the neighborhood. Buildings are required to line streets, and a variety of housing types are encouraged. DPZ's original Traditional Neighborhood Development consisted of generic descriptions of Block Types, Open Space Types, and Thoroughfare Types, all elements which evolved subsequently into their *Lexicon*. The TND ordinance is simple and reductive because it is intended as a collection of guidelines, not designs. The best designers have challenged and transformed them into specific formal proposals containing variety and ambiguity. It is too early too tell, however, if the development industry will simply replace one set of norms (conventional suburban design) with another (traditional neighborhood design).

Sometimes the rewriting of the codes is presented as a rhetorical device for displaying the relative value of Traditional Neighborhood Development in general, and specific regulatory revisions in particular. For instance, Dover Kohl designed two versions of a hypothetical build-out of a 583 acre site in Mt. Pleasant, South Carolina: a "sprawl scenario" and a "town scenario." A computer model was developed by the Charleston Harbor Project, a group funded by the National Oceanic and Atmospheric Administration and administered by the South Carolina Department of Health and Environmental Control, to test surface water pollution by simulating runoff, or nonpoint source pollution. The sprawl scenario was developed using conventional suburban techniques: all of the

developable land was utilized and uses were separated. Housing in zones of single-family houses were separated from commercial areas. Conventional road widths, parking requirements, and lot sizes were assumed. The town scenario, on the other hand, assumed the same amounts of residential, commercial, and industrial space, but increased the housing densities and mixed uses in keeping with Traditional Neighborhood Development principles. The open space of 400 acres under the town scenario was over ten times greater than that of the sprawl scenario. The experiment also determined that surface water pollution was greatly reduced in the town scenario. The advocates of this project hope that the regional government will revise its codes to reflect the Traditional Neighborhood Development principles as a means of best accommodating an expected increase of 170,000 people by 2015. At a federal level, they hope better water runoff policies, linked to development patterns, will be implemented to reduce nonpoint source pollution. (figs. 5–8)

In the early 1990s the Regional Plan Association (RPA) developed similar "visual sim-

5–8. Comparison of two types of development. Using the same amounts of program, a "sprawl scenario" of a neighborhood and its mall (figs. 5, 6) were compared to a "town scenario" configured around a town center (figs. 7, 8). The comparison was intended to study and compare surface water pollution for a 583 acre site, Belle Hall, in Mt. Pleasant, South Carolina. (Dover Kohl and Partners, 1995)

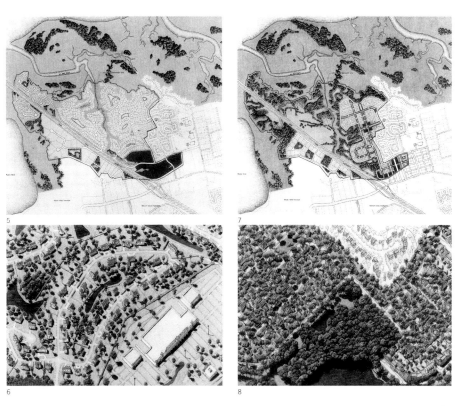

5

6

7

8

Regional Design Program
Regional Plan Association

11A

Suburban Commercial Strip Before Development: Commercial strip along a suburban state highway. Super markets, fast-food restaurants, small office buildings and gas stations compete loudly with neon signs and billboards for the dwindling business along the roadway. Traffic congestion is severe as a result of the many individual access roads creating chaotic driving conditions. Several of the stores have recently gone out of business and the strip is suffering from a decline resulting, in part, from the visual blight, traffic congestion and poor overall shopping environment that results from a prior lack of good planning and design.

Regional Design Program
Regional Plan Association

Suburban Commercial Strip After Typical Development: While s undeveloped land further on down the highway, which is zoned strip commercia as homes, fields and woodlands are removed to create new expanses of aspha congested and less safe as a result of total dependence on the automobile and overhead utility wires, and glaring floodlights destroy, in a frenzy of unrestra enjoyed by this formerly civilized landscape.

a

11B

Copyright © Regional Plan Association/Dodson Associates 1991

ousiness in the foreground, new shopping centers are established on previously
h. The commercial strip continues to invade nearby residential neighborhoods
ractive commercial buildings. Traffic along the state highway becomes more
w more commercial access drives onto the main road. Billboards, neon signs,
he little remaining beauty, environmental quality and historic character once

Regional Design Program
Regional Plan Association

11C

Suburban Commercial Strip After Recommended Development: To accommodate the same amount of development shown in the previous panel, increased development densities are allowed in distinct centers along the highway, shown in the foreground and the distance, separated by expanses of rural or low density development. Increased zoning densities, investments in infrastructure and site planning and design guidelines in the development centers designated along the former strip provide incentives for landowners and developers to build a mix of new commercial, office and multi-family residential buildings organized around a new system of internal streets. Many of the existing commericial buildings are kept and renovated to fit into the new commercial center. Access roads to businesses along the highway are organized at key intersections, helping to reduce traffic congestion. Additional parking required by the expanded commercial center is handled through a combination of structured parking garages and carefully screened parking lots located behind the buildings. Placement and design of buildings creates a strong edge of buildings along streets to provide enclosure and scale.

b

c

Previous pages:
9 a–c. Suburban
Commercial Strip,
Regional Plan Association
(RPA), New York, 1990.
These diagrams are
typical of a series of
triptychs by the RPA
to illustrate the
consequences of future
conventional suburban
development, and the
superiority of new
regulations they
recommended. For this
"suburban commercial
strip," the RPA shows the
existing conditions (a),
a scenario after typical
development (b) in which
the parking lots further
erode the street,
and a scenario
of buildings and streets
after recommended
development (c).

ulations" for growth in the states of New York, New Jersey, and Connecticut. Based on real sites that ranged from urban to rural, the RPA represented in aerial perspectives existing conditions, scenarios for continued growth based on conventional development, and growth scenarios according to the RPA's recommended development guidelines. Each vision for recommended development was accompanied by a description of the revised codes.[20] (figs. 9 a–c)

New Project Codes

Coding has been adopted by many architects as the generative armature of master plans for new projects. The code translates the intentions of the master plan into a collection of specific guidelines for builders and architects. Particularly in new towns and neighborhoods, where there are very few existing conditions or constituencies, the vision of the design team as translated through the code is most uncompromisingly realized. Seaside, for example, is essentially a physical embodiment of its code. Yet the variation within the code, and the interpretation by different designers, produce a remarkable amount of variety within.[21]

The projects which most clearly follow the code and conform to the original master plan vision tend to be those implemented under the auspices of a benevolent developer, or "town founder" in New Urbanist parlance, such as Robert Davis at Seaside, or Vince Graham at I'on outside Charleston, South Carolina. These are developers who intimately understand all aspects of making a place, including the design of buildings, public spaces and streets, as well as implementation and financing strategies to facilitate these anomalous (to developers) projects. Few developers are professionally trained to produce these kinds of places. While Robert Davis gained much of his knowledge from studying the evolution of Siena on a Rome Prize sojourn, Vince Graham measured the streets of his favorite historic towns in South Carolina for inspiration.

For the majority of projects which lack such a benevolent developer, the build-outs most consistent with the intent of the plan occur under the guidance of a "town architect" who oversees and approves all projects and ensures conformance to the code. DPZ has successfully installed such an office in their projects at Windsor and Kentlands, for example. The urban design firm Urban Strategies, author of numerous master plans, also advocates the idea of "community design centers" which are semiautonomous organizations which help implement the principles of their urban strategic plans over the course of years.

The use of a code to integrate and govern the design of Seaside was a significant departure from the recent history of modern architecture. Although technical codes were accepted as necessary for efficient urban development, design codes were viewed by architects as "suspect and philistine devices of control" that undermined the creative genius of individual architects.[22] But the simple one-page code of Seaside (fig. 10) was remarkable for its brevity and abstraction, and actually encouraged a fair amount of architectural interpretation. The code, even in its architectural details, was primarily in support of an *urban* vision. Like Olmsted one hundred years earlier, DPZ recognized the importance of the aggregate of private dwellings in creating the public and communal aspects of a place. The Seaside Code creates the public spaces, particularly those of the street (fig. 11), by stipulating particular "urban regulations" for the architecture. Within particular lots, or "classes" of lots, development is regulated within five categories: yard, front porch, out-buildings, parking, and building height. Another code, the "architectural regulations," was produced primarily at the insistence of the developer, but it too was brief and relatively abstract. It does not govern styles, but stipulates aspects of roofing (pitch and material), windows (vertical proportions), and materials (only natural materials—"no material may imitate another"). The code allows for architectural experimentation and diversity (figs. 12, 13), and any general conformity to a vernacular style has been initiated by clients, not the code.[23]

The emphasis on developing projects through codes can be seen as both a radical adjustment in the representation of architecture and town planning, as well as a conceptual change in the conception of the "project." Codes do not stipulate an entire "designed" project, with each building designed in detail. Rather, the code fixes certain infrastructural aspects of the design, such as streets, blocks, platting, and open spaces, and governs the parameters of others. The establishment of the urban infrastructure, whether of small urban infill or a large new town, allows for a project's realization by many participants over a long duration of time. A level of conformity to the original vision is thereby ensured through the interpretations and expressions of individually designed elements.

These codes can therefore be seen as an attempt at a new synthetic proposal for balancing the community (unity through parameters of code) with the individual (freedom of architectural expression). In a similar vein, the codes indicate a resolution between two alternative tendencies in American suburb design: mass-produced housing in masterplanned subdivisions and the custom design of single-family houses. The new towns stipulated by codes reflect both the lineage of Levittown as well as the more rural Jeffersonian emphasis on individual dwellings. New Urbanists believe that codes will provide, in the words of noted town planner John Nolen, "safeguards against incongruity."

The evolution of codes since Seaside has primarily been developed by New Urbanist architects, and particularly DPZ, who have strived most persistently to standardize code conventions. Their codes are often taken as standards for other architects and planners, especially after the publishing of their *Lexicon*. The fixed aspects of a project are typically presented in a *regulating plan* which establishes the infrastructure of the plan, such as the pattern of streets and blocks, platting (the size and allocation of lots), "public spaces" (streets, squares, parks, etc.), and the location of any "public" buildings. (fig. 15) Platting is often color coded by use—different kinds of residential (low and high density), commercial, and civic, etc. This vision of neighborhoods as a mosaic of separate uses, however, is still very much a typical modernist diagram, and falls short of representing New Urbanist claims of more complex and integrated neighborhoods. The transect zoning of DPZ, based on type not use, is an attempt to overcome this representational shortcoming. An *illustrative plan* (fig. 14) is an example of a hypothetical development of the site according to the code and standards.

The *urban standards*, like those of the original Seaside Code, establish certain guidelines for buildings that physically define the public realm as well as "influence social behavior."[24] Thresholds between public and private, such as garages and driveways, porches and entrances, etc. are emphasized. Physical guidelines, such as setbacks, encroachments, height, and frontage lines are ascribed to different building types. These guidelines are typically represented in a matrix or series of diagrams.

The *thoroughfare standards* determine the design of the streets as both public spaces and transportation conduits. Typically, the stan-dards stipulate type (boulevard, street, alley, etc.), design speed of car movement, number of lanes, kind of parking, right-of-way width (between property lines), lane width, curb radius, planter and sidewalk width, type of curb, and type and spacing of street trees. They are often based on the best examples of existing local streets. Such references help clients understand the physical parameters of the new streets, as well as serve as an effective counter to traffic engineer's who claim such new streets are substandard. (figs. 16, 17)

Other standards that can be incorporated into a code are *architectural standards*, which in the best examples are short (one-page) suggestions for particular abstract qualities of building form and material. Landscape standards, use standards, environmental guidelines, and frontage standards are suggested as code conventions in DPZ's *Lexicon*.

The pattern book has reemerged as a device that combines abstract code issues with specific architectural guidelines. Urban Design Associates has developed a number of these pattern books, including for projects they did not masterplan. UDA's pattern books combine architectural details and form with guidelines for the urban disposition of building in a larger plan. There are also more prosaic examples, simply catalogs of building plans, typically emphasizing "traditional" styles. The architectural conservatism associated with New Urbanist town planning is clearly evident in these pattern books. (figs. 18, 19)

Establishing New Conventions

Another target for those interested in the reformation of settlement patterns are the conventions of existing professional and policy-making organizations. Over the past decade, advocacy groups interested in stopping what they see as the devastating effects of sprawl have increasingly garnered national support and attention. These groups include, besides the Congress for New Urbanism, Livable Communities, Smart Growth, and national environmental organizations. They advocate systematic policy changes to manuals, bylaws, educational programs, and other means of institutionalizing and disseminating knowledge.

The ubiquitous manual of architectural convention, *Graphic Standards*, now has a seven page category describing the forms and processes of town planning. Architects from the Congress for New Urbanism have worked with Henry Cisneros and Andrew Cuomo, consec-

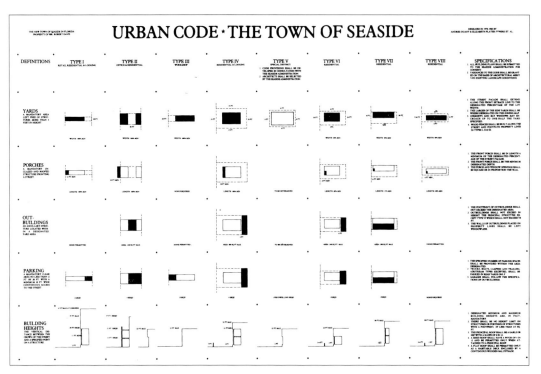

10. The "Urban Code" for the Town of Seaside, by Duany Plater-Zyberk and Company, 1982, stipulates requirements for different building types. The code is primarily concerned with those building elements that "directly affect the public realm."

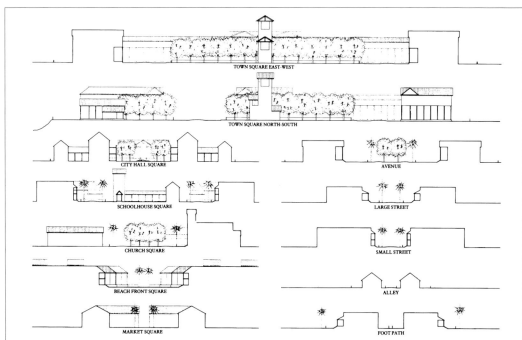

11. Prototypical Street Sections, by Duany Plater-Zyberk and Company, 1982, accompany the Seaside Code and reveal the emphasis on the town's public spaces, ranging from a central square to pedestrian footpaths at the center of blocks.

12. Appell House at Seaside, Victoria Casasco, Architect, 1987–89. (Photo: Stephen Brooke)

13. Chatham House at Seaside, Walter Chatham, Architect, 1987–88. (Photo: Stephen Brooke)

utive heads of the Department of Housing and Urban Development (HUD), to rewrite the guidelines for new public housing in America. These new guidelines, known as Hope VI, are having an impact not just on social housing policy, but on urban infill and renewal in general. The Urban Land Institute, a powerful and conservative organization which establishes building conventions for developers, has now incorporated traditional neighborhood development into its handbooks. A small group of progressive traffic engineers led by Walter Kulash have rewritten the Institute of Traffic Engineers' (ITE) manual with New Urbanist principles, undermining some of the most entrenched professional standards that affect our cities and suburbs today.

Since the policies of municipalities affect development patterns at a local level, a number of architectural and planning practices are oriented to assisting municipalities gain the tools and knowledge to better structure and direct future growth, as well as ameliorate the effects of past sprawl. They include small firms, such as Thomas Comita Associates in Pennsylvania, larger firms, such as Urban Strategies in Toronto, and non-profit institutes such as The Design Center for American Urban Landscape, associated with the University of Minnesota. William Morrish and Catherine Brown of the Design Center co-authored *Planning to Stay*, which teaches residents and merchants to see and as-

sess their neighborhood environment, and provides specific steps for community planning.

Reestablishing architectural conventions is the goal of much of the Congress for New Urbanism (CNU). As discussed in more detail in Chapter Two, the CNU is attempting to redefine the practice and methods of the architectural profession. Their principles are disseminated in books, reports, seminars, and annual congresses, where, like CIAM half-century ago, case studies are presented and discussed. The *Lexicon of the New Urbanism*, written by DPZ, is among the most grandiose attempts at restructuring the language and ideas of urban development in recent decades. (See Case Studies) But in aiming at a wholesale restructuring of development patterns and representational techniques, the *Lexicon* and codes presented by the New Urbanists are confronting the tremendous inertia of existing conventions. Although definite inroads have been made, it is still too early to assess their impact. Perhaps the most far-reaching effect will be the revelation of the relationship between policy conventions and physical form.

14. Illustrative plan
of neighborhood center,
Quemazon, Los Alamos,
New Mexico (Moule
and Polyzoides Architects
and Urbanists with Lloyd
Tryk Architects, 1997).

15. Regulating plan,
Quemazon, Los Alamos,
New Mexico (Moule
and Polyzoides Architects
and Urbanists with Lloyd
Tryk Architects, 1997).

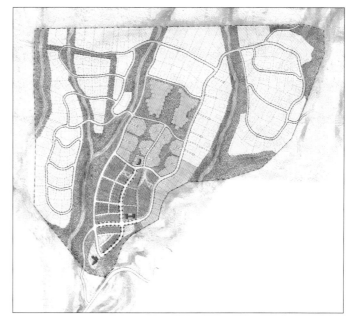

[1] See especially the first chapters of Eric Mumford, *The CIAM Discourse on Urbanism, 1928–1960* (Cambridge, Mass.: The MIT Press, 2000).

[2] From the La Sarraz Declaration of CIAM, reprinted in José Lluís Sert, *Can Our Cities Survive? An ABC of Urban Problems, Their Analysis, Their Solutions* (Cambridge, Mass.: Harvard University Press, 1942), 242.

[3] Witold Rybczynski, *City Life: Urban Expectations in a New World* (New York: Scribner, 1995), 29, 44, 58.

[4] Leonardo Benevolo, *The Birth of Modern Town Planning*, 4th ed., trans. Judith Landry (Cambridge, Mass.: The MIT Press, 1980), xi.

[5] *Ibid.*, 44–50.

[6] Raymond Unwin, *Town Planning in Practice* (1909; reprint, New York: Princeton Architectural Press, 1994), 4.

[7] See letter from Frederick Law Olmsted to the Riverside Improvement Company, September 1, 1868 in S.B. Sutton, *Civilizing American Cities: Writings on City Landscape* (New York: Da Capo Press, 1997), 302–303.

[8] Gwendolyn Wright discusses this history of private architecture and public domestic environment. See Gwendolyn Wright, *Building the American Dream* (Cambridge, Mass.: The MIT Press, 1995), xv.

[9] Kenneth T. Jackson, *Crabgrass Frontier* (New York: Oxford University Press, 1987), 177–178.

[10] For a comparison of Perry's "neighborhood unit" with New Urbanism's "traditional neighborhood district," see Chapter One, illust. 3.

[11] Michael Southworth and Eran Ben-Joseph, *Streets and the Shaping of Towns and Cities* (New York: McGraw Hill, 1997), 89–91.

[12] The 1939 Underwriters Manual declared that "crowded neighborhoods lessen desirability" and "older properties in a neighborhood have a tendency to accelerate the transition to lower class occupancy." As quoted in Kenneth T. Jackson, *Crabgrass Frontier* (New York: Oxford University Press, 1987), 207.

[13] Jackson, 205–209.

[14] Michael Southworth and Eran Ben-Joseph, *Streets and the Shaping of Towns and Cities* (New York: McGraw Hill, 1997), 89–91.

[15] The first zoning code was created in Los Angeles in 1907. New York's code was created in 1916. But the mindset of use separation is really from CIAM.

[16] The traffic engineer who has most advanced these notions, which are slowly gaining widespread acceptance, is Walter Kulash of Glatting Jackson.

[17] Joel Garreau, *Edge Cities: Life on the New Frontier* (New York: Doubleday, 1991), appendix.

[18] From the report issued by Solomon Architecture for the Residential Design Guidelines of San Jose, 1986.

[19] Andres Duany and Elizabeth Plater-Zyberk, "The Traditional Neighborhood Ordinance," *The New City* 2 (1994), 142–151.

[20] Regional Plan Association with Introduction by Raymond Gastil, "Visual Simulations: The Future of the Tri-State Region," *The New City* 2 (1994), 128–141.

[21] As the town in the movie *The Truman Show*, Seaside was misrepresented as more uniform, and traditional, than it actually is. No modern buildings were shown, for example, and the rather sublime and unruly native landscape was replaced by lawns (prohibited at Seaside).

[22] Neil Levine, "Questioning the View: Seaside's Critique of the Gaze of Modern Architecture," in David Mohney and Keller Easterling, *Seaside* (New York: Princeton Architectural Press, 1991), 240–255.

[23] "The code for Seaside is strong typologically and weak architecturally; most people don't realize that. The architectural code is very informal, having to do with the use of real materials, minimum sizes for the rafters, and so on. Seaside looks the way it does largely because individual residents have commissioned certain styles. There are some modernist buildings at Seaside—but they're not very popular. In our experience, what happens when you free up the architectural code is that people tend to choose vernacular architecture." Andres Duany interviewed for "Urban or Suburban?," A discussion held at the Graduate School of Design in July 1996, and published in *Harvard Design Magazine* (winter–spring 1997), 47.

[24] See *The Lexicon of the New Urbanism* (Duany Plater-Zyberk & Company, 1999), M-2.

83

16, 17. Example of Thoroughfare Standards for Miles Point in St. Michaels, Maryland, that are based on local street precedents (Duany Plater-Zyberk and Company, 1998).

 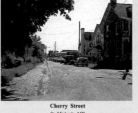  

	Talbot Street St. Michaels, MD	Cherry Street St. Michaels, MD	Grace Street St. Michaels, MD	Locust Street St. Michaels, MD
Type	Commercial street	Residential street	Residential street	Residential road
Movement	Free movement	Free movement	Yield movement	Yield movement
Traffic Lanes	Two way	Two way	Two way	Two way
Parking Lanes	One side	One side	One side	One side
R.O.W. Width	59 ft.	33.5 ft.	24 ft.	18 ft.
Pavement Width	34 ft. +/-	28.5 ft.	20 ft.	18 ft.
Curb Type	Header	Header	Header	Open section
Curb Radius	25 ft.	15 ft.	5 ft.	5 ft.
Vehicular Design Speed	30 m.p.h.	30 m.p.h.	15 m.p.h.	15 m.p.h.
Pedestrian Crossing Time	8 seconds	4.4 seconds	4.4 seconds	4 seconds
Sidewalk Width	9 ft. & 14 ft.	5 ft.	N/A	N/A
Planter Width	4 ft.	N/A	N/A	N/A
Planter Type	4 x 6 ft.	N/A	N/A	N/A
Tree Pattern	30 ft. on center	Varies	Varies	Varies
Tree Species	Varies	Varies	Varies	Varies
Ground Cover	Varies	N/A	N/A	Lawn

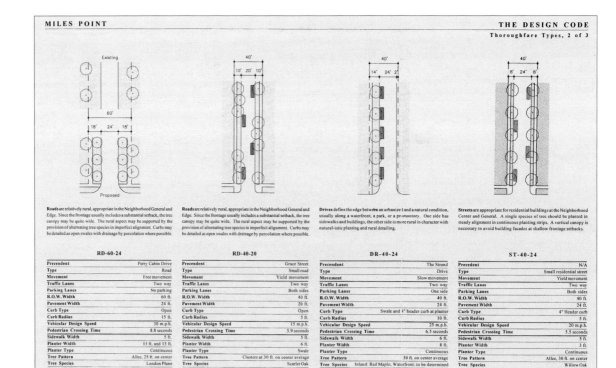

Roads are relatively rural, appropriate in the Neighborhood General and Edge. Since the frontage usually includes a substantial setback, the tree canopy may be quite wide. The rural aspect may be supported by the provision of alternating tree species in imperfect alignment. Curbs may be detailed as open swales with drainage by percolation where possible.

Roads are relatively rural, appropriate in the Neighborhood General and Edge. Since the frontage usually includes a substantial setback, the tree canopy may be quite wide. The rural aspect may be supported by the provision of alternating tree species in imperfect alignment. Curbs may be detailed as open swales with drainage by percolation where possible.

Drives define the edge between an urbanized and a natural condition, usually along a waterfront, a park, or a promontory. One side has sidewalks and buildings, the other side is more rural in character with natural-istic planting and rural detailing.

Streets are appropriate for residential buildings at the Neighborhood Center and General. A single species of tree should be planted in steady alignment in continuous planting strips. A vertical canopy is necessary to avoid building facades at shallow frontage setbacks.

	RD-60-24	RD-40-20	DR-40-24	ST-40-24
Precedent	Perry Cabin Drive	Grace Street	The Strand	N/A
Type	Road	Small road	Drive	Small residential street
Movement	Free movement	Yield movement	Slow movement	Yield movement
Traffic Lanes	Two way	Two way	Two way	Two way
Parking Lanes	No parking	Both sides	One side	Both sides
R.O.W. Width	60 ft.	40 ft.	40 ft.	40 ft.
Pavement Width	24 ft.	20 ft.	24 ft.	24 ft.
Curb Type	Open	Open	Swale and 4" header curb at planter	4" header curb
Curb Radius	15 ft.	5 ft.	10 ft.	5 ft.
Vehicular Design Speed	30 m.p.h.	15 m.p.h.	25 m.p.h.	20 m.p.h.
Pedestrian Crossing Time	8.8 seconds	3.9 seconds	6.5 seconds	5.5 seconds
Sidewalk Width	5 ft.	5 ft.	6 ft.	5 ft.
Planter Width	13 ft. and 13 ft.	6 ft.	8 ft.	3 ft.
Planter Type	Continuous	Swale	Continuous	Continuous
Tree Pattern	Allee, 25 ft. on center	Clusters at 30 ft. on center average	30 ft. on center average	Allee, 30 ft. on center
Tree Species	London Plane	Scarlet Oak	Inland: Red Maple; Waterfront: to be determined	Willow Oak
Ground Cover	Lawn	Lawn	Lawn	Lawn

© 1998 Duany Plater-Zyberk & Company
Revision Date August 27, 1998

40

18, 19. Excerpts from the pattern book for Liberty, on Lake Elsinore in California. The pages describe the location, placement, and guidelines for the "Cottage Lots." (Urban Design Associates, 1999)

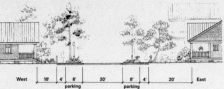

The Cottage District

The Cottage District is a two-block-long street, lined with cottages, that runs from the beach to the lake. The corners of streets are defined with two-story houses, that serve as gateways and make the transition from the larger buildings at each end of the street. The front porches and landscape provide shade and an intimate neighborhood character.

West Side (Cottage Lots)

Main Body Types
For (**A**) lots, one- or one-and-one-half-story Single cottages; for (**C**) lots, two-story Side Hall houses

House Placement
Front porches are to be placed on the Front Yard Setback Line, 10 feet from the front property line. Wrap-around porches, towers and tall elements are encouraged on corner (**C**) lots.

Colors
A range of gray and neutral colors, from cool to warm, with trim and special elements in more colorful tones; see Section E.

East Side (Cottage Lots)

Main Body Types
For (**A1**) lots, one- or one-and-one-half-story Single cottages; for (**C**) lots, two-story Side Hall houses

House Placement
Front porches must be built on the Front Yard Setback Line. Corner lots (**C**) have a 10-foot Front Yard Setback. Mid-block houses on the east side of the street (**A1**) have a 20-foot Front Yard Setback. Wrap-around porches, towers and tall elements are encouraged on corner (**C**) lots.

Addresses – The Cottage District

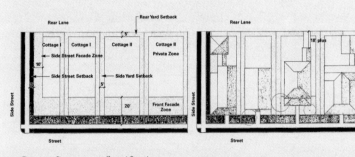

Cottage Lots I & II Specifications

Lot Size
Cottage I lots are 40 feet wide. Cottage II lots are 50.

Main Body
The width of the Main Body of the house shall be a maximum of 30 feet for Cottage I and 40 feet for Cottage II lots.

Front Yard Setback
Front Facade Zone
The depth of the Front Yard is typically 10 feet from the front property line to the Front Yard Setback Line, unless noted otherwise in the Address section. The Front Facade Zone extends 20 feet from the Front Yard Setback Line. The

front porch shall be placed as close to the Front Yard Setback Line while siting the house to preserve as many trees as possible.

Side Yard Setback
Minimum 5-foot setback from the side property line

Side Street Setback
Side Street Facade Zone
Structures shall be set back a minimum of 5 feet from the side street property line, unless noted otherwise in the Address section. The Side Street Facade shall be defined by the side facades of the Main Body and any Rear Wings or Out-buildings. Wraparound porches are

encouraged on the Main Body. Where there is no building structure, the Side Street Facade shall be delineated by a fence or hedge. Houses on corner lots shall have a garage, carport, or other out building placed on the Rear Yard Setback line within the Side Street Facade Zone.

Rear Yard Setback
All structures shall be set back a minimum of 5 feet from the rear lane right-of-way.

Encroachments
Only porch steps may extend into the Front Yard and Side Street Setback Zone.

Out Building Requirements
Garages and carports shall be set back either 5 feet from the rear property line or a minimum of 18 feet. Garages may be either detached or attached to the Main Body by a one-story rear wing. Garage doors opening onto public streets are not permitted.

Building Placement – Cottage Lots

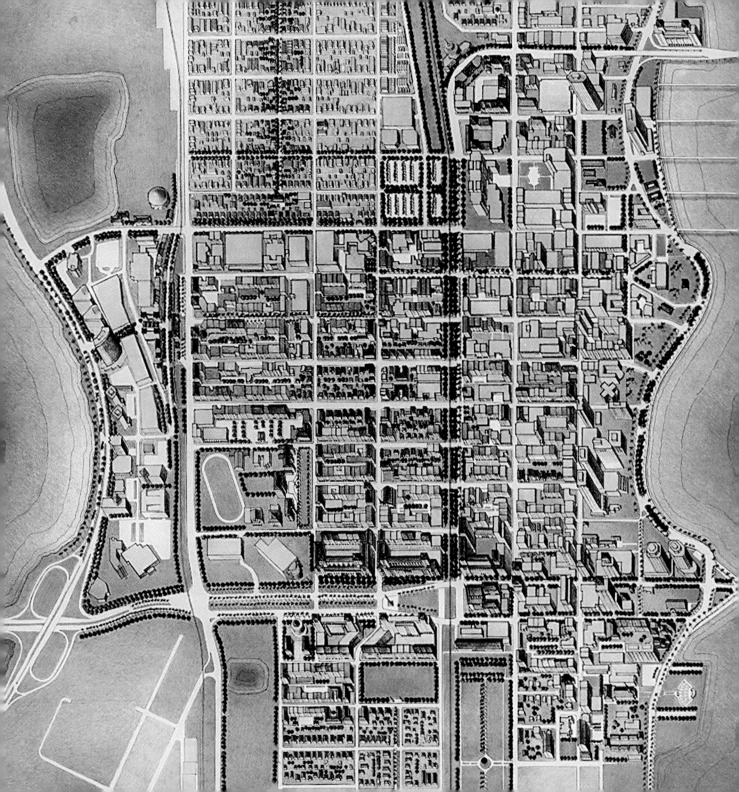

Chapter Five

Insertions, Deletions, Edits:
Retrofitting Suburbs and Cities

For much of the post-World War II era, the conventional method of urban reconstruction has been a simple yet crude policy of wholesale clearance and rebuilding. In the last two decades, however, as architects have reexamined their profession's relationship to the city and suburb, new kinds of architectural interventions have emerged. These are projects in which contemporary urban planners and architects attempt to restructure the existing urban and suburban patterns and establish new models of incremental growth for future urbanization.

Significantly, architects and planners have begun focusing their attention not only on cities, which have long been the site of modern attempts at reform, but on suburbs. New Urbanists in particular, by establishing a scaled "transect" of development based on density, from agrarian hinterland and villages to metropolitan regions and cities, have expanded the site of architectural intervention to include all forms of settlement patterns. Suburbs, dismissed by Le Corbusier and CIAM (Congrès Internationaux d'Architecture Moderne) as insignificant development, are now recognized by architects as important embodiments of late twentieth-century culture that require similar architectural methodologies and practices as cities.

As the suburban model became the dominant form of development over the past decades, its patterns of development have invaded traditional urban areas. Certainly there still exist traditional urban cores as well as classic low-density residential suburbs. Yet more frequently traditional forms of land development are overlapping and coalescing with sprawl development into hybrid forms of urbanity.[1] The hierarchy of city center and periphery, so important in defining the original suburbs, is dissolving in many places. Although some core cities have remained powerful job centers and coveted locations to live, others have imploded under disinvestment and the flight of capital and jobs to the periphery. How then do architects build in this new kind of sub-

urban/urban melange? This chapter will look at the various strategies for intervening in this suburban metropolis.

A growing number of architects, engineers, and planners have begun reconceiving the design of cities and suburbs as an integrated design process balancing many functions (ecology, built form, housing, open space distribution, transit, etc.). Although the re-emphasis on town-planning ideas by New Urbanists is based on a traditional notion of a unified whole, a kind of ideal "town" like Seaside, its principles and priorities are also being applied to the reformation of the more inchoate places existing today. This chapter will explore different approaches to reforming this suburban metropolis through interventions at various scales—from the entire city to a commercial center or corridor to a block or building. Indeed, because connections are implied between the region, the city, the block and the building, operating at one scale necessarily affects the others. At each of these scales, the idea of retrofitting, of selective and nuanced editing, stands in contrast to the large-scale clearance of late-modernist planning. Such a policy valorized large architectural projects—projects the size of blocks and greater— over incremental rebuilding of the selective parts of the city.

The projects in this chapter approach the reformation of the existing built environment in two ways; restructuring and interventions. The first term relates to strategic alterations of existing policies that affect the overall urban infrastructure. Restructuring can also be initiated through the creation of new strategic visions that generate a framework for future growth. The first part of this chapter will examine these attempts in the form of strategic master plans. The second part of the chapter focuses on interventions, that is infill projects that incrementally rebuild a suburb or city. These interventions, usually one or a few buildings, contribute to a larger urban reform, and can serve as a catalyst and example for future development. Finally, the chapter will conclude by look-

Axonometric plan for West Palm Beach, Florida, by Duany Plater-Zyberk and Company, 1993, as part of their neighborhood revitalization plan.

ing at the transformation of some new suburban types that have emerged in the last half-century. In particular, the single-use suburban pods of malls, public housing, and office parks represent some of the most challenging and topical sites today.

Strategic Master Plans

A strategic plan is a vision for a place which balances a wide range of issues, such as housing, transportation, and economic development, within a physical framework of design. It is typically a compilation of diagrams, analyses, plans, proposals, and implementation strategies. This kind of broad reformist vision, presented under the auspices of urban design and architecture, is a legacy of modernist planning ideals. The New Urbanist strategic plans in particular balance technical demands of the functional city with the aesthetic aspirations of making places. They are a hybrid between the abstract and analytical methodologies of late-modern planning and the picturesque and vernacular tendencies of the English Garden City Movement.

The implementation of the strategic plan occurs through numerous incremental projects, rather than one large master project. Yet the size of the individual projects can be misleading. Strategic plans leverage a disproportionate amount of work: they can be completed within one year, but may direct development for years and decades to follow. The process of consensus building means that a constituency will more likely assume responsibility for the implementation of the plan, long after the departure of the architects. The numerous public workshops and presentations are used to educate the constituents, teaching them to see their city in new ways.

Strategic plans therefore depend on a multitude of people, from residents to government officials, who have a hand in shaping the plan. Such a diverse constituency, as well as the need to balance competing goals (social housing, economic development, downtown revitalization, traffic flow, homelessness, crime, etc.) leave the plan open to political and architectural compromise. Even plans that are adopted can prove difficult or contentious to implement. For this reason, the best plans are often open-ended and adaptable. Because these plans, unlike urban renewal, are implemented in piecemeal fashion—plot by plot, building by building, street by street—they tend to be flexible. This allows for reassessment and changes in strate-

gic investment over time. For each project within the scope of a strategic plan, individual owners, developers, and architects add their own interpretation rather than constructing *a priori* determined designs.

New Urbanists in particular use Strategic Plans as an effective means of promoting their urban agenda. Although each plan is different and addresses a unique set of conditions, they reinforce similar goals: identify and reinforce neighborhood identities, clarify hierarchy and pattern of streets and open spaces, balance the demands of automobiles with other forms of mobility (pedestrian, transit, etc.), respect historic building typologies, and encourage a mix of housing types and uses. Strategies for future infill are proposed, usually structured around a code. Sometimes specific *catalytic projects* are suggested, which are exemplary individual projects intended to spark development.

Urban Strategic Plans

Compared to the more disruptive proposals of urban renewal, recent strategic plans are inherently conservative. They seek to preserve the traditional urban structure and enhance the identity of existing neighborhoods. The policy of sanitization and clearance, so prevalent with urban renewal, has been replaced with a more complex orchestration of strategies within a given urban fabric.

Clients of urban strategic plan are typically large municipalities who have suffered over the past decades because of the flight to the suburbs and the subsequent disinvestment in their metropolitan area. The plans are often instigated by a coalition of downtown merchants and residents, as opposed to a governmentally imposed policy. Past decisions regarding freeway and roadway building, public housing projects, rigid zoning of uses, and new buildings, which destroyed the historic fabric of a place, are commonly cited in the plans as typical problems. In many cases, a large single-use district has become obsolete—a military base, factory, industrial waterfront, or hospital, for example—and becomes the impetus for rethinking a city's future growth.

In the strategic plan for St. Paul, Minnesota, Ken Greenberg of Urban Strategies reconnected the city's downtown to the Mississippi River to fill the void after its waterfront industries had relocated. Greenberg proposed extending the city block structure to accommodate new mixed-use, high-density neighborhoods. Through public workshops, his

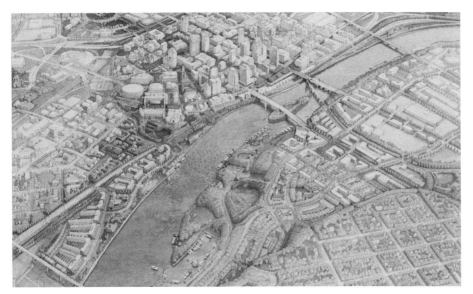

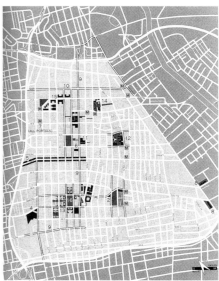

1. Aerial perspective
of Saint Paul, Minnesota,
by Urban Strategies,
1996–97.
The Strategic Plan focuses
on redeveloping the areas
along the river after
the waterfront industries
had relocated.

2. Diagram of catalytic
projects for Downtown
Strategic Plan,
Los Angeles, by Moule
& Polyzoides Architects
and Urbanists, 1993.
These sixteen mixed-use
projects are intended
to stimulate the social,
physical and economic
transformation
of downtown Los Angeles
as part of a larger
strategic plan.

"Framework Plan" developed goals in four areas: the environment, urban structure, movement networks, and the public realm. Precinct plans for key areas in the downtown and along the waterfront were developed, and specific development opportunities were identified block by block. (fig. 1)

For the Strategic Plan of downtown Los Angeles, Moule & Polyzoides and a team of consultants also established a framework for future development. Their plan enhanced the identity of six neighborhoods, and created a system of open space and street connections to promote pedestrian movement between them. With the infrastructure established, they then proposed "catalytic projects" for the neighborhoods to spark private development and urban identity. (fig. 2)

Duany Plater-Zyberk created the strategic plan for the City of West Palm Beach in 1993. The plan first calls for the preservation of the vast heritage of historic buildings and trees, as well as preserving and enhancing existing neighborhoods, districts, and corridors identified in the charrette. Proposals for the redesign of streets, including paving, lighting, street trees, and façade guidelines, were intended to make them more comfortable and attractive for pedestrians. Infill housing was encouraged, and architectural proposals were made for the infill of particular sites. Such proposals also including block restructuring and suggestions for specific housing types. Retail

strategies were coupled with these urban and architectural guidelines in an effort to revitalize the downtown shopping district. (opening illustration)

Neighborhood Revitalization

Similar to urban strategic plans are neighborhood revitalization strategies for towns and older suburbs. These projects often focus on places which are having difficulty absorbing changing retail and residential patterns of development—often the "sprawl" development that New Urbanists criticize. The revitalization plans are not attempts to stop development, but to channel it into particular forms and locations. The kinds of complaints that a community commonly makes when engaging a neighborhood revitalization plan are diverse but often share common themes: new shopping centers, strip malls, or office parks that disrupt the form and pattern of the community; street improvements geared to the car, which have led to increased traffic and paved areas that erode the original scale and pedestrian quality of a community; new residential cul-de-sac development of monotonous and poorly designed housing with little connection to the original community; new houses in existing neighborhoods that dramatically flout neighborhood scale and character; no central public spaces or sense of "downtown;" decaying public infrastructure; and the demise of the original business district due to the draw of regional malls at the periphery. Often there is pressure from demographic changes which demand different forms of housing or public space for their needs. As strategic plans, these projects balance the goals of educating a community, establishing principles, reworking neighborhood infrastructure, and proposing specific architectural interventions.

Facilitating discussion and action at the local level in small towns and suburbs has been the focus of the Design Center for American Urban Landscape, founded by architects Catherine Brown and William Morrish, at the University of Minnesota. The Center educates communities so they can make their own choices regarding preservation and development. Through handbooks, workshops, and analytic studies, the Design Center teaches people how to "see" the structure of their own community, particularly the relationship of physical design to a larger environmental, social, and economic context. Similar Design Centers that focus on local communities exist throughout America, often in association with universities, like those at the University of Kentucky, University of Mississippi, and the former Urban Innovations Group founded by Charles Moore at UCLA. But the Design Center has perhaps been the most successful at connecting theories of community design to practice, and has subtly but critically shifted the focus from specific physical designs to giving communities the methodological tools and insight necessary to create future projects for themselves.

In their community handbook, *Planning to Stay*, Morrish and Brown teach residents to analyze their own neighborhoods in terms of houses, gardens, streets, "anchoring institutions" and "neighborhood niches." The book leads the reader through a series of questions and explanations that help residents understand the structure of their particular town or suburb, from general planning issues to specific architectural issues. Under the chapter "Homes and Gardens," for example, the authors ask questions that pertain to house location and siting, scale, building types, and movement between the house and the town. The larger scale questions are oriented around the neighborhood: where is your neighborhood located? Is it near downtown, clustered with other neighborhoods? Are there primary destinations nearby? How does the neighborhood's location affect its residential quality of life?[2]

In recent work, the Center has focused on the question of first-ring suburbs. These res-idential enclaves that originally surrounded downtowns now find themselves in a geographic middle between older, often decaying, downtowns and newer suburban development and edge cities at the periphery. Such a position has significant physical and social implications. "The first ring faces, among other pressures, an aging built environment, degraded natural systems, and increasingly anaemic demographics. Yet it also enjoys a wealth of resources, and now sits in an ideal spot in the region—halfway to jobs and amenities in both directions."[3] The Center assists these suburban communities in coordinating economic, housing, land-use, natural resources, and transportation policies, such as in their North Metro I-35W Corridor Study of seven communities outside of Minneapolis. Through research, analysis, public workshops and discussions, the Design Center established principles for these communities to better plan neighborhoods and housing. At the end of the study, GIS mapping, sociodemographic profiles, natural feature analysis, and analyses of development patterns revealed specific redesign opportunities. Sites for housing infill, new town center locations, street corridor enhancement, and landscape restoration opportunities were identified.

An example of an older neighborhood on the urban periphery suffering from high vacancy and disinvestment is Greenlaw-Manassas, in Memphis, Tennessee. A plan for this 160 square block neighborhood, just north of downtown, was designed by Looney Ricks Kiss (LRK). Greenlaw-Manassas is an area of mainly working-class residents who commute the short distance downtown. LRK's plan calls for the renovation of existing housing stock, the construction of new single-family and multifamily housing in a variety of types, maintaining and restoring where necessary the historic block structure and street grid, and better defining the edges of the neighborhoods through boulevards and greenways. Besides housing, the architectural proposals include a new community center, a light-rail station, and street and pedestrian furnishings and enhancements. (fig. 3)

Similar principles were developed for the South Carolina city of Port Royal, where Dover Kohl prepared a code for infill development based on the historic fabric of the town. Their code calls for new infill housing that conforms to local historic building types, size, form, architectural language, and relationship to the street. All new streets are designed with sidewalks, and garages are situated off rear alleys.

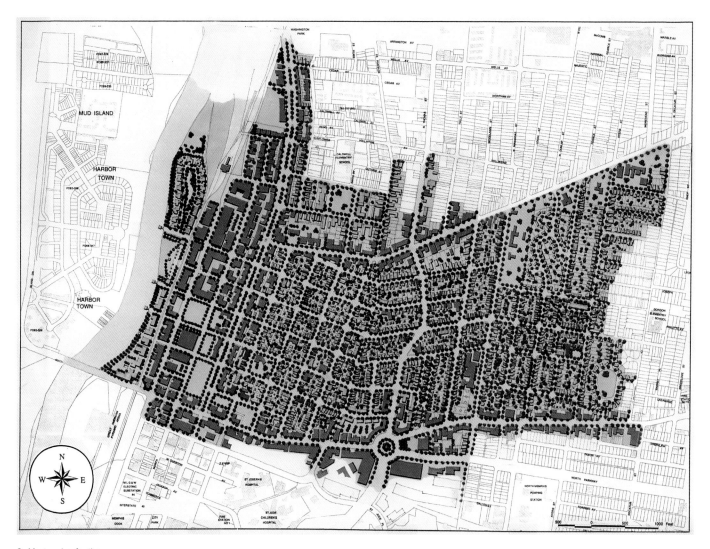

3. Master plan for the revitalization of Greenlaw-Manassas neighborhood, Memphis, Tennessee, by Looney Ricks Kiss Architects, 1997–98.

The Master Plan for
PORT ROYAL

IDEALIZED BUILDOUT

TOWN OF PORT ROYAL, SOUTH CAROLINA
Founded 1562
DOVER, KOHL & PARTNERS
Urban Design

.1995.

Dover Kohl strengthened the importance of the main strip as a civic place through landscape and redesign of the right-of-way, the placement of civic buildings, and architectural guidelines for future infill that require minimal setbacks from the street. (fig. 4)

Addressing the devastating effects of the construction of highways and widening of roadways through towns is a common goal in these neighborhood revitalization plans. Duany Plater-Zyberk (DPZ) confronted two such situations in pilot projects for a regional plan for Onondaga County, New York. In the town of Liverpool, the historic downtown has been split in two by a roadway previously widened and straightened to accommodate high-speed through-traffic. Similarly, a "parkway" along the adjacent river formed a barrier between the town and the river. DPZ's plan to restore the town center focused almost entirely on these two roadways. First, they proposed to create a bypass around the town from the parkway to a parallel interstate. In this way the riverfront area can be reclaimed as a linear waterfront park accessible from town. Secondly, in an effort to make the center of town more pedestrian friendly, they narrowed the number and size of lanes of the wide downtown roadway and pro-

vided head-in parking. Minor adjustments to the street grid also created a second triangular green, better pedestrian connections between the adjacent neighborhoods and downtown, and a prominent site reserved for a future civic building. (fig. 5) In a second pilot project, for the town of Bayberry, a large arterial bordered by strip malls created a vast chasm between the two sides of the town that was only traversable by automobile. This roadway was transformed into a boulevard section with coordinated access points to the vast parking lots bordering the roadway. Most ingeniously, a large shopping center, set back hundreds of feet from the arterial behind a parking lot, was turned around to face a new "Main Street" at the back. The design of this new street created two triangular greens, like at Liverpool, and provided pedestrian connections to the adjacent residential neighborhoods. (fig. 6)

Campus Master Plans

The principles and methodologies of strategic plans are equally applicable to the college campus. Superb examples of historic American urbanism can be found in the balanced design of buildings and open spaces of campuses such as University of Virginia, Union

5. Master plan for
Liverpool, New York,
by Duany Plater-Zyberk
and Company, 1999.

6. Detailed plan for
Bayberry, New York,
by Duany Plater-Zyberk
and Company, 1999.
The scheme turns existing
"big box" retail around
so it faces a new street
and park instead
of a parking lot.

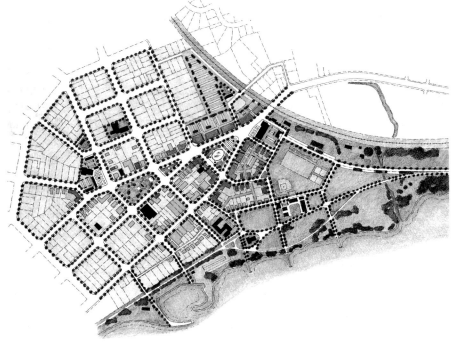

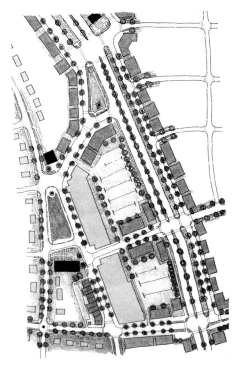

College, or Scripps College. In the past decades, many campuses have experienced the same problem as towns and cities. Planning policies have encouraged "object-buildings" that have eroded the carefully defined relationship of building, fabric, and pedestrian-intensive open spaces, like the college quadrangle. The dominance of the car and the influence of suburban planning often result in campuses of isolated buildings surrounded by parking lots connected to internal access roads. Many of the architects interested in town planning are, not surprisingly, engaged in campus design. There are, of course, many architects beside those strictly labeled New Urbanists, like Machado and Silvetti, Koetter Kim, or Michael Dennis, who have a deep appreciation of urban space and create sensitive and intelligent campus plans. In fact, the idiom of modern architecture has been able to be absorbed into the traditional college campus much more easily than in American suburbs and town centers. (figs. 7–11)

Infill
Transit-oriented Districts

Transit Oriented Districts (TOD's), as introduced in Chapter One, are dense, mixed-use developments oriented around transit stations. Their size and features generally resemble the New Urbanist's "Traditional Neighborhood Design." In their ideal embodiment, TOD's are conceived as urban nodes linked by transit to form larger regional networks. Presently, such regional plans are difficult to implement for most metropolitan areas, however, because of a lack of regional authority, municipal coordination, and public support.

Peter Calthorpe is perhaps the best known and most persistent advocate of TOD's. Most of his larger regional plans are structured on the improvement or creation of lightrail and other transit, and the selective densification of areas along transit lines. Such a policy, Calthorpe claims, maximizes the amount of people who can function without a car, and most efficiently develops land so that large areas can remain undeveloped as open space and ecological resources.

For Clackamas Town Center, presently consisting of two large shopping malls surrounded by surface parking, Calthorpe proposed a TOD as part of his Portland 2040 Regional Plan (see Case Studies). Calthorpe's plan presents two scenarios for development along a proposed light-rail route. (figs. 12–14) A low-intensity scenario is based on the introduction

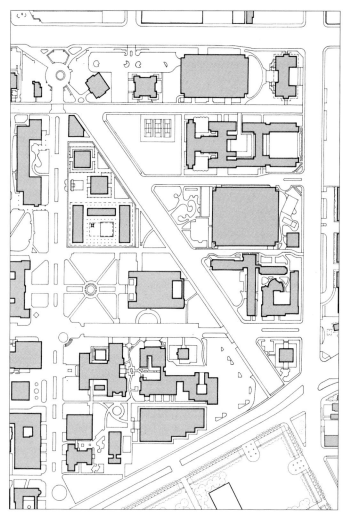

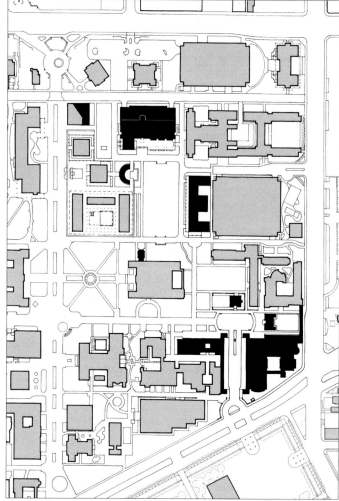

7. Existing campus plan
of the University of
Southern California,
Michael Dennis
and Associates.

8. Proposed campus plan
of the University
of Southern California,
Michael Dennis
and Associates,
1992–93.
The project reorganizes
the public open space
by locating new buildings
to provide two new
quadrants
of the university.

9. Figure ground analysis of the master plan for University Park, Massachusetts Institute of Technology, Koetter Kim & Associates, 1988.

10. Master plan for the new 43 acre Mission Bay campus of the University of California, San Francisco, Machado & Silvetti Associates, 1999.

11. View of new building as part of the University Park master plan, Massachusetts Institute of Technology, Koetter Kim & Associates. Completed 1990. (Courtesy: Koetter Kim & Associates)

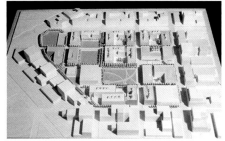

12. Existing Plan
of Clackamas,
a suburb whose center
is defined by two large
malls, Calthorpe
& Associates.

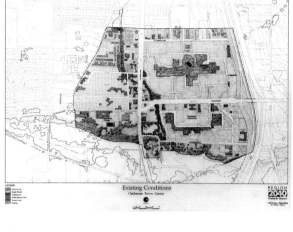

13. Lower intensity plan
for suburban infill,
Clackamas Town Center,
Oregon, Calthorpe
& Associates, 1994.

14. Higher intensity plan
for suburban infill,
Clackamas Town Center,
Oregon, Calthorpe
& Associates, 1994.

of 1,800 dwelling units and 3,900 jobs, and a high-level intensity plan projects 29,000 dwelling units and 4,600 jobs. The lower-intensity plan focuses on a series of moderate interventions on empty parcels and parking lots, and leaves most of the existing parcelization and street configuration. The plan connects the two malls into a continuous pedestrian "Main Street" supported by the surrounding surface parking. Mixed-use buildings are gathered and distributed along the primary streets.

The high-intensity plan, on the other hand, envisions much greater structural changes to the parcelization and streets. The two mall sites are broken up into smaller blocks; parking is located in structures lined by commercial buildings at their perimeter; and defined open spaces, such as parks and squares, are distributed throughout. The seven-lane arterial is split into a one-way couplet to make the street less of a barrier, as well as to create a "transit and civic center" between the two halves of the couplet.

Large-scale Infill

Three projects illustrate the approach to large-scale urban infill. The first is Liberty Harbor North in Jersey City, designed by Duany Plater-Zyberk (DPZ). (fig. 15) The project is located on an 80 acre brownfield site on the Morris Canal across the Hudson River from lower Manhattan and the Statue of Liberty. It will contain housing of urban density (100 units per acre), commercial, entertainment, and hotel uses, as well as two schools. The second is Crawford Square, a 500 unit mixed-income housing redevelopment on the edge of downtown Pittsburgh by Urban Design Associates (UDA). (figs. 16, 17) The third is a reconstruction plan for downtown South Miami by Dover Kohl and Partners. (figs. 18, 19) Similar principles and methodologies were used in all three projects, yet they represent three different intensities of infill: South Miami is fairly urbanized already, Crawford Square, immediately adjacent to downtown, had few existing buildings and many vacant lots, and Liberty Harbor is almost entirely new construction.

The existing street and block structure is maintained in the Crawford Square and South Miami projects, although a few new streets were necessary to restore continuity in the grid and to break up over-sized blocks. In the case of Crawford Square, the existing street grid was fairly intact, and only one street was added. UDA used this opportunity to design a small median park, bordered on each side of the street with a continuous wall of townhouses. South Miami has a street and block network that is also relatively intact. One large superblock to the north is broken up with new streets that connect to the existing surrounding streets. Alleys were also added for service and access to parking within the block. Although the street grid was maintained at Crawford Square and South Miami, the right-of-ways were entirely redesigned: reconfigured travel and parking lanes, new planter strips, sidewalks, street trees, furniture and lighting, and revised setbacks for building fronts. On the other extreme is Liberty Harbor, with no existing network of streets. DPZ employed a street grid similar in scale to nearby Greenwich Village, and oriented it toward views of the canal, the World Trade Center, and the Statue of Liberty.

In all three schemes, buildings are given continuous and minimal setbacks to reinforce the primacy of the street as a public space. UDA uses the rhythm of closely spaced single-family houses, duplexes, and rowhouses to define the streets and a new park at the center of the neighborhood. Dover Kohl's scheme relies on a finer grain of judicious infill, as well as perimeter-block buildings to mask surface parking lots within the block. Dover Kohl also "wraps" the existing buildings to create more unified frontages along the street. The continuous fabric of buildings helps define smaller dedicated squares and plazas in lieu of the existing diffuse and unformed open spaces and parking lots. DPZ tested the principles and flexibility of their code with outside architects during the charrette. (figs. 20, 22)

Of the three, Liberty Harbor North is the most urban in character and scale, although Dover Kohl's scheme has an intensity appropriate for Miami's suburban-scaled metropolis. Crawford Square is the least dense, and relies on a more traditional image of low-density urban neighborhoods and first-ring suburbs. One has to remember, however, that urban density can be realized just as easily through continuous three and four-story buildings, as evidenced in San Francisco, Boston's Back Bay, or Manhattan's West Village.

Infill at the Scale of Building and Block

Infill at the scale of the building and block incrementally lays the foundation of urban space. Elizabeth Moule, one of the founders of New Urbanism, has said that two buildings next to each other are an architectural project, but two buildings across from each other are an urban project, for it begins to define the public space of the street. Although New Urbanists clearly promote the relationship between small-scale infill and town planning, many architects have practiced urban architecture that is sensitive to a larger urban context. The urbanism of infill depends on typological sensitivity, and can accommodate a wide range of architectural styles. In European cities today, with their rich, layered history of urban structure, juxtapositions of styles are often harmoniously accommodated in the urban fabric. Design issues such as streetwall, circulation, access, massing, height, and setbacks, for example, are not the domain of any one style.

The examples of infill presented here all are mixed-use buildings, primarily residential with some street-level retail. In each case, buildings are positioned at the street edge, which allows for an urban consistency that is either echoed in the continuity of the façade, as in Solomon's Vermont Village, or permits more dramatic manipulation of building massing, as in Rob Wellington Quigley's 202 Island Inn. RTKL's Cole's Corner holds the block's corner as a solid mass, while Vermont Village and Michael Pyatok's Hsmin Nu have permeable façades with walkways leading to interior courts. (figs. 21, 23–27)

Street and Corridor Renovation

Streets and corridors are another site of architectural intervention in recent American urbanism. The design of streets is no longer automatically relegated to traffic engineers, who have been the professionals with perhaps the greatest impact on the form and character of post-World War II American towns and cities. With their single-minded goal of moving traffic as efficiently as possible, traffic engineers have created vast systems of roadways designed from manuals of performance standards. Most are inhospitable to pedestrians and active street life. Now, more progressive traffic engineers and designers are collaborating on the design of streets in more sophisticated and subtle ways. Right-of-way design might include reconfiguring the number of lanes devoted to traffic, the addition of on-street parking, the size of sidewalks and planter strips, the selection of street trees, and the design of street furniture like light poles, seating, trash cans, etc. Malls, surprisingly, with their absolute control over the aesthetics of their interior spaces, have greatly influenced street design and helped set

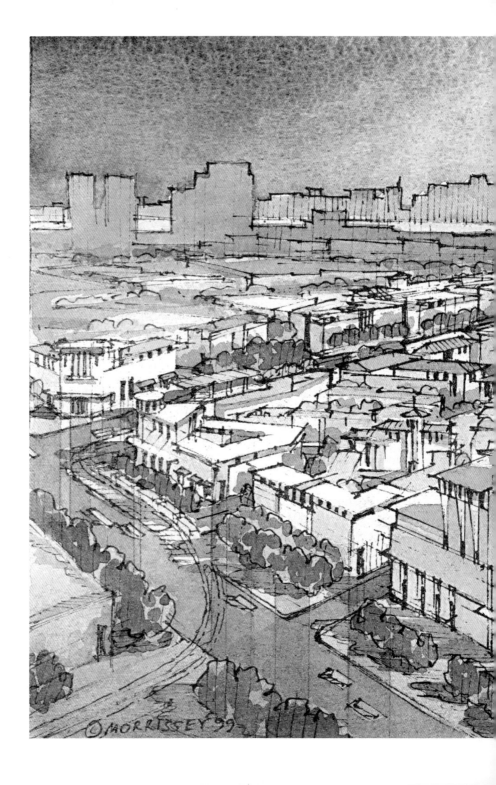

15. Aerial perspective of Liberty Harbor, New Jersey, by Duany Plater-Zyberk and Company, 1999. This 80 acre brownfield site is developed with high, urban densities.

16. Previous conditions of Crawford Square, Pittsburgh, Pennsylvania, Urban Design Associates.

17. Completed infill development of 500 mixed-income housing units at Crawford Square, Pittsburgh, Pennsylvania, Urban Design Associates. Completed 2000.

18. Existing plan of downtown South Miami, Florida, by Dover Kohl and Partners.

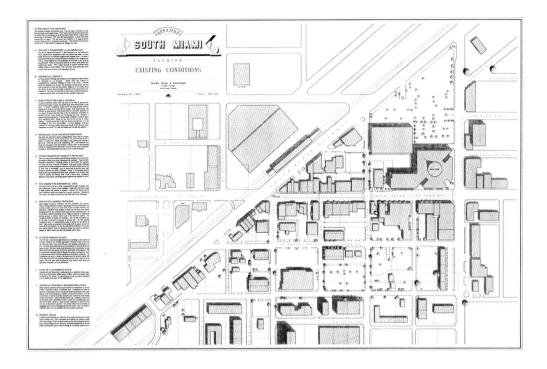

19. Hypothetical roof plan showing urban infill strategies, downtown South Miami, Dover Kohl and Partners, 1993.

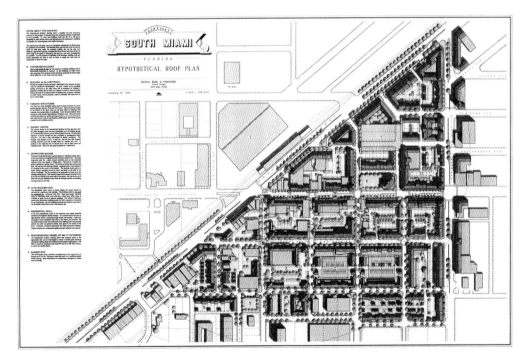

20. Rowhouses designed according to proposed code, Liberty Harbor, Alexander Gorlin Architects, 1999.

21. 202 Island Inn, San Diego, California, Rob Wellington Quigley. Completed 1992. (Photo: David Hewitt/Anne Garrison)

22. Typical waterfront blocks designed according to proposed code, Liberty Harbor, Victoria Casasco, 1999.

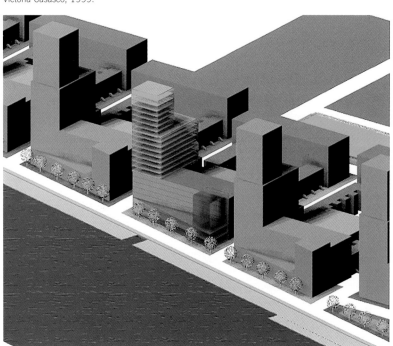 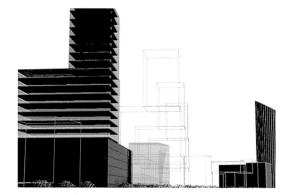 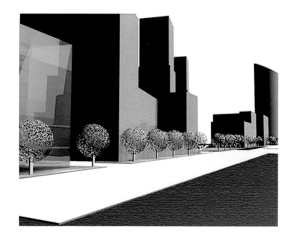

23. Plan of Vermont Village, South Central Los Angeles by Solomon Architecture. The project includes 36 owner-occupied houses and townhouses arranged around a series of walkways and courtyards, and ground-level retail facing the street.

24. View from street of Vermont Village by Solomon Architecture. Completed 1998. (Photo: Grant Mudford)

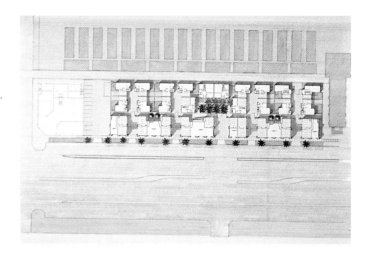

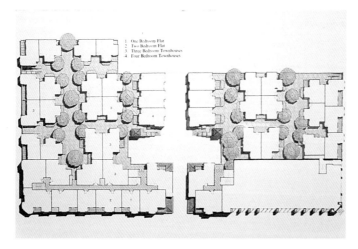

25. Plan of Hsmin Hin-Nu, Oakland, California, Michael Pyatok Associates. This block-sized building with interior courtyards contains 92 units of senior and low-income housing, small vendor retail space along the street, a daycare center, and a community center.

26. View from street of Hsmin Hin-Nu, Oakland, California, Michael Pyatok Associates. Completed 1995.

27. View of Cole's Corner, Texas, by RTKL, a four-story mixed-use development. Completed 1997. (Courtesy: RTKL)

new standards for the current pedestrian-oriented districts. (figs. 29, 30)

The redesign of corridors, including not just the street but the buildings along it, also demonstrates the newfound importance of streets as public urban spaces and structure. Corridor plans can allow for incremental growth of infill in diverse urban situations. A collection of smaller projects are more easily phased over time, often by different developers and architects. The West Main Street Corridor redesign in Charlottesville, for example, connects the University of Virginia to downtown. The designers, William Rawn Associates, knitted together University uses, such as residential colleges, with community uses, such as a community center, a park, a hotel, a new train station, and parking. (fig. 28)

Reworking Existing Pieces of the Suburban Metropolis

A number of large, single-use types have emerged in the past decades that are currently undergoing transformation. These isolated, often car-oriented, projects have proven to be untenable, and the architectural response has been to transform them into connected parts of an urban structure. They tend to be comprised of large, inflexible buildings on vast lots, and so require wholesale transformations rather than the incremental changes which prove more effective for existing cities and suburbs. New Urbanists in particular have identified these sites as important targets of architectural reformation. Their goal has been to transform these large single-use projects into complex, mixed-use, and fine-grained neighborhoods.

Public Housing

With the advent of the Hope VI program, the Department of Housing and Urban Development (HUD) ended its policy of isolating public housing urbanistically and architecturally from the rest of the city. The Secretary of the Department at the time, Henry Cisneros, was a founding signer of the Congress for New Urbanism's Charter and borrowed its principles as public housing guidelines. The Hope VI program funds replacement housing as part of new neighborhoods that integrate themselves into their urban context. The requirement for a mix of housing types and the goal of attracting residents from different income levels, standard New Urbanist principles, does mean, however, that there is often a shortfall of low-income replacement units. Although the success of the

DOWNTOWN
CHARLOTTESVILLE

WEST MAIN STREET
DISTRICT

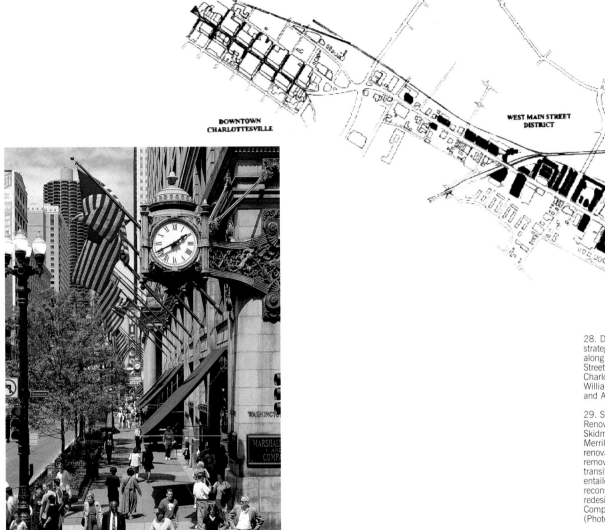

WASHINGTON

MARSHALL
AND
COMPA

28. Diagram showing strategic interventions along the West Main Street Corridor, Charlottesville, Virginia, William Rawn and Associates, 1993.

29. State Street Renovation, Chicago, Skidmore Owings & Merrill. The nine block renovation project, which removed the unsuccessful transit mall built in 1979, entailed a complete reconstruction and redesign of the roadway. Completed 1999. (Photo: James Steinkamp)

30. Plan of Canon Drive, Beverly Hills District Enhancement, Moule & Polyzoides Architects and Urbanists, 1993.

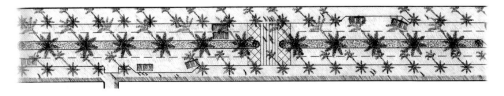

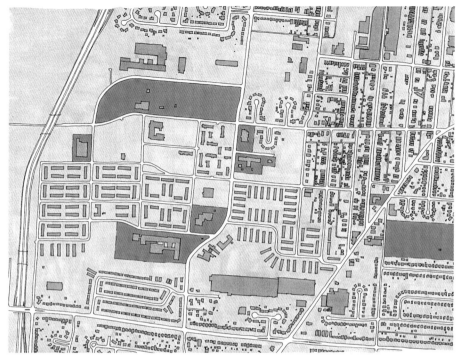

31. Existing plan of Park Du Valle, Louisville, Kentucky, by Urban Design Associates.
The site was dominated by two urban-renewal era public housing projects and a badly deteriorating apartment complex.

32. Master plan of Park Du Valle, Louisville, Kentucky, by Urban Design Associates, 1995.
The form of the new infill public housing, inspired by traditional Louisville neighborhoods, has a street and block structure supporting smaller-scale residential and mixed-use development.

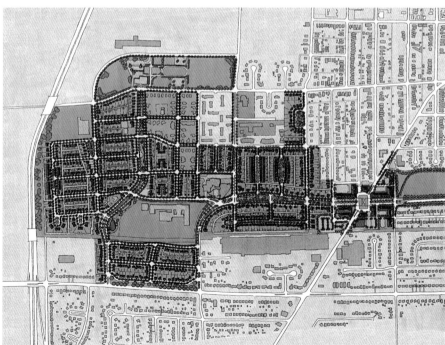

33. Existing plan of Churchill Neighborhood, Holyoke, Massachusetts, Calthorpe & Associates with The Community Builders and Dietz Architects

34. Proposed Plan of Churchill Neighborhood, Calthorpe & Associates, 1996–97. This project, part of the federal Hope VI program, seeks to revitalize not just the failed public housing projects, but the entire inner-city neighborhood.

program is still too young to gauge, the lack of sufficient replacement social housing indicates the limits of a strictly architectural solution to ameliorating social conditions.

The dramatic differences between the existing projects and the new Hope VI projects is illustrated by Park Du Valle in Louisville, Kentucky, designed by Urban Design Associates; Churchill Neighborhood Revitalization Plan in Holyoke, Massachusetts, designed by Calthorpe Associates; and Pleasant View Gardens and Lexington Terraces, two projects in downtown Baltimore, Maryland, designed by Torti Gallas CHK. (figs. 31–37)

In each case, the original public housing was comprised of isolated slabs or towers within large "superblocks," legacies of urban renewal inspired by Le Corbusier's early vision of tower slabs floating in landscaped open space. These public housing projects were designed to have little if any relationship to the existing street and block network. The original city structure, usually dismissed as "slums," was cleared and "sanitized" in service of a grand urban vision. This heroic view of isolated housing blocks as architecturally progressive solutions to social housing crises crumbled with the demolition of the failed flagship housing project Pruitt-Igoe. Its death was officially proclaimed with the launching of Hope VI.

Each of the Hope VI projects illustrated here aims to create a new but integrated piece of the city to erase the physical and social barriers previously separating social housing from the rest of the city. In contrast to the diffuse space surrounding isolated buildings in the original public housing projects, the Hope VI plans employ smaller, continuous pieces of multifamily housing to form new streets, blocks, and open spaces. For example, Torti Gallas CHK uses rowhousing, a traditional housing type in Baltimore, as a contiguous form to shape new streets in Lexington Terrace and a central square at Pleasant View Gardens. Rowhousing also allows for some private space behind each unit. Park Du Valle and Churchill use a larger variety of housing types, including rowhouses, duplexes, and triplexes, to a similar effect. These projects also provide neighborhood amenities such as community centers, schools, and parks. As is particularly clear in Park Du Valle, parking is usually located behind the buildings in garages, accessed from a new network of alleys. In all three projects, streets are treated as public spaces, generously planted and designed to encourage comfortable walking, and, where possible, connect to the adjacent street grid of the city. Active pedestrian life and dwelling units facing the street also give residents a heightened sense of security.

The restructuring of public housing does not necessarily require wholesale rebuilding of portions of the city. Urban Design Associates' Diggstown project in Norfolk, Virginia, uses a more subtle approach. (figs. 38–41) The existing site consisted of rows of brick barrack-like buildings distributed within superblocks. The most dramatic transformation came from the renovation of the surrounding open space, a barren no-man's land between the buildings, avoided by the residents because of crime and drug problems. Landscaped streets were added between the buildings, with sidewalks and on-street parking. Each unit was given its own address with front entrance facing the new street. The architectural renovation was

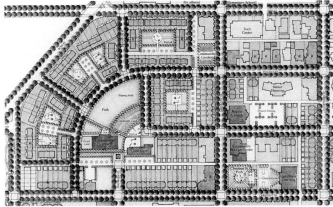

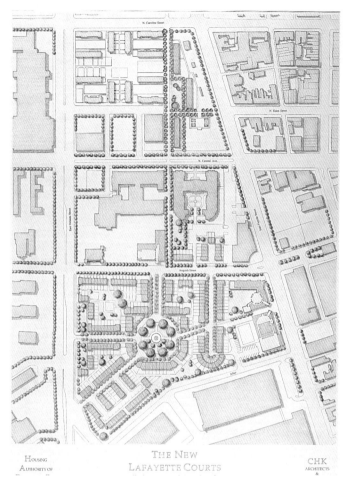

35. Master plan for
Pleasant View Gardens,
Baltimore, Maryland, by
Torti Gallas CHK. This
urban housing project
in Baltimore, Maryland
uses streets, rowhouses,
and open space to create
a new neighborhood
that is organized around
a community square.
Designed 1994.

36. View of Pleasant View
Gardens, Baltimore,
Maryland, Torti Gallas
CHK. Completed 1998.
(Courtesy: Torti Gallas
CHK)

37. Master plan for
Lexington Terraces by Torti
Gallas CHK, a public
housing project in
Baltimore, Maryland,
creates a street and block
pattern that connects
to that of the adjacent
rowhouse neighborhoods.
An existing school, new
recreation/community
center, and square have
become the focal point
of this new neighborhood.
Designed 1994,
completed 2000.

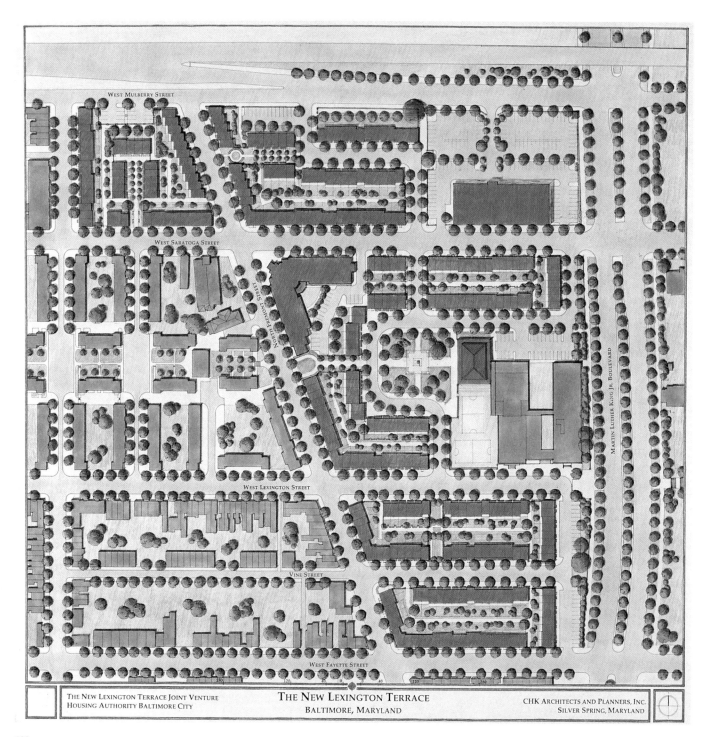

WEST MULBERRY STREET

WEST SARATOGA STREET

NORTH FREMONT STREET

MARTIN LUTHER KING, JR. BOULEVARD

WEST LEXINGTON STREET

VINE STREET

WEST FAYETTE STREET

THE NEW LEXINGTON TERRACE JOINT VENTURE
HOUSING AUTHORITY BALTIMORE CITY

THE NEW LEXINGTON TERRACE
BALTIMORE, MARYLAND

CHK ARCHITECTS AND PLANNERS, INC.
SILVER SPRING, MARYLAND

109

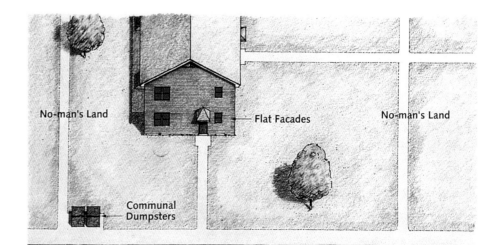

38. Diagram of previous conditions of public housing project, Diggstown, Norfolk, Virginia, Urban Design Associates.

No-man's Land

Flat Facades

No-man's Land

Communal Dumpsters

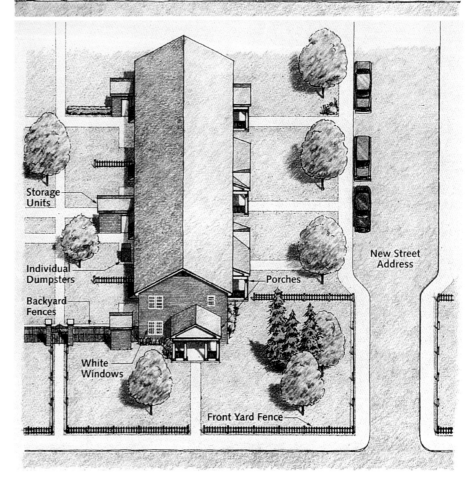

39. Diagram showing the strategic alterations, Diggstown, Norfolk, Virginia, Urban Design Associates, 1992.

Storage Units

Individual Dumpsters

Backyard Fences

White Windows

Porches

New Street Address

Front Yard Fence

40. View of Diggstown before renovations.

41. View of Diggstown after renovations, 1996.

simply the addition of large porches at each unit entrance. This threshold space of the porch provides a semiprivate gathering space for the family as well as a place to survey the neighborhood. And although porches may seem like nostalgic symbols of bygone times to many architects, they were coveted by the lower income families of Diggstown as symbols of middle class respectability. As the social critic Nathan Glazer warns, "one must avoid the danger of building for the poor under regulations or in a style very different from that to which the middle class is accustomed."[4]

Malls and Shopping Center Conversions

Malls and other large shopping centers present potential for dramatically reshaping the suburban landscape. Currently an estimated 20 percent of malls fail annually.[5] There are numerous reasons for their failure, including market usurpation by larger and newer malls further out on the suburban periphery, as well as recent shifts in retail trends toward street retail districts. The failing malls typically occupy large, highly accessible parcels adjacent to existing suburbs. Their accessibility and proximity to existing neighborhoods have made them desirable sites for redevelopment. But malls are often isolated on superblocks, or giant parcels of undivided land, surrounded by great expanses of paved space (parking lots, access drives, loading docks, etc.). They are designed to be accessible only by automobile.

The goal of many of the mall renovations has been the transformation from single-use and isolated structures to mixed-use neighborhoods integrated with the adjacent city or suburb. So far there have been two methods: adaptation of existing structures, and the complete replacement of the mall with new development.[6] In both cases, as in Hope VI projects, the first important action of the designer has been the division of land into an assemblage of urban pieces that can accommodate incremental growth and phased development.

The wholesale reurbanization of Clackamas Town Center (figs. 12–14) and The Crossings (figs. 43, 45), both by Calthorpe Associates, illustrate the strategy of wholesale replacement of the mall. At The Crossings, the mall site was adjacent to a transit line, and so Calthorpe was able to create a Transit Oriented Development around a new transit station. Dover Kohl's plan for Downtown Kendall outside of Miami is an example of adapting the existing mall structure. (figs. 44, 46) The new streets and blocks surrounding the mall correspond to the entrances and pedestrian streets of the mall. New frontage buildings wrap the existing mall to turn it inside out and integrate it with the new neighborhood. The development, previously contained within the interior box of the mall, now focuses on tree-lined streets, small parks, and a river that bisects the site.

A third method of mall revitalization ingeniously combines the two aforementioned strategies. Dover Kohl and Robert Gibbs' plan for Eastgate Mall redevelopment in Chattanooga, Tennessee, outlines a five-phase strategy for slowly altering and selectively demolishing the existing mall, turning it ultimately into a dense, mixed-use urban place. The project turns the mall inside out through incremental reconstructions. The vast parking lots which created a paved moat separating the mall from the adjacent neighborhoods, are developed into connective urban tissue. Both big box and small-scale retail are accommodated in the new urban structure. (fig. 47)

Where new malls are being built, such as Mizner Park in Boca Raton, Florida, similar principles of neighborhood design are being employed. Municipalities are also beginning to demand housing as part of shopping center developments. Big box retailers like Wal Mart, in reaction to mounting community criticism, have tried to develop new models of smaller scaled, street-oriented buildings, that respect the urban quality of a particular place. The Redmond Town Center (fig. 48) is an example of a new mall designed as a pedestrian oriented development that emphasizes outdoor streets instead of interior atriums and promenades. Parking lots are hidden behind stores and offices that line new streets, or in parking structures wrapped in retail space at the street level. The project reflects a more sophisticated way of recasting typical mall elements into new forms with other uses, like office space and hotels. The program is almost identical to that of a small edge city, and is indeed still an isolated "project" primarily accessible by car in its present context. Viewed from within, the image and scale of Redmond is that of Main Street, but an aerial photograph belies the character of small-town romance. (figs. 49, 50)

Office Parks

The proliferation of office space over the past decades has mainly been located within suburbia or on the outskirts of metropolitan cores in "edge cities." The office park, an iso-

42. Previous conditions plan, The Crossings, Mountainview, California, Calthorpe & Associates.

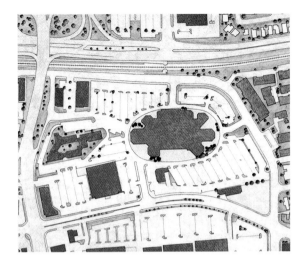

43. Master plan for Crossings, Mountainview, California, Calthorpe & Associates.
The shopping center was replaced with a neighborhood of many housing types, parks and squares, and a new transit station.

44. Master plan for Downtown Kendall, Florida, Dover Kohl and Partners with Duany Plater-Zyberk and Company, 1998. The plan absorbs the mall into a larger urban context.

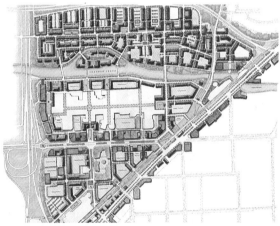

45. Photograph of the Crossings, Mountainview, California, Calthorpe & Associates. Completed 1999. (Photo: author)

46. Aerial view of existing conditions of Downtown Kendall, Florida. The area contains four heavily-traveled, regional roadways that crisscross a high intensity development of mall retail, office buildings, and hotels. (Courtesy: Dover Kohl and Partners)

112

47. Phasing Diagrams
indicating steps
in the conversion
of Eastgate Mall,
Chattanooga, Tennessee,
by Dover Kohl
and Partners
with Robert Gibbs, 1997.

lated, single-use, car-oriented project of generic office space, has formal qualities analogous to the mall, and therefore similar methodologies of urban transformation. Like malls, office parks are emerging as sites to be reworked into mixed-use centers of activity that provide more than just jobs. The loft-like character of the building shells and the immense amounts of appended land (primarily parking lots), should assimilate easily into larger, complex urban neighborhoods. Advocates of this approach claim that with housing, some retail, and transit connections, office parks could be reformed into viable communities.

The Regional Plan Association (RPA) studied the conversion of the office park Forrestal Center in Princeton, New Jersey. (fig. 54) Groups of office buildings along an access drive became the basis for a series of larger neigh-borhoods. In Somerset County, the RPA reworked edge city conditions into a more connected and cohesive urban space. Streets, open space, and new building were designed to transition from large-scale use by the highway to smaller-scale infill development in the residential neighborhoods. (figs. 51, 52) Similarly, the RPA is trying to guide the creation of "suburban centers" which accept much of the existing suburban-scaled development. These centers focus on transit, and although they attempt to provide a level of pedestrian comfort, there is no small-town nostalgia, but rather the pragmatic adaptation of automobile-scaled suburbia.(fig. 53)

The same principles can be applied to new construction in edge cities. RTKL's Addison Circle brings a high density urban neighborhood to an edge city context. The 80 acre

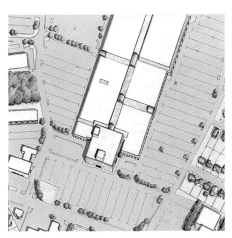
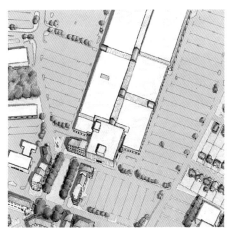
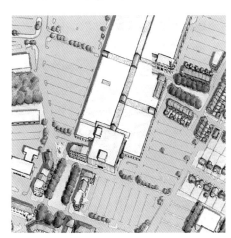

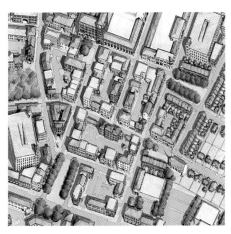

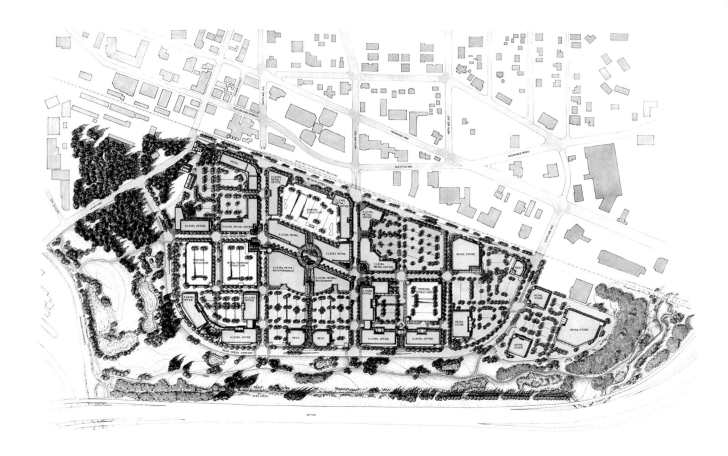

48. Master plan
of Redmond Town Center,
Washington, LMN
Architects, 1999.
Reconfiguring the mall
into a street-retail district,
this complex contains
1.49 million square feet
of retail, as well as office,
entertainment
and commercial uses,
and a hotel.

development attempts to create a community focal point where none previously existed. Open space, usually diffused around free-standing buildings, has been framed as public space by the continuous frontages of new buildings. Streets, usually relegated as access drives and parking lanes in edge cities, become public spaces, lined by retail and residential buildings. (figs. 55–57)

The examples in this chapter indicate the challenges of infilling the suburban metropolis. Sprawl is, by its very nature, difficult to reform. Urban grids usually have a rather fine grain of buildings and street network that can accept any number of building types and uses. But suburbia is built as single-use, isolated structures connected by access roads. It is also typically constructed for short-term occu-

pation by a particular client rather than a long-term commitment to a community. The challenge is to turn such monolithic structures into more heterogeneous, flexible, and permanent parts of neighborhoods. The difficulty of this endeavor is that not only do the forms of sprawl resist easy manipulation, but the urban effects of the transformation to a post-industrial economy are considerable and difficult to sway. Although the New Urbanist predilection for small-scale commercial buildings is compelling for a new generation of entrepreneurs and net-commuters, there is still a need to accommodate the large-scale requirements of the new economy. By starting to address edge cities, big-box retail, malls, etc., urban infill reaches a new scale of structural intervention and contemporary relevance.

49. View of street
in Redmond Town Center.
(Photo: John Gallagher)

50. Aerial view of the
Redmond Town Center
reveals the structural
similarities to a mall
or large edge-city.
(Photo: Skyview Aerial
Surveys)

[1] According to Joel Garreau, 92 percent of people living in
the New York metropolitan area do not live in Manhattan.
The "urbanized" areas are not urban in the traditional sense
at all, with the central city only comprising a fraction of the
larger metropolis. *Edge Cities: Life on the New Frontier* (New
York: Doubleday, 1991), 6
[2] See William Morrish and Catherine R. Brown, *Planning to
Stay* (Minneapolis: Milkweed Editions, 1994).
[3] From *Report on First Ring Suburbs* by The Design Center
for American Urban Landscapes.
[4] Witold Rybczynski, *City Life: Urban Expectations in a New
World* (New York: Scribner, 1995), 168.
[5] "Reviving Dead Malls," *New Urban News* 5, no. 1 (Janu-
ary–February 2000), 10.
[6] *Ibid.*, 10–13.

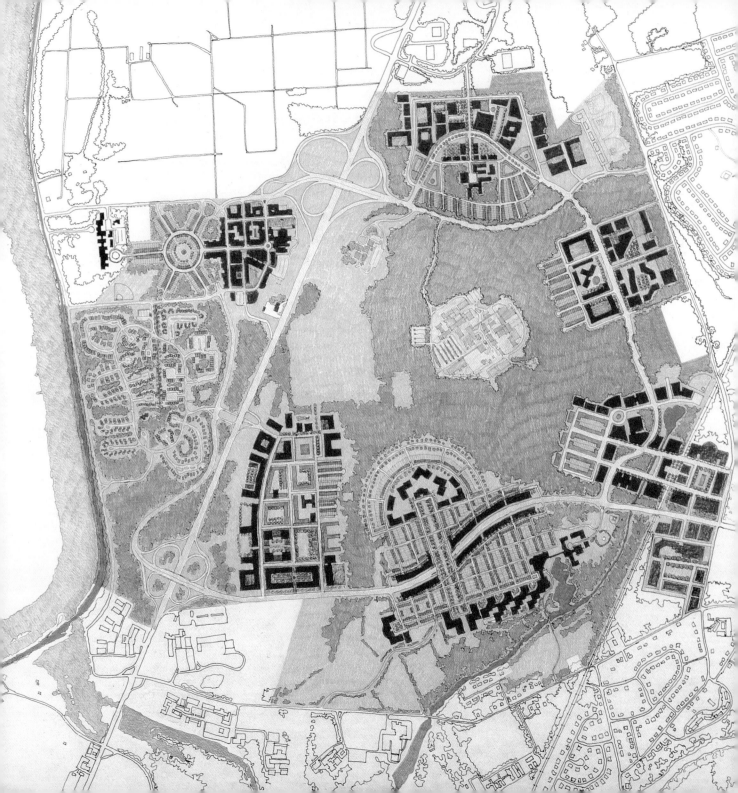

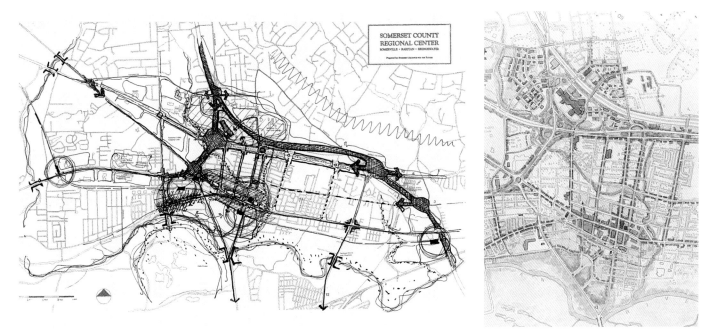

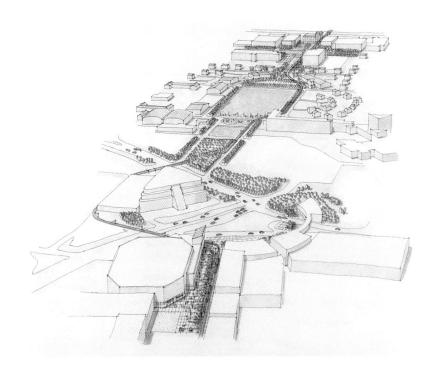

51. Sketch analysis of creating suburban infill, Somerset County Regional Center, New Jersey, Regional Plan Association with Robert Lane, 1999.

52. Master plan for new suburban infill, Somerset County Regional Center, New Jersey, Regional Plan Association with Robert Lane, 1999.

53. Aerial perspective of suburban infill proposal, Nassau Hub, New Jersey, Regional Plan Association with Robert Lane, 1999.

54. Plan for Princeton Forrestal Center, New Jersey, 1994. The study by the Regional Plan Association focused on converting suburban edge city developments into neighborhood centers.

55, 56. Addison Circle,
Texas, RTKL.

57. Aerial perspective of Addison Circle, Texas, RTKL, 1999. This 80-acre, high-density, mixed-use district is an attempt to reconceive the edge city development.

Chapter Six

New Towns and their Fragments

The renaissance of town planning principles in America has seen its most legible and seductive embodiment in large-scale developments in which the multiple aspects of urban design are subjected to a unifying vision. In such projects, the two strands of modern planning, technical and utopian, are synthesized. As evidenced in the last chapter, these town planning principles are equally applicable to the piecemeal redesign of existing places, but the ideal vision has a better possibility of realization on a tabula rasa, a site unencumbered by such existing interests and context as street networks, buildings, private property division, and community influence. Ebenezer Howard, the progenitor of the modernist town planning vision, exhorted the obvious utopian aspects to such endeavors when he asked in 1898:

"Can better results be obtained by starting on a bold plan on comparatively virgin soil than by attempting to adapt our old cities to our newer and higher needs? Thus fairly faced, the question can only be answered in one way; and when that simple fact is well grasped, the social revolution will speedily commence."[1]

Almost all new towns built by American architects over the past decade that have attempted to make mixed-use, compact, and walkable neighborhoods (as opposed to suburban subdivisions or edge cities) have been designed or influenced by New Urbanists. How is this legacy associated with one particular school of thought? Primarily because faced with the seemingly invincible march of suburban sprawl and the apparent collapse of traditional relationships between center and periphery, city and suburb, New Urbanists have most fervently and convincingly postulated a response that reinstates neighborhoods and towns as the fundamental unit of urban development. Their monopoly on new towns can also be attributed to the Congress for New Urbanism's rapid ascent as a powerful institution—both as an effective distributor and marketer of its ideas, and as a forger of alliances between architects, planners, banks, developers, and builders. The abil-

ity to disseminate and market ideas was in no small measure a factor in the success of previous town planners in the modern era, including Camille Sitte, Frederick Law Olmsted, Ebenezer Howard, Raymond Unwin, John Nolen, and Clarence Stein.

These new American towns can also be seen as reinvigorated visions of what Robert Fishman, the astute historian of the Anglo-American suburb, calls "bourgeois utopias."[2] But if the current embodiments of these ideals represent the cultural imperatives of an expanded and powerful middle class after a half-century of economic expansion, the designers of these towns are careful to point out that their principles of town planning can be found throughout the history of cities. Like the work of Kevin Lynch or Christopher Alexander, there is an attempt to abstract principles governing urban form that are manifest in Western cultures across time. But as designers of actual places for contemporary America, they also have made an attempt to create specific normative standards appropriate for today. These norms are presented, particularly by New Urbanists, as applicable for all communities regardless of income, race, and cultural heritage. New Urbanist rhetoric makes the almost indisputable claim that diverse choices of housing, places for children to play, streets safe and comfortable to walk on, "third places" of social gathering other than home and work, and preserved natural resources should be rights available to all without discrimination.

Yet New Urbanist towns have been criticized as havens for the wealthy. Studies have indicated that New Urbanist houses do indeed command a premium compared to houses in conventional suburbia,[3] and their demand has fueled skyrocketing value. An original lot at Seaside, for example, which sold for $20,000 now sells for as much as $400,000. Most New Urbanist towns, however, because of the variety of housing types, have an unusually wide range of house prices. Certainly some projects are oriented toward particular markets, such as Hope

Aerial perspective, Monte Vista, Arizona, Duany Plater-Zyberk and Company, 1991. In their plan for a community of manufactured housing, DPZ designed the public realm and then developed architectural designs that subtly transformed standard manufactured housing.

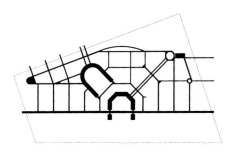

1. Street grid diagram for the town of Seaside, Florida, Duany Plater-Zyberk and Company. The street grid connects to the existing grid of Seagrove Beach to the east, and provides points of connection for future development to the north. (See illust. 2.6 of the adjacent Watercolor development)

VI public housing, or exclusive resorts like Windsor, Florida, but the majority of new towns are aimed at diverse residents. The town-planning principles of the New Urbanism are meant to be able to be applied to any kind and scale of development, from vast new towns of primarily custom houses to small, compact manufactured housing developments. (opening illustration) To counter the increasingly expensive lot and rental prices, New Urbanists call for more development to combat the exclusivity of their product in the market. In other words, New Urbanists, like Olmsted a century ago, invite emulation of their models. In this way, expanded production of New Urbanist neighborhoods may both ameliorate such unintended exclusivity and promote more diverse residents.[4]

Unlike the construction of contemporary suburban subdivisions, the development of most New Urbanist towns are phased over long periods of time which allows for flexibility. The design is never fixed by the architects, but guided by a master plan and code. The red brick streets of Seaside, for example, one of its signature attributes, was not specified by Duany Plater-Zyberk (DPZ) during planning, but by the homeowners organization years later. Phased growth also allows developers to leverage initial development as its value increases. The developers of most New Urbanist towns have made long-term commitments to creating a place, as opposed to typical suburban developers whose timeline is often based on quick financial pay-offs of short-term mortgage loans. Since phasing, growth, evolution, and change occur slowly over generations, the true measure of these towns and their claims won't be assessable for decades.

What are the common design principles and physical components of these new American towns? They are predominantly composed of walkable neighborhoods of approximately 1/4 to 1/2 mile in radius; they have a dense mixed-use center or multiple centers; their density tends to decrease from center to periphery; they are knitted by a network of streets designed as walkable public spaces; houses and other buildings reinforce the space of the street with garage and service access typically from alleys; multiple housing types are intermixed; civic buildings are dispersed on prominent sites; and open spaces and parks are distributed within walking distance of all residents. Parking for town centers and commercial areas is usually accommodated within the block behind buildings, in structured parking over street-level re-

tail, and on the street in parking lanes.[5] Although each of the projects in this chapter are designed with these same components and principles, there is great variety in their application as well as in the design of the components. Identity and idiosyncrasies vary with topography and site, client demands, program, parking or traffic concerns, and of course the individual design solutions of the architect's team.

New Urbanist towns and neighborhoods emphasize connectivity, not just within their own borders, but to adjacent neighborhoods. The street grid, where possible, extends to join adjacent streets (fig. 1), in contrast to cul-de-sac suburbs as well as the more recent "gated communities." New Urbanist towns also encourage visitors to their public spaces and town center. Some projects, like DPZ's Riverside outside of Atlanta, have become regional attractions. Seaside's grand lawn hosts festivals and concerts during the summer for local residents.

Streets designed as public spaces to encourage pedestrian activity contrast to the streets of most contemporary suburbs which at best discourage walking, and at worst prove lethal to the daring, stray pedestrian. Conventional suburban streets are conduits arrayed in a "sparse hierarchy" to efficiently move automobile traffic. In these suburbs, the safest streets for playing children are cul-de-sacs, but these often trap children on their own street, since fear of the high capacity collector beyond keeps them from walking to the rest of the neighborhood. Conventional suburban development also typically builds long blocks, up to 600', or more than twice as long as blocks in New Urbanist towns. This makes walking more difficult because the route between two places tends to be longer and less direct. The emphasis on pedestrian connectivity in New Urbanist towns leads some towns, like Kentlands, to add walking paths where a road might not be buildable. (fig. 2)

The connected and shared street network is a rejection of urban designer Clarence Stein's influence on suburban planning. In his 1957 book, *Toward New Towns for America*, Stein sought ways to live "in spite of" the automobile through the "complete separation of pedestrian and automobile." In his design for Radburn, for example, Stein first achieved this separation by creating 30–50 acre superblocks encircled by high capacity roadways. (The entire town of Seaside, 23 blocks in 80 acres, would fit into two Radburn superblocks.) Where roads and walkways did intersect, they did so at different levels using underpasses and

2. Houses fronting on walking paths, Kentlands, Maryland. (Photo: author)

overpasses. Roadways were categorized by use ("movement, collection, service, parking, and visiting") rather than imagined as public spaces that accommodate multiple uses. Finally, because the streets were mere service conduits, houses were "turned around" to face rear gardens in the interior of the superblock. In New Urbanist towns, by contrast, street frontages of buildings are important public gestures.[6]

As the conceptual unit of development, the neighborhood is both its own structure and part of a larger ensemble. The figural legibility of neighborhoods varies among new town projects. Early DPZ plans, for example, are almost diagrammatic in their emphasis on neighborhoods as semiautonomous, discreetly defined elements linked to one another. A master plan drawing of McKenzie Town from 1991, shows each neighborhood with a definite boundary, center, and connecting roadway to adjacent but separate neighborhoods. (fig. 3) Street and block structure are indicated in detail in a few exemplary cases, but otherwise simply implied. Greenways of open parkland act as divisions between the neighborhoods. Other designers, and indeed DPZ in their later projects, tend to overlap the neighborhoods into more ambiguous and complex compositions.

Site and topography are usually the first considerations for the layout of a plan. In Hueco, a 436 acre new community outside of El Pa-

so jointly designed by Moule and Polyzoides and Duany Plater-Zyberk, a 300 foot square block grid is oriented north-south to maximize solar exposure. (fig. 4) The east-west streets are continuous to permit views of the distant mountain ranges, whereas the north-south streets are deliberately unaligned to mitigate the extreme southerly winds. In Bahcesehir, a new project in Istanbul by Torti Gallas CHK, the steep topography of the site was the primary factor in the design of the town. Public stairways and terraced gardens connect the site, and link a park and two towers at the top of the site with the main commercial plaza at the bottom. The slope allows for units to be naturally ventilated, and have parking accommodated in terraced and tuck-under garages. (figs. 5, 6)

Greenfield Developments

Projects for new towns and neighborhoods tend to be located in areas that both have ample space for development, and are subject to economic pressures that make such development tenable. Most of these locations are either greenfield or brownfield sites. Greenfield sites are undeveloped areas, usually on the outskirts of an urbanized area, or in some cases isolated from any adjacent urbanization. They are developed typically into self-sufficient residential communities, ranging from a single neighborhood with only local amenities to larg-

123

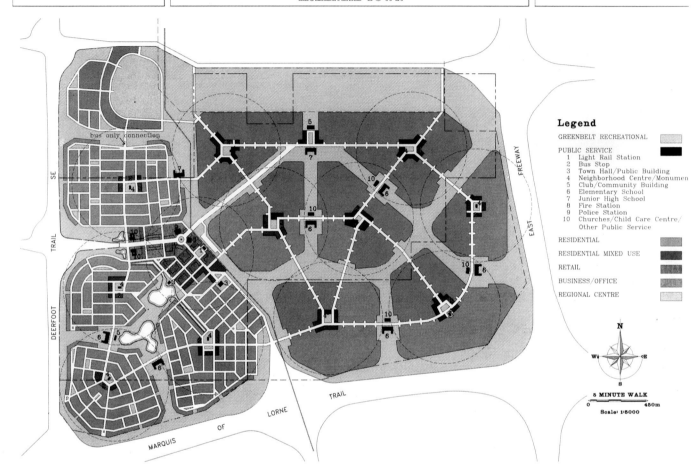

OWNER
CARMA DEVELOPERS LTD.
CALGARY, ALBERTA

MASTER PLAN
McKENZIE TOWN

TOWN PLANNERS
ANDRES DUANY & ELIZABETH PLATER-ZYBERK
ET AL

Legend

GREENBELT RECREATIONAL

PUBLIC SERVICE
1 Light Rail Station
2 Bus Stop
3 Town Hall/Public Building
4 Neighborhood Centre/Monumen
5 Club/Community Building
6 Elementary School
7 Junior High School
8 Fire Station
9 Police Station
10 Churches/Child Care Centre/
   Other Public Service

RESIDENTIAL

RESIDENTIAL MIXED USE

RETAIL

BUSINESS/OFFICE

REGIONAL CENTRE

5 MINUTE WALK
0   450m
Scale: 1:5000

3. Plan for McKenzie
Town, Calgary, Alberta,
Duany Plater-Zyberk
and Company.
In this 1991 plan,
neighborhoods
are designed
with diagrammatic clarity,
separated from each other
by greenbelts.

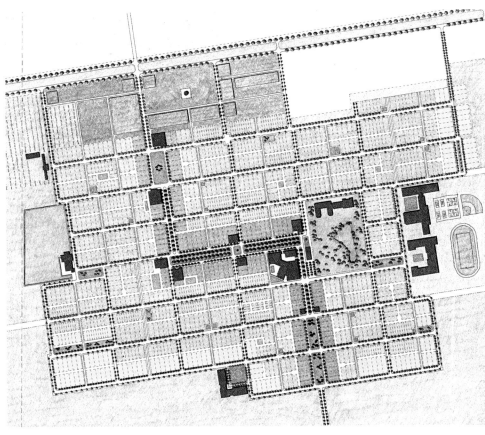

4. Regulating Plan
for new town of Hueco
in El Paso, Texas,
by Moule & Polyzoides
Architects and Urbanists,
Duany Plater-Zyberk
and Company, 1991.
The original plan
of the 436-acre project
is based on early Spanish
settlement towns
governed by the Laws
of the Indies. (The plan
is being significantly
revised.)

5. The master plan
for Bahcesehir, Istanbul,
Turkey, by Torti Gallas
CHK, 1996–97,
incorporates
the infrastructure
and architectural design
for over thirty housing
types (2,300 units)
and numerous
educational and public
facilities on a steep site.

6. Perspective rendering
of Bahcesehir,
Istanbul, Turkey,
by Torti Gallas CHK.

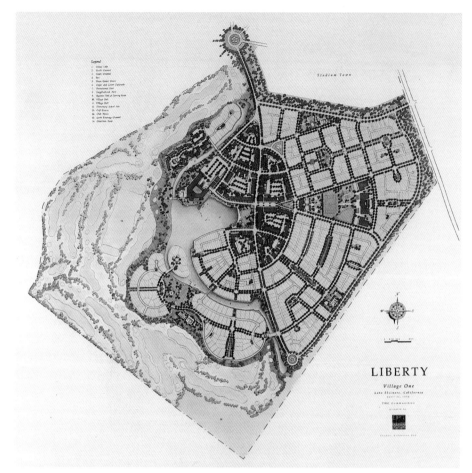

Legend
1. *School Lake*
2. *North Channel*
3. *South Channel*
4. *Park*
5. *Town Green Grove*
6. *Upper and Lower Esplanade*
7. *Recreational Area*
8. *Neighborhood Park*
9. *Reserve Park of Turning Basin*
10. *Village Hall*
11. *Elementary School Site*
12. *Golf Course*
13. *Club House*
14. *Earth Drainage Channel*
15. *Downtown Town*

Stadium Town

LIBERTY

Village One
Lake Elsinore, California
April 20, 1998

TMC Communities

prepared by

Cooper, Robertson Ltd.

7. The master plan
of the first phase
of the new town of Liberty
by Cooper Robertson,
1998, a 2,907 acre
community located
on Southern California's
largest natural lake.
(Drawing by EPT,
landscape architects)

er towns with multiple neighborhoods and major employment centers. They are the most controversial projects from an environmentalist perspective, as they contribute to the rapid disappearance of farmland and other open lands. To some critics, greenfield projects are just a better form of suburban sprawl. Others claim that the compact development patterns are environmentally and socially superior to the blanket of single-use suburbia that would otherwise be constructed.

Many greenfield projects are located adjacent to newly constructed highways, which makes the adjacent land suddenly accessible and valuable. In the examples of greenfield development presented here, each is bordered on at least one side by a regional highway. (figs. 7–19) While Liberty and Celebration both depend on the highway for access, they also stand in isolation from it. Coffee Creek allows for multiple connections from the surrounding arterials, but in each case the access is minimized as a pragmatic entry point. Williamsburg New Town bridges a highway which bisects the site. Rosemary Beach is also bisected by a highway, but DPZ, in a move similar but bolder than their plan for Seaside a few miles down the road, tame the highway through traffic calming measures, like stop signs, landscaping, and a large entry square that affords drivers views within.[7] Harbortown also places large public spaces on the highway to mark the entrance, from which the primary avenues radiate inward as formal devices to divide the site.

Some form of a connected street system is evident in each of the schemes. There is a slightly more rigid grid in Coffee Creek, where two parallel main streets, one primarily residential and the other primarily commercial, are situated on either side of a preserved wetlands. A street grid deforms into radiating patterns at Liberty and Celebration, suggesting a deference to the town centers and providing a means of dividing up the site into smaller neighborhoods. The residual space formed by the radiating geometries become landscaped parks or, in the case of Liberty, a school site just east of the town center.

The grid of Harbortown bridges a park-like band of marshland that divides the site into an inner "island" and surrounding areas. Unlike Coffee Creek, in which the two grids on either side of the wetlands are connected almost incidentally (and more in keeping with the midwestern history of a banal imposition of a grid on landscape), Harbortown's grid is oriented around three boulevards which connect the entry plazas at the edge of the site with three squares on the center island. These streets also subtly define single-family, multifamily, and commercial areas. This division is one of the few weaknesses of the plan, but as one of the earliest New Urbanist projects Harbortown no doubt suffered great builder resistance to mixing housing types. Celebration, in contrast, has a much greater mix of single-family and multifamily housing. Large mixed-use buildings of apartments over stores form the town center, while apartments, duplexes, and rowhouses line the principle avenues and neighborhood parks.

The plan of Williamsburg New Town elegantly transforms itself across the site from a rigid pattern at the commercial district, designed to accommodate big box retail and large amounts of parking, to the curvilinear streets adapting to the hillside topography. Inspired by the historic Williamsburg a few miles away, a few perpendicular grand streets serve as axes to connect the disparate neighborhoods and to link the smaller squares and civic buildings distributed throughout the plan. A large park of preserved wetlands and woods at the center of the plan serves as a buffer between the commercial and residential areas.

Deviating from a strict adherence to their own town planning principles, DPZ created two separate grids at Rosemary Beach: streets and walking paths. Unlike Seaside, in which the streets are the primary public spaces[8]—always filled with walkers and bicycle riders—cars and pedestrians are often separated at Rosemary Beach. The exceptions are the main streets that connect through the site. These streets feed the two other networks: car lanes (often cul-de-sacs) that give access to garages at the rears of houses, and walking paths and boardwalks which pass by the fronts of houses and extend to the beach. There are multiple connections across the highway in an attempt to weave the two halves of Rosemary Beach together.

Suburban Greenfield Developments
   Greenfield developments often exist as isolated ersatz villages surrounded by nature. A more provocative and challenging setting for these town planning principles is existing suburbia, particularly the subdivision. Here, the contrast with conventional suburban development becomes most apparent. The subdivision has been the principle unit of suburban development in America since the 1920s. Contrary to the often simplistic dismissal of the subur-

8. Aerial view of the new town of Celebration, master plan by Cooper Robertson and Partners and Robert A.M. Stern Architects, 1994. (Photo: Smith Aerial Photography)

View of a street in the town center, Celebration, Florida. (Photo: author)

10. View of the lake and town center, Celebration, Florida. (Photo: author)

11. Master plan for Coffee
Creek, Michigan,
William McDonough
Architects, 1998.

12. Aerial perspective of
town center, Coffee Creek,
Michigan, William
McDonough Architects.

13. Aerial perspective of
residential neighborhood
in Coffee Creek, Michigan,
William McDonough
Architects.

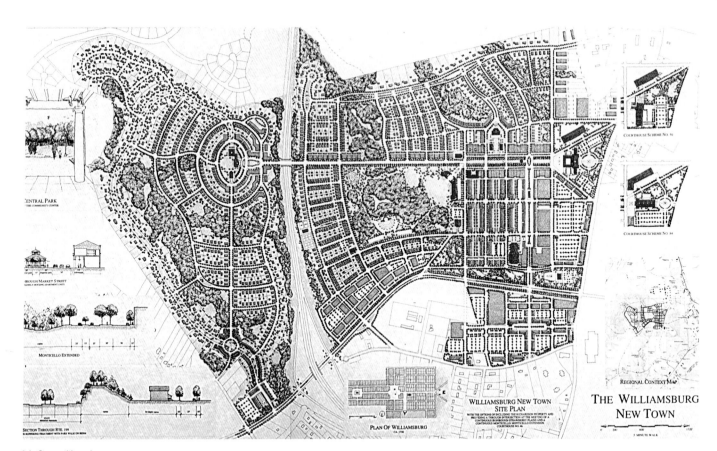

CENTRAL PARK
THE COMMUNITY CENTER

BOROUGH MARKET STREET
LEVEL 3 HOUSING APARTMENT UNITS

MONTICELLO EXTENDED

SECTION THROUGH RTE. 199
BUFFERING TREATMENT WITH PARK WALK ON BERM

PLAN OF WILLIAMSBURG
CA. 1780

WILLIAMSBURG NEW TOWN SITE PLAN
WITH THE OPTIONS OF INCLUDING THE RICHARDSON PROPERTY AND
PROVIDING A THROUGH INTERSECTION AT THE MEETING OF A
CONTINUOUS IRONBOUND STRAWBERRY PLAINS AND A
CONTINUOUS MONTICELLO MONTICELLO EXTENSION.
COURTHOUSE NO. 46.

COURTHOUSE SCHEME NO. 50

COURTHOUSE SCHEME NO. 44

REGIONAL CONTEXT MAP

THE WILLIAMSBURG NEW TOWN

0   200'   600'   1120'
5 MINUTE WALK

14. Competition plan
for extension
of Williamsburg, Virginia,
Paul Mortensen
and Robert Goodill,
1994.

130

WOLF RIVER

MISSISSIPPI RIVER

15. Master plan for Harbortown, Memphis, Tennessee, by RTKL, 1989, a residential community set between the Mississippi and Wolf rivers comprising 800 dwelling units (attached and detached), retail, restaurants, a Montessori school, and marina.

16. Aerial view of Harbortown, Memphis, Tennessee. (Photo: Jim Hilliard, Looney Ricks Kiss Architects)

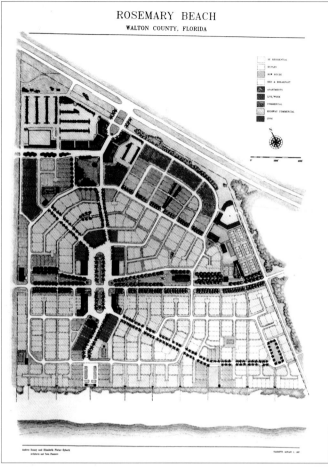

17. Master plan for
Rosemary Beach,
Walton County, Florida,
by Duany Plater-Zyberk
and Company, 1995–96.

18. Aerial perspective
of Rosemary Beach,
Walton County, Florida,
by Duany Plater-Zyberk
and Company.

19. View of houses from walking path, Rosemary Beach, Walton County, Florida. (Photo: author)

ban social landscape, much of which is warranted in contemporary development, the first developers of subdivisions often had a more complex understanding of their endeavors. They imagined new models of community throughout an expanding region that defied easy categorization as city or suburb, center or edge.[9] To one important planner in Los Angeles in the 1920s, "the subdivision ... is that upon which a city is fashioned or molded and contains practically all the elements for the successful planning thereof. The formation of a city plan can hardly be conceived to be complete in itself at its inception, but by the coalescing or joining together of subdivisions a city or town is gradually erected. ..."[10]

Combating the entrenched regulations of subdivision codes is difficult, and these "suburban greenfield" projects are often affected by existing codes and zoning in a way that more isolated new development is not. DPZ's Charleston Place (fig. 20) , surrounded by gated communities, was not permitted by subdivision codes to have street connections to adjacent properties, including a shopping center "behind." So instead of crossing a street to the stores, residents must drive out of Charleston Place to a collector road, then to an arterial road, back to another collector road, and finally into the shopping center's sprawling parking lot. To circumvent the requirement for unnecessarily wide roads within the subdivision, DPZ labeled the landscaped lanes "driveways" to gain municipal approval of their "substandard" roadways.

Ironically, a shopping center (a residual commercial requirement from the original subdivision zoning) marks the main entrance to DPZ's Kentlands, a 352 acre development in the greater suburban Washington, D.C., area. (figs. 21–23) Assuming its inevitable demise, the architects dimensioned the shopping center's parking lots into blocks that can be later "urbanized" and incorporated into the Kentlands plan. The impact of the shopping center on the plan is also mitigated by a "main street" that connects the conventional shopping center with the rest of Kentlands neighborhoods. Surrounding Kentlands are typical, large, single-use, suburban developments: office parks, townhouse subdivisions, and strip shopping centers. Within Kentlands, the designers were able to create a diverse range of judiciously mixed housing types and uses. The juxtaposition of houses, rowhouses, live/work units, commercial space, and community buildings is among the most mixed of New Urbanist

towns. The street grid deforms to the slightly sloping topography and is oriented around two large civic spaces, one containing a church and school and the other a recreational park and community center. Subtle manipulation of the streets and block structure create a surprising array of small public parks and greens.

Nearby in Maryland is King Farm, a subdivision developed into a series of mixed-use neighborhoods designed by Torti Gallas CHK. (fig. 24) While King Farm connects to adjacent subdivisions where possible, it is intended to be (and represented in the plan drawing as) self-sufficient. Its proposed 3 million square feet of office space, 125,000 square feet of neighborhood retail, and 3,200 units of housing, usually zoned into different areas of a subdivision, are intricately combined, absorbed by a clear urban structure.

Both the 192 acre Orenco Station Village outside of Portland, Oregon (one of the case studies of Calthorpe's 2040 regional plan), and the over 400 acre Civano in Tucson, Arizona, are situated on the periphery of cities being rapidly developed into subdivision suburbia. (figs. 25–29) Both are presented as an alternative form of development in stark contrast to the surrounding landscape of condominiums, shopping centers, and single-house suburbia. Fletcher Urban Designers and Architects Farr Ayotte oriented the Orenco Station neighborhood around a main avenue and pedestrian "promenade" that connects a transit station in the south to a community park in the north. Dense, mixed-use buildings including retail, office space, and live-work units, line the avenue. The master plan of Civano, a joint project by Duany Plater-Zyberk and Moule and Polyzoides, creates a primarily residential neighborhood with a rich variety of housing types that reflect the history and climate of the region. In the design of the buildings, Moule and Polyzoides employed alternative construction materials (straw bale, foam block, adobe), and intelligent site-planning in an effort to mitigate the effects of the harsh desert climate. A small neighborhood center containing stores, offices, a restaurant and a community meeting room, all situated around a large courtyard, has been built in the center of the development, within walking distance of all the residents.

I'on is a 243 acre development situated amongst low density suburbs outside of Charleston, South Carolina. (figs. 30, 31) Each of its six neighborhoods is focused on a natural feature, such as a lake or park. The original

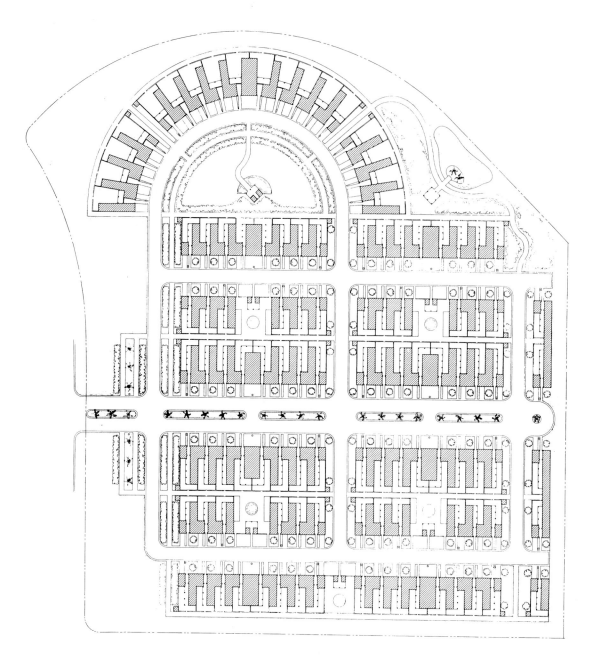

20. Master plan
for Charleston Place,
Boca Raton, Florida, by
by Duany Plater-Zyberk
and Company, 1980.
The plan attempts
to be an alternative
to the surrounding gated
subdivisions.

21. Master plan
for Kentlands, Maryland,
by Duany Plater-Zyberk
and Company, 1988.
This 356 acre
development includes
1,600 residential units
with a population of over
5,000 total residents.

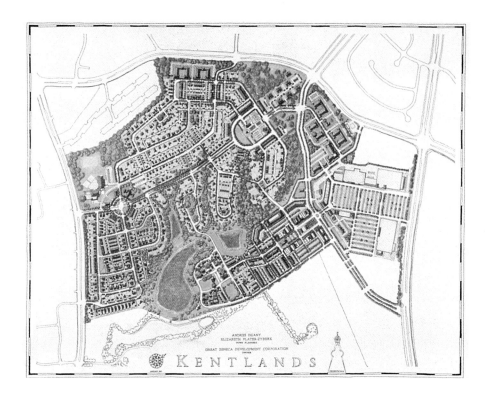

22. Aerial view of part of
Kentlands, Maryland.

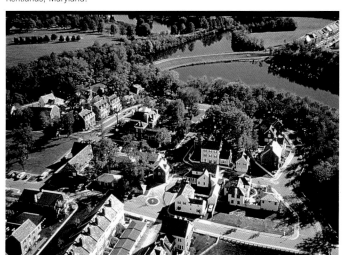

23. View of street of
single-family houses
in Kentlands, Maryland.
Duany Plater-Zyberk and
Company.

KING FARM

CITY OF ROCKVILLE, MARYLAND

OWNER:
KING FARM ASSOCIATES LLC.
C/O PENROSE GROUP
8330 BOONE BOULEVARD
VIENNA, VIRGINIA 22182

ARCHITECT AND LAND PLANNER:

CHK ARCHITECTS & PLANNERS
1300 SPRING STREET
SILVER SPRING, MARYLAND 20910

0   200'   400'   800'

24. The master plan for King Farm, Montgomery County, Maryland, by Torti Gallas CHK, 1996, includes approximately 3.17 million square feet of office/employment space, 125,000 square feet of neighborhood retail space and 3,200 dwelling units.

project contained more multifamily housing and a larger commercial center, but neighbor opposition from the adjacent single-family subdivisions forced the developer to scale back its density and mixed-use composition. The houses vary significantly in size and type, including some live/work buildings. Developer Vince Graham of Civitas, like in his earlier Newpoint, drew from the physical qualities of historic towns in South Carolina, like Beaufort and Charleston. The self-contained adjacent subdivisions made it difficult to connect I'on to a larger suburban context. It is therefore rather self-contained, but with a small commercial center at its entrance as a means of attracting neighboring residents. A simple eight page code requires minimal front setbacks, rear garages (typically fed by alleys), and traditional southern architectural elements like deep front and side porches.

Brownfield Developments

 Brownfields are former industrial sites— airports, docklands, railyards, factories, etc.— converted to post-industrial uses, usually housing and office space. The shift from an industrial to a service-oriented economy has the potential to radically transform American cities. With the increasing demand for flexible office space and housing, once isolated brownfield sites have become opportunities for reclamation

and reurbanization. Although these sites face similar issues seen in town planning insertions in suburban subdivisions, there are notable differences: unlike the expansiveness of greenfields, brownfields tend to be limited and awkwardly shaped by the exigencies of past industrial needs. Often they are on "leftover" sites adjacent to major transportation infrastructure.

 Carlyle, a development of 1,800 units of housing and 4,500,000 square feet of retail and offices designed by Cooper Robertson, is located on an 80 acre former railyard in Alexandria, Virginia. (fig. 32) The grand, City Beautiful-inspired imagery suggests more a corporate campus, perhaps, than a neighborhood. Carlyle's broad streets form a refined grid that makes connections where possible to the adjacent city. Low-rise buildings line the perimeter of the blocks, both reinforcing the space of the street and serving as podiums for the many office towers. Open space consists of grand public circuses, crescents, and symmetrical squares.

 Victory District in Dallas, Texas, located on an old utility and industrial site just outside of downtown, is identical in size to Carlyle, but with a very different urban disposition. (figs. 33, 34) Here the designers, Koetter Kim Associates, specified only the essential infrastructure of primary streets and building parcels to form what they call "a dynamic and resilient frame-

25. Aerial view of Orenco Station, Oregon, looking toward the neighborhood center and park. (Photo: J. Douglas Macy)

26. Master plan for Orenco Station by Fletcher Farr Ayotte, 1995.

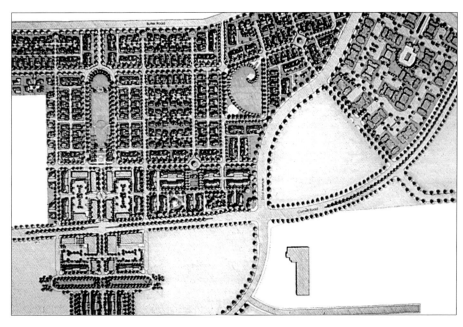

27. Neighborhood center
of Civano, Moule
and Polyzoides
with GRP Architects,
1999.

28. Houses in Civano,
by Moule and Polyzoides,
1999.

29. Master plan of
Civano, Tucson, Arizona,
by Duany Plater-Zyberk,
Moule and Polyzoides,
and Wayne Moody, 1997.

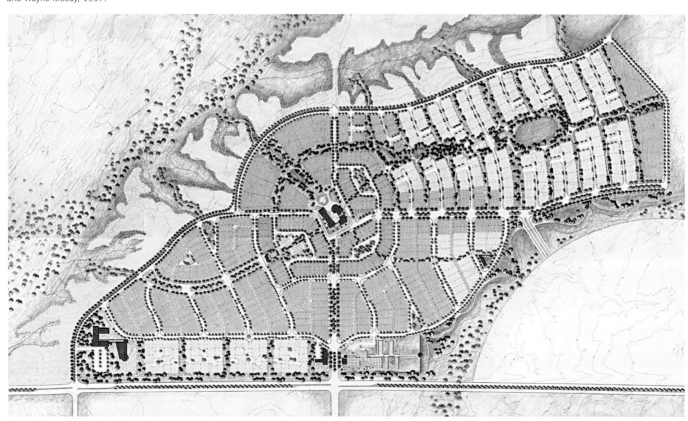

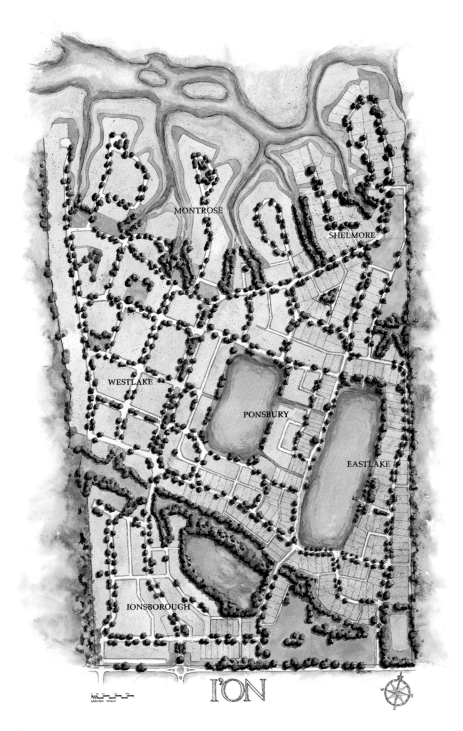

MONTROSE

SHELMORE

WESTLAKE

PONSBURY

EASTLAKE

IONSBOROUGH

I'ON

GRAPHIC SCALE

30. Master plan for I'on,
South Carolina,
by Duany Plater-Zyberk,
Dover Kohl, and Vince
Graham, 1997.

31. View of I'on's first
neighborhood of Eastlake.
(Courtesy: Civitas)

work for development."[11] Major streets are designed with lane configurations, parking, sidewalk width, and plantings, and important building parcels have specified "street walls," "build-
to-lines," and frontage configurations, like ar-
cades. But the rest of the site is left open for
development according to a few simple guidelines. These secondary parcels can be assembled
and built in a variety of sizes and configurations.
To give a sense of identity and control to what
is otherwise a deliberate embrace of ambiguity and possibility, the designers provide the urban elements distributed throughout the site:
sidewalk patterns and material, street lights, and
signage. Though it lacks the formal balance of
Carlyle, Victory District nonetheless holds
strong view and street axes and represents well
its marginal site along a freeway.

Since the end of the Cold War, America
has closed a number of military bases which
have become brownfield sites for development.
Some are located in urbanized areas, such as the
Orlando Naval Training Center. A 1998 competition for the redevelopment of this base presented a catalog of design solutions employing
New Urbanist principles. (figs. 35–38) More
remote military bases are transformed into self-
contained and self-sufficient neighborhoods. At
the former Glenview Naval Air Station in Illinois, Skidmore Owings and Merrill are de-

signing a 1,100 acre master plan for multiple
residential neighborhoods, a town center, parks
and recreational facilities, and a 150 acre of-
fice/industrial campus. (fig. 39)

The New Urbanist Commodity and Its Future
In the tradition of some of the most influential and successful suburban designers,
from John Nash to John Nolen, the New Urbanists have carefully packaged and sold their
towns as commodities that can be produced in-
definitely. Like any architectural firm that spe-
cializes in a product (office buildings, retail,
health care, etc.), many New Urbanist firms
have focused and streamlined their methods of
designing towns and neighborhoods. A talent-
ed and efficient firm like DPZ, for example, can
design a regulating plan and code for a new
town of hundreds of acres in a one-week charrette. Standardizing the conventions of production and representation have enabled this
efficiency. New Urbanist firms continue to build
upon the professionalization of town planning
that began over a century ago, when the crisis
of the modern city first emerged. Olmsted was
the first American designer to structure a na-
tionally-recognized consultancy of town planning, creating a professional legacy benefiting
Daniel Burnham, John Nolen, and, now, many
New Urbanists.[12]

33. Aerial perspective
of Victory District, Texas,
by Koetter Kim
& Associates, 1999.

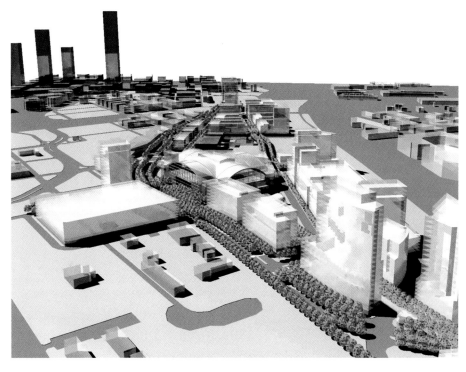

34. Street perspective
of Victory District
by Koetter Kim
& Associates.

As the forces of globalization take hold, the form and problems of the post-modern city are increasingly similar across borders. With conditions of American-type sprawl confronting other parts of the world, it is not surprising that New Urbanist ideas of urban reformation are being applied outside the States. (figs. 40, 41) The American practice of New Urbanism has certain affinities with urbanist practices in other countries, notably that of Leon Krier, but the ability to easily commodify New Urbanist towns may make them formidable exports in the coming decades. It may also indicate a nascent stage in the globalization of New Urbanism, which would echo CIAM (Congrès Internationaux d'Architecture Moderne)'s international aspirations. How New Urbanists balance the internationalism of urban conditions with their emphasis on local context and "place" will be one of their greater challenges.

The term "New Urbanism" has garnered considerable cache among developers, making it a term of marketable value. Neighborhoods designed with New Urbanist principles command a premium in price. It is not surprising, therefore, that conventional suburban developments simplistically strive for the New Urbanist mantle by adding front porches, sidewalks, or other elements of "traditional" architecture, while altogether ignoring more sophisticated, and important, urban and typological patterns. Indeed the "dilution" of the New Urbanist product is a challenge being actively debated within the CNU. Some argue that "hybrid" forms of neighborhoods are at least superior to "purely" conventional suburbia, while others argue for protecting the New Urbanist designation against all pretenders.

Ultimately, like the suburbs of Nash, Olmsted or Nolen, New Urbanist towns will evolve beyond the control of their creators as they are emulated, diluted, and subsumed by the larger momentum of American and international land development. It appears likely that New Urbanism will, however, affect the direction of this evolution, rather than be a footnote to it. For New Urbanism to remain viable, however, it will have to balance the inherent "freezing" of its principles into a commodity with the need to evolve, adjust, and transmute with changing contemporary conditions. Already New Urbanism has adjusted its focus to important urban issues such as infill, gentrification, community life, and environmental decay.

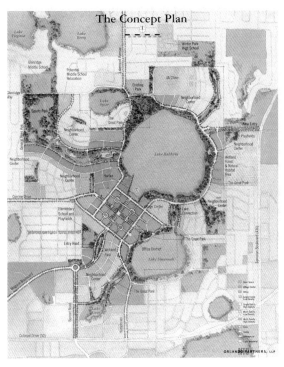

The Concept Plan

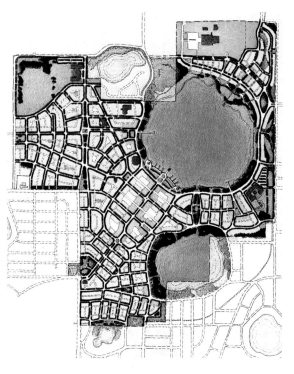

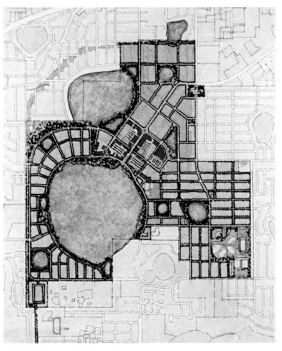

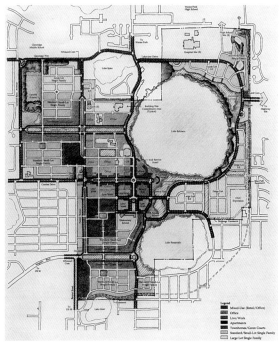

35. Master plan for
Orlando Naval Training
Center, Florida,
by Skidmore Owings
& Merrill, 1998.

36. Master plan for
Orlando Naval Training
Center, Florida, by Duany
Plater-Zyberk
and Company, 1998.

37. Master plan for
Orlando Naval Training
Center, Florida, by Cooper
Robertson Associates,
Urban Design Associates,
and Glatting Jackson,
1998.

38. Master plan for
Orlando Naval Training
Center, Florida,
by Calthorpe
& Associates, 1998.

39. Aerial perspective
of redevelopment of
Glenview Naval Station,
Illinois, by Skidmore
Owings & Merrill, 1998.

To some critics, the New Urbanist promise rings false. Architectural historian Margaret Crawford compares New Urbanist towns to company towns of the first part of the century, both of which offered "certainty, reassurance and the image of a coherent social order—comforting illusions for a nation again undergoing radical social, economic, and ethnic transformations."[13] Yet, as architectural historian Robert Fishman points out, this emulation of a mythologized past is part of the paradox of the suburb's origins:

"For in suburbia, the conquering bourgeoisie had chosen to recreate an invented version of the 'feudal, patriarchal, idyllic' village environment it was destroying. … At the same time that bourgeois economic initiatives were swelling the metropolis and undermining the traditional balance between man and nature, this class was creating a private retreat that expressed tradition, domesticity, and union with nature."[14]

With the saturation of sprawl development, American suburbs have reached the limits of the myth of suburbs as pre-industrial, rural villages. Although New Urbanism (and other contemporary suburban development) still appeals to this ingrained sentiment, they have also, significantly, focused their attention on the city. As the global economy threatens to erase notions of place and community in this post-industrial era, the American public is turning to sanitized, romanticized incarnations of the early industrial city. Warehouse districts, factories, meat packing plants, piers, docklands and other remnants of the industrial city become the basis for an urban recolonization by the middle class. New Urbanists, with their emphasis on urban structure, are well positioned to affect this next evolution of city making.

Some critics contend that these new developments are creating a New Suburbanism, a traditionally-styled version of sprawl. But it can be argued that New Urbanist towns actually reflect a return toward more traditional forms of urbanism. Just as the origins of suburbia began with "weekend villas" as the incremental step away from the cities, New Urbanist towns like Seaside might indicate the trend in reverse, creating "halfway houses for recovering suburbanites."[15] It may be that we are witnessing the end of the suburbs as they were envisioned over a century ago. Having reached the practical limits of suburban expansion, new forms of urbanism will inevitably replace low-density forms of development. In this way New Urbanist towns can be understood as part of a century-long search for new settlement patterns and a continued assertion of the inherent relationship between built environment and social well-being.

The question of whose well-being the urban patterns support is a significant one. Especially with the New Urbanist dependence on coding, a practice widely used in the past to exclude whole segments of the population, the control of "undesirables," whether aesthetics or peoples, assumes an ideological stance that cannot be ignored. As architectural historian Gwendolyn Wright remarks, "the New Urbanists must acknowledge the subtext of conformity and hostility that usually underlies any kind of code or guideline." This is not to say, she continues, that "throwing away controls releases us from these problems."[16] Indeed, New Urbanist practices have highlighted past practices of suburban control, and brought to bear new debates on the role of town-planning in forming any kind of community. The social, political, and economic conditions of the post-industrial era will no doubt bring their own challenges. New Urbanism may or may not ultimately prove to be the answer, but it has laid claim to the importance of the questions, and critique, of contemporary development patterns. As the costs of sprawl are increasingly recognized by a wider public and by authorities, New Urbanism will assume an increasing important role in the search for alternative forms of urbanism. Whether it will possess the flexibility and stewardship to enable these urbanisms, or whether it will, like CIAM, be a victim of its own success by becoming a parody of well-intentioned efforts, remains to be seen.

[1] Ebenezer Howard, *Garden Cities of To-morrow* (1898; reprint, Cambridge, Mass.: The MIT Press, 1965), p. 146.
[2] This is the title of Robert Fishman's seminal history of the Anglo-American suburb, *Bourgeois Utopias: The Rise and Fall of Suburbia* (New York: Basic Books, 1987).
[3] Studies reported in "Sales and consumer response to the New Urbanism," in *New Urbanism and Traditional Neighborhood Development: Comprehensive Report and Best Practices Guide* (Ithaca: New Urban News, 2000), 16.1–16.10.
[4] Olmsted was aware that his residential developments would be inhabited by the rich, but believed his towns would be emulated and thereby made accessible to the middle class. Fishman, *Bourgeois Utopias*, 133.
[5] For descriptions of the physical design strategies of New Urbanist towns and neighborhoods see Duany Plater-Zyberk, *The Lexicon of the New Urbanism*; Andres Duany, Elizabeth Plater-Zyberk, and Jeff Speck, *Suburban Nation, The Rise of Sprawl and the Decline of the American Dream* (New York: Northpoint Press, 2000), 245–252, "The Traditional Neighborhood Checklist"; Peter Calthorpe, *The Next American*

40. Master plan for
Cayman Island
development, by Moore
Ruble Yudell Architects,
1997.

41. Master plan for
Heulebrug, in Knokke-
Heist, Belgium,
by Duany Plater-Zyberk
and Company
and Leon Krier, 1998.

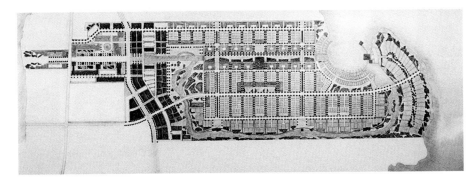

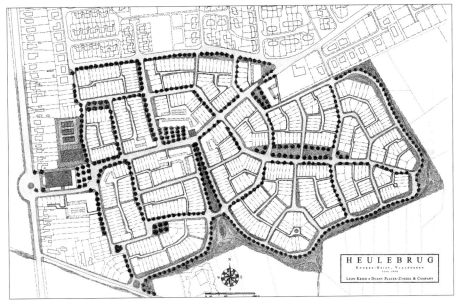

Metropolis (New York: Princeton Architectural Press, 1993); and Michael Leccese and Kathleen McCormick, eds., *Charter of the New Urbanism* (New York: McGraw Hill, 2000).

⁶ Clarence S. Stein, *Toward New Towns for America* (1957; reprint, Cambridge Mass.: The MIT Press, 1989), 41–44.

⁷ In the earliest Seaside Schemes, DPZ proposed diverting the coastal highway around their project. It was only as their ideas developed about streets as multifaceted public spaces, and not specialized conduits (as in Stein's new towns, or much of modern suburbia), that the highway was slowed down and incorporated, even celebrated, as a fundamental part of their design.

⁸ The original plan for Seaside provided for walking paths at mid-block, but after the first few were built the developer opted to encourage pedestrians to use the streets instead. "Rose Walk" will give the visitor an indication of what Seaside would have been like.

⁹ Greg Hise, *Magnetic Los Angeles: Planning the Twentieth-Century Metropolis* (Baltimore: Johns Hopkins University Press, 1997). See particularly the Introduction.

¹⁰ John R. Prince, regional chairman of subdivisions for the Los Angeles County Regional Planning Commission. From the commission's first conference (1922) proceedings as quoted in Hise, 6.

¹¹ From the *Victory District Guidelines*, as written by Koetter, Kim and Associates for the Hillwood Development Corporation, 1999.

¹² Witold Rybczynski, *City Life: Urban Expectations in a New World* (New York: Scribner, 1995), 133.

¹³ Margaret Crawford, "The New Company Town," *Perspecta: The Yale Architecture Journal* 30 (1999), 57.

¹⁴ Fishman, *Bourgeois Utopia*, 71.

¹⁵ Alex Krieger in "Urban or Suburban?" A discussion held at the Graduate School of Design in July 1996, and published in *Harvard Design Magazine* (winter–spring 1997), 55.

¹⁶ Gwendolyn Wright in "Urban or Suburban?" A discussion held at the Graduate School of Design in July 1996, and published in *Harvard Design Magazine* (winter–spring 1997), 49.

Case Studies

The previous chapters presented illustrative examples of principles and themes that form the basis of recent American urbanism and town planning. To follow are more complete case studies that are intended to give the reader a sense of how these themes and principles are applied. These projects are selected as examples, not paradigms, of this urbanism. Together they give the reader a sense of a diverse but connected scope of work. They share a common approach to design that addresses the interrelationship of all scales of design, from a regional plan (Portland 2040) to a floor plan (Dos Rios).

The first project, *The Lexicon of the New Urbanism*, is not a project per se, but a manual that attempts to reshape the practice and representation of architecture and town planning. The second project, the Region 2040 study for Portland, is an example of a regional plan. The Charleston Downtown plan is a strategic plan focusing on a metropolitan area. The master plan for the Alvarado Transportation Center area in Albuquerque is an example of a large urban infill project. Finally, two projects, Karow Nord and Dos Rios, represent the international application of these urban ideas by American firms.

The Lexicon
of the New Urbanism,
1999

The *Lexicon of the New Urbanism*, written and compiled by Duany Plater-Zyberk & Co. attempts no less than the analysis, compilation, and categorization of urban space and its relationship to buildings. The standards it sets forth are intended to create a common language of urbanism and to supplant the pervasive conventions of suburban design which have, according to the authors, led to sprawl. The *Lexicon* attempts to control urban ideology through the control of language, to clarify and enrich urban design by clarifying and enriching the language of urbanism. Chapters are divided according to a taxonomy of urbanism, with glossaries of terminology presented with each chapter. The *Lexicon* concludes with a chapter on implementation which describes means of representing urban plans, creating "transect zoning" maps, and establishing standards (landscape, environmental, frontage, etc.) through codes.

The *Lexicon* has been critiqued for its essentialism as well as its hubris in defining "appropriate" urban vocabulary and sanctioning "correct" forms of urbanism. It is defended for its encyclopedic scope and a rigorous compilation of abstracted pieces of urbanism. Yet the richness of urban space is never denied in the *Lexicon*. Rather, urban form is clearly abstracted into constituent concepts—landscape, open space, thoroughfares, building typology, block patterns etc., which, in turn, can be recombined in countless permutations.

The endeavor can be seen as the latest attempt by architects to understand and catalog the modern city, including such figures as J.N.L. Durand, Ebenezer Howard, Hegemann and Peets, Le Corbusier, and Leon Krier.

General Index
by Taxonomy.

The Transect Diagram
showing an analysis
of the Neighborhood
Structure. The Transect
is a scalar section through
the urban condition
and is meant
to be the underlying
structure of any
neighborhood.
It established appropriate
ranges of urban elements
according to position
on the transect.

• **The Transect:** a system of classification deploying the conceptual range rural-to-urban to arrange in useful order the typical elements of urbanism. The transect is a natural ordering system, as every urban element easily finds a place within its continuum. For example, a street is more urban than a road, a curb more urban than a swale, a brick wall more urban than a wooden one, an allee of trees more urban than a cluster. Even the character of streetlights can be assigned in the transect according to their fabrication from cast iron, extruded pipe, or wood posts.

© 1999 DUANY PLATER-ZYBERK & COMPANY (6/3/99)

◄ R U R A L ||||| | | | | | |||| || || |||| | | | | | || || || ||||| || U R B A N ►

RURAL ZONE ►

EDGE ZONE ►

GENERAL ZONE ►

CENTER & CORE ZONE ►

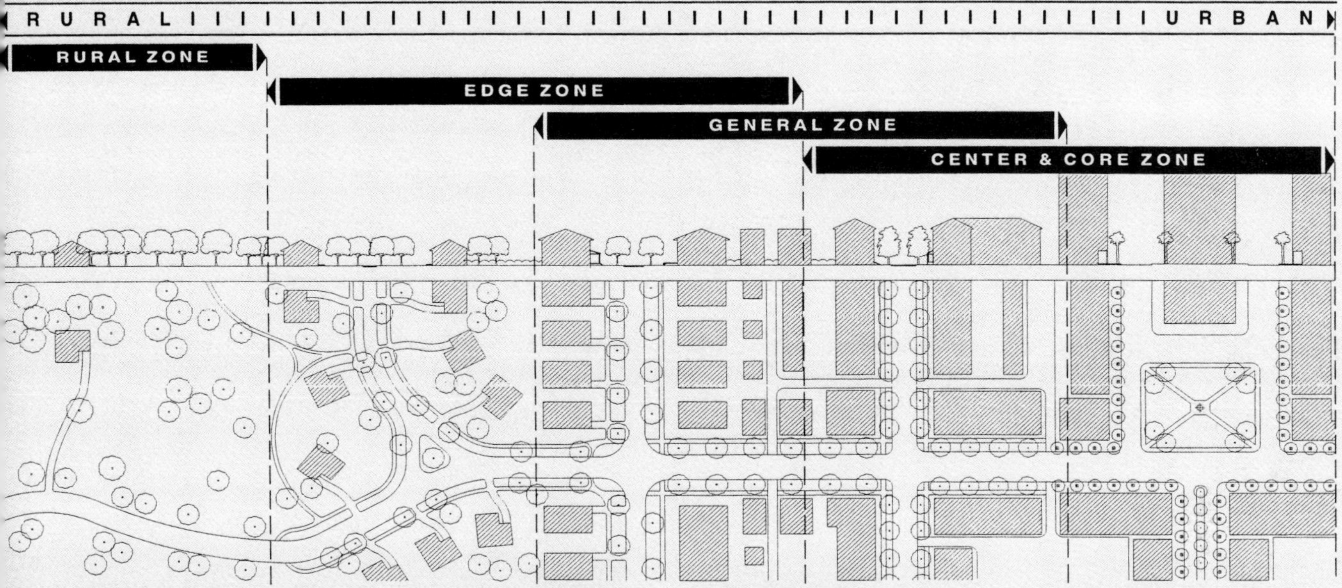

LESS DENSITY	MORE DENSITY
PRIMARILY RESIDENTIAL USE	PRIMARILY FLEXIBLE USE
SMALLER BUILDINGS	LARGER BUILDINGS
MOST BUILDINGS DETACHED	MOST BUILDINGS ATTACHED
ROTATED FRONTAGES	ALIGNED FRONTAGES
ARTICULATED MASSING	SIMPLE MASSING
WOODEN BUILDINGS	MASONRY BUILDINGS
PITCHED ROOFS	FLAT ROOFS
OVERHANGING EAVES	TAUT CORNICES
DEEP SETBACKS	SHALLOW SETBACKS
FENCES	STREET WALLS
LOCAL GATHERING PLACES	REGIONAL INSTITUTIONS
ROAD & LANE SECTIONS	STREET & ALLEY SECTIONS
PATHS & TRAILS	CROSS-BLOCK PASSAGES
NARROW MOVING LANES	WIDE MOVING LANES
CURVILINEAR TRAJECTORIES	RECTILINEAR TRAJECTORIES
THREE-WAY INTERSECTIONS	FOUR-WAY INTERSECTIONS
OPPORTUNISTIC PARKING	DEDICATED PARKING
LARGER CURB RADIUS	SMALLER CURB RADIUS
NARROW SIDEWALKS	WIDE SIDEWALKS
OPEN SWALES	RAISED CURBS
SPORADIC TASK LIGHTING	EVEN STREET LIGHTING
PICTURESQUE LANDSCAPING	ALLEE PLANTING
MIXED TREE CLUSTERS	SINGLE TREE SPECIES
PARKS & MEADOWS	PLAZAS & SQUARES

NEIGHBORHOOD STRUCTURE

THE TRANSECT 1 | C | 1

- **Transect Zoning:** A system of classification based on the correlation of the various elements by a common rural-to-urban Transect. Five segments calibrate the Transect to the neighborhood structure. These are the Rural, Edge, General, Center, and Core Zones. There is an additional category, Civic, that is an overlay zone applicable anywhere on the five standard zones.

Three categories (Edge, General, and Center) follow the natural internal structure of the neighborhood. The Core is assigned to the intensification that occurs where several neighborhoods conjoin, and the Rural is outside the urbanized area.

Each zone is an immersive environment, a place where all the component elements reinforce each other to create and intensify a specific urban character. Several such immersive environments within a single neighborhood provide variegation, in contrast to the homogenous tracts of conventional suburbia. This integrated system of zoning discourages the prescription of specialists.

BUILDING KEY (See M1)

Zoning Categories

N^E Neighborhood Edge
N^G Neighborhood General
N^C Neighborhood Center
C^T Town Core

OVERVIEW OF APPROPRIATE ELEMENTS FOR EACH ZONE

◀ R U R A L I I I I I I I I I I I I I I I I I I T R

EDGE ZONE

GENERAL

- **Edge Zone:** the least dense, most purely residential sector of the neighborhood. The size varies in proportion depending on whether the model is more rural (village-like) or more urban (town-like).

- **General Zone:** the sector that is mixed in but principally residential. It has a general character, and is usually the largest area neighborhood.

	EDGE ZONE	GENERAL
Land Use	Land use is restricted, combining residential with certain other uses.	Land use is limited, permitting the combination of residential with other uses
Building	Buildings of the low density freestanding **edge yard** type.	Buildings of the medium density freestanding **yard** and **edgeyard** types.
Frontage	Frontages which weakly define the public space with deep setbacks: **common lawn** and **porch & fence.**	Frontages which are variegated with medium setbacks: **dooryard,** and **porch & fence.**
Streetscape	Streetscapes which create the most rural conditions: **parkway, road,** and **lane.**	Streetscapes which create a variety of conditions: **road, residential street,** and **avenue.**
Thoroughfare	Thoroughfares are **roads** and **drives.** Buildings may be served by rear **lanes,** though wider lots may dispense with them.	Thoroughfares are **avenues, streets, and** Most buildings are served by rear **lanes.**
Open Space	Open space may be **parks** within the proximate **greenbelt.**	Open space is organized as **parks** and g

154

Analysis of appropriate
elements and zoning
categories for the
Neighborhood Structure.

ECTIIIIIIIIIIIIIIIIIIIIURBAN▶

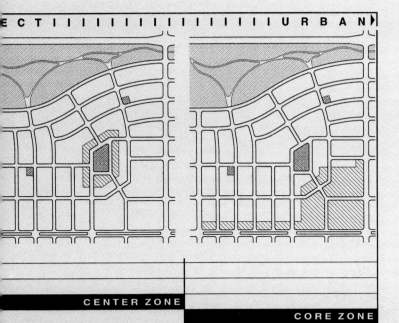

CENTER ZONE	CORE ZONE
nter Zone: the dense multifunctional social ndenser of a neighborhood. It is usually at a ntral location, within walking distance of the sur- unding, primarily residential areas.	• Core Zone: the most dense business, service, and institutional center. It is usually shared by several neighborhoods. It always straddles thor- oughfares at their most active intersection. It is usually within walking distance of a large residen- tial catchment.
nd use is open, encouraging the combination of sidential and other uses.	Land use is open, encouraging the combina- tion of residential and other uses.
ildings of the higher density attached courtyard, ar yard, and also side yard types.	Buildings only of the high density attached court- yard and rear yard types.
ntages which define continuous streetwalls with allow setbacks: arcade, shopfront, stoop, and recourt.	Frontages which define continuous streetwalls with shallow setbacks: arcade, shopfront, stoop, and forecourt.
eetscapes which create urban conditions: resi- ntial street, commercial street, enue, and boulevard.	Streetscapes which create the most urban condi- tions: commercial street, avenue, and boule- vard.
oroughfares are avenues and streets. All build- s are served by rear alleys.	Thoroughfares are streets and boulevards. All buildings are served by rear alleys.
en space is organized as plazas or squares.	Open space is organized as plazas or squares.

- **Network:** the pattern of thoroughfares. The principal structuring device of the urban pattern. Six models constitute the range of options available; five manifest a web pattern. The sixth, Radburn, is a stem pattern.

SAVANNAH PATTERN

Advantages
Excellent directional orientation
Controllable lot depth
Provides end grain of blocks for fast traffic
Even dispersal of traffic through the web
Straight lines enhance rolling terrain
Efficient double-loading of alleys and utilities

Disadvantages
Monotonous unless periodically interrupted
Does not easily absorb environmental interruptions
Unresponsive to steep terrain
Syn.: **orthogonal grid, gridiron**

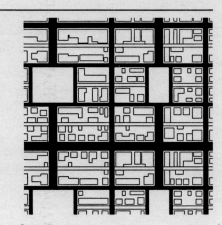

MARIEMONT PATTERN

Advantages
Hierarchy with diagonals for through traffic
Even dispersal of traffic through the web
Monotony interrupted by deflected vistas
Diagonal intersections spatially well-defined

Disadvantages
Tends to be disorienting
Syn.: **unwin model, spider web**

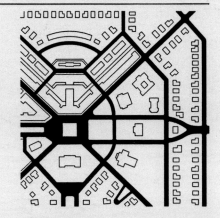

RIVERSIDE PATTERN

Advantages
Monotony interrupted by deflected vistas
Easily absorbs environmental interruptions
Highly responsive to terrain
Even dispersal of traffic through the web

Disadvantages
Highly disorienting
Uncontrollable variety of lots
No intrinsic hierarchy
Syn.: **olmstedian**

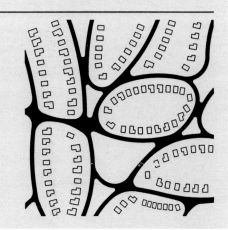

NANTUCKET PATTERN

Advantages
Hierarchy with long routes for through traffic
Even dispersal of traffic through web
Responsive to terrain
Easily absorbs environmental interruptions
Monotony eliminated by terminated vistas
Follows traces on the landscape

Disadvantages
Uncontrollable variety of blocks and lots

Syn.: **sitte model, townscape**

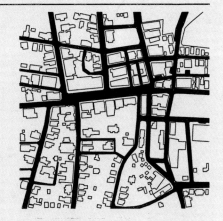

WASHINGTON PATTERN

Advantages
Hierarchy with diagonals for through traffic
Even dispersal of traffic through the grid
Diagonals focus on terrain features
Diagonals interrupt monotony of the grid

Disadvantages
Uncontrollable variety of lots
High number of awkward lot shapes
Diagonal intersections spatially ill-defined
Syn.: **city beautiful, haussmann model**

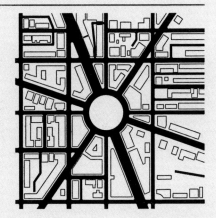

RADBURN PATTERN

Advantages
Good street hierarchy for locals and collectors
Controllable variety of blocks and lots
Easily absorbs environmental interruptions
Responsive to terrain

Disadvantages
Congestion of traffic by absence of web
Syn.: **cul-de-sac**

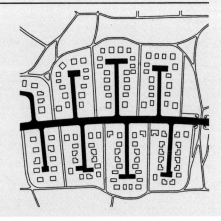

157

• **Block:** the aggregate of lots and tracts, circumscribed by thoroughfares.

The block is the middle scale of town planning. While it is not the determinant of the network nor of the building type, it strongly affects both.

There are a large number of block forms as implied by the six models of network; however, analysis reduces the variety to three categories: square, elongated, and irregular.

Each block type has distinct technical implications, and all types are useful even within a single neighborhood. For example, the square block accommodates the additional parking of a civic building within itself, useful at the Center Zone. The General Zone usually requires the normative lot sizes easily provided by the elongated block. The rural aspect, desirable at the Edge Zone is supported by the picturesque qualities of the irregular block.

SQUARE BLOCK

The Square Block was an early model for planned settlements in America. It was sometimes associated with agricultural communities with four large lots per block, each with a house at its center. When the growth of the community produced additional subdivision, the replatting inevitably created irregular lots (Figure 1).

While this may provide a useful variety, it is more often regarded as a nuisance by a building industry accustomed to standardized products.

A disadvantage is that discontinuous rear lot lines prevent double-loaded alleys and rear-access utilities. Despite these shortcomings, the square block is useful as a specialized type. The forced variety of platting assures a range of lot prices. When platted only at its perimeter with the center open (Figure 2), it can accommodate the high parking requirements of civic buildings. The open center may also be used as a common garden or a playground, insulated from traffic.

Figure

ELONGATED BLOCK

The Elongated Block is an evolution of the square block which overcomes some of its drawbacks. The elongated block eliminates the uncontrollable variable of lot depth, while maintaining the option of altering the lot width. Elongated blocks provide economical double-loaded alleys with short utility runs. The alley may be placed eccentrically, varying the depth of the lot (Figure 3-1). By adjusting the block length, it is possible to reduce cross-streets at the rural edges and to add them at the urban centers. This adjustment alters the pedestrian permeability of the grid, and controls the ratio of street parking to the building capacity of the block.

The elongated block can bend somewhat along its length, giving a limited ability to shape space and to negotiate slopes (Figure 4). Unlike the square block, it provides two distinct types of frontage. With the short side or end grain assigned to the higher traffic thoroughfare, most buildings can front the quieter long side of the block (Figure 3-2). For commercial buildings, the end grain can be platted to take advantage of the traffic while the amount of parking behind is controlled by the variable depth (Figure 3-3).

Figure

IRREGULAR BLOCK

The Irregular Block is characterized by its unlimited variations. The original organic block was created by the subdivision of land residual between well-worn paths.

It was later rationalized by Sitte, Cullen, Krier, and Olmsted to achieve a controllable picturesque effect and to organically negotiate sloping terrain. An important technique in the layout of irregular blocks is that the frontages of adjacent blocks need not be parallel (Figure 5).The irregular block, despite its variety, generates certain recurring conditions which must be resolved by sophisticated platting. At shallow curves, it is desirable to have the facades follow the frontage smoothly. This is achieved by maintaining the side

lot lines perpendicular to the frontage line (Figure 6-1). It is important that the rear lot line be wide enough to permit vehicular access (Figure 6-2). At sharper curves, it is desirable to have the axis of a single lot bisect the acute angle (Figure 6-3). In the event of excessive block depth it is possible to access the interior of the block by means of a close (Figure 6-4). *Syn.:* **organic block**
(note: discuss topography)

Figure

URBAN — TRANSECT — RURAL

158

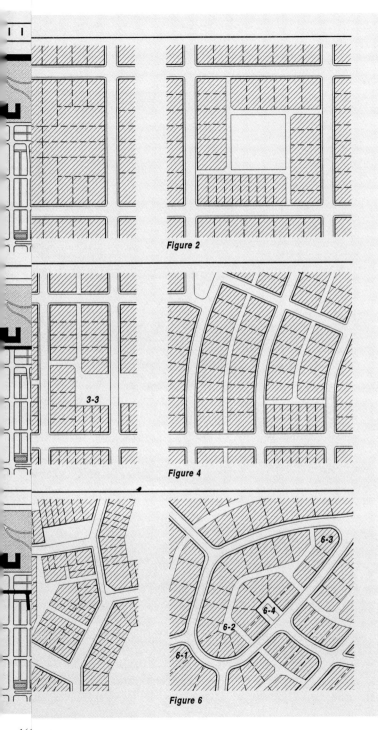

Figure 2

3-3

Figure 4

6-3

6-4

6-2

6-1

Figure 6

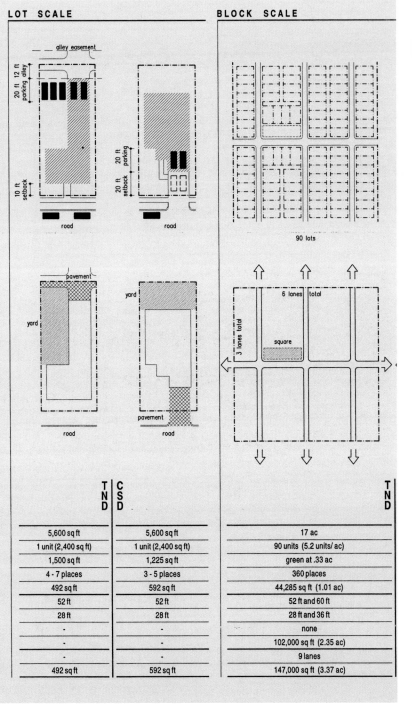

Analysis of thoroughfare design on lot, block and neighborhood scale.

Infrastructure Cost: the cost of service improvements on a given site, including utilities, streetscapes, and thoroughfares but excluding common amenities and buildings. The cost of infrastructure of Traditional Neighborhood Development should be equal to or less than that of Conventional Suburban Development for the following reasons:

- the elimination of CSD front-loaded driveways compensates for the rear lanes, providing the latter are built to driveway standards.

- the TNDs narrower thoroughfare widths compensate for the shorter length of cul-de-sacs.

- TNDs use of simple open sections for drainage wherever roads are appropriate.

- TNDs on-street parking consumes substantially less pavement than off-street parking by double-use of the moving lane as access lane.

- since the TNDs network system has much greater connectivity than the CSDs stem system, there is a near-complete elimination of costly collectors that do not provide developable frontage;

- TNDs increment of phasing is much smaller, as all market segments are accommodated within a single neighborhood as opposed to carrying the infrastructure costs of many homogeneous pods;

- lot width based on an off-street parking module (12, 24, 36, 48, 60, 72 etc.) increases the density of TNDs by eliminating slivers of wasted land (parking controls density).

	TND	CSD	TND
Total Area (constant)	5,600 sq ft	5,600 sq ft	17 ac
Units (constant)	1 unit (2,400 sq ft)	1 unit (2,400 sq ft)	90 units (5.2 units/ ac)
Open Space	1,500 sq ft	1,225 sq ft	green at .33 ac
Total Parking	4 - 7 places	3 - 5 places	360 places
Driveway / Alley Pavement	492 sq ft	592 sq ft	44,285 sq ft (1.01 ac)
Street ROW (constant)	52 ft	52 ft	52 ft and 60 ft
Pavement Width (constant)	28 ft	28 ft	28 ft and 36 ft
Cul-de-sac Radius	-	-	none
Pavement Area	-	-	102,000 sq ft (2.35 ac)
Total Connective Lanes	-	-	9 lanes
Total Pavement	492 sq ft	592 sq ft	147,000 sq ft (3.37 ac)

Diagrams showing
block typologies.

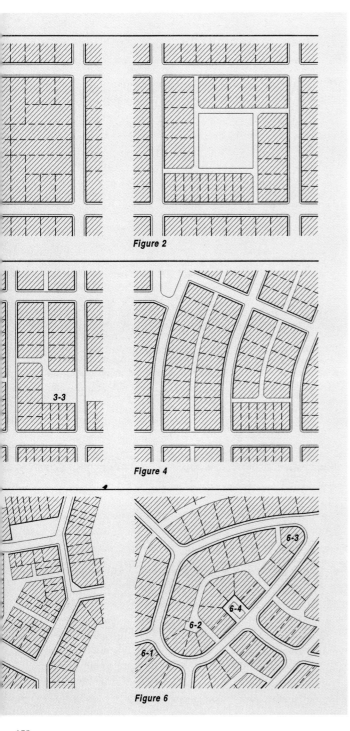

Figure 2

3-3

Figure 4

6-3

6-4

6-2

6-1

Figure 6

159

- **Thoroughfare** is an urban element that provides the major part of the public open space as well as moving lanes for vehicles. A thoroughfare is endowed with two attributes: capacity and character.

- **Capacity** is the number of vehicles that can move safely through a segment of a thoroughfare within a give time period. It is physically manifested by the number of lanes and their width, by the centerline radius, the curb radius, and the superelevation of the pavement.

- **Character** is the suitability of a thoroughfare as a setting for pedestrian activities and as a location for a variety of building types. Character is physically manifested by the associated frontage types as determined by the location within the Transect.

◀ R U R A L I I I I I I

- **Highway:** a long-distance, speed-movement tl fare traversing open countryside. A highway s relatively free of intersections, driveways, and buildings, otherwise it becomes strip developm interferes with traffic flow and human comfo **townless highway**

  Variants include **Expressway** and **Parkway** pressway is a highway with grade-separated tions. A parkway is a highway designed in co with naturalistic landscaping, including a varia median.

- **Drive:** a thoroughfare along the boundary be urbanized and a natural condition, usually alon front, a park, or a promontory. One side of a driv urban character of a street or boulevard, with and buildings, while the other has the qualities or parkway, with naturalistic planting and rural

- **Road:** a local, slow-movement thoroughfare su Edge and Rural Zones. Roads provide frontag density buildings such as houses. A road tends in character without curbs or striped on-street p may have clustered plantings and paths instea walks. The degree of rural or rustic character may be adjusted by the manipulation of such e

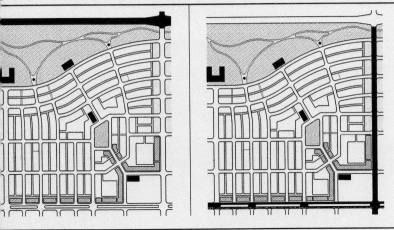

- **Boulevard:** a long-distance, free movement thorough-fare traversing an urbanized area. A boulevard is flanked by parking, sidewalks, and planters buffering the buildings along the sides.

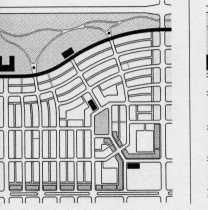 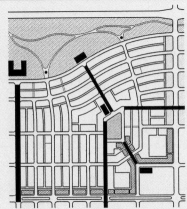

- **Avenue:** a limited distance, free-movement thorough-fare connecting civic locations within an urbanized area. Unlike a boulevard, its length is finite and its axis is terminated. An avenue may be conceived as an elongated square. *Syn.:* **connector** (from TOD usage)

  Variant: **allée.** a rural thoroughfare, free of fronting buildings, except at the terminus, where only trees in alignment define the space. Over time, an allée may become urbanized, evolving into an avenue.

 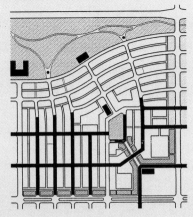

- **Street:** a local, slow-movement thoroughfare suitable for General, Center, and Core Zones. Streets provide frontage for higher-density buildings such as offices, shops, apartment buildings, and rowhouses. A street is urban in character, with raised curbs, closed drainage, wide sidewalks, parallel parking, and trees in individual planting areas. Character may vary somewhat, however, responding to the enfronting commercial or residential uses.

Infrastructure Cost: the cost of service improvements on a given site, including utilities, streetscapes, and thoroughfares but excluding common amenities and buildings. The cost of infrastructure of Traditional Neighborhood Development should be equal to or less than that of Conventional Suburban Development for the following reasons:

- the elimination of CSD front-loaded driveways compensates for the rear lanes, providing the latter are built to driveway standards.

- the TNDs narrower thoroughfare widths compensate for the shorter length of cul-de-sacs.

- TNDs use of simple open sections for drainage wherever roads are appropriate.

- TNDs on-street parking consumes substantially less pavement than off-street parking by double-use of the moving lane as access lane.

- since the TNDs network system has much greater connectivity than the CSDs stem system, there is a near-complete elimination of costly collectors that do not provide developable frontage;

- TNDs increment of phasing is much smaller, as all market segments are accommodated within a single neighborhood as opposed to carrying the infrastructure costs of many homogeneous pods;

- lot width based on an off-street parking module (12, 24, 36, 48, 60, 72 etc.) increases the density of TNDs by eliminating slivers of wasted land (parking controls density).

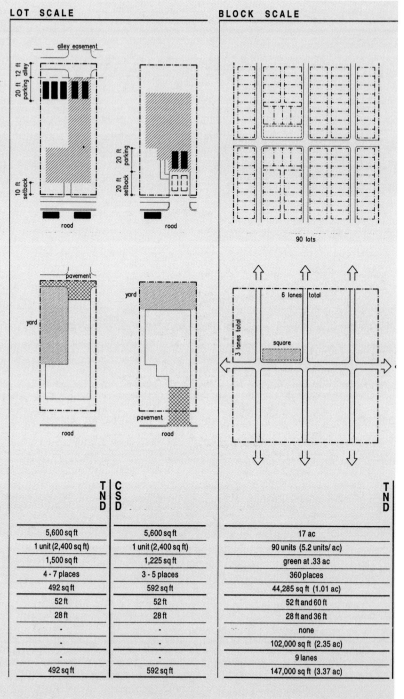

	TND	CSD	TND
Total Area (constant)	5,600 sq ft	5,600 sq ft	17 ac
Units (constant)	1 unit (2,400 sq ft)	1 unit (2,400 sq ft)	90 units (5.2 units/ ac)
Open Space	1,500 sq ft	1,225 sq ft	green at .33 ac
Total Parking	4 - 7 places	3 - 5 places	360 places
Driveway / Alley Pavement	492 sq ft	592 sq ft	44,285 sq ft (1.01 ac)
Street ROW (constant)	52 ft	52 ft	52 ft and 60 ft
Pavement Width (constant)	28 ft	28 ft	28 ft and 36 ft
Cul-de-sac Radius	-	-	none
Pavement Area	-	-	102,000 sq ft (2.35 ac)
Total Connective Lanes	-	-	9 lanes
Total Pavement	492 sq ft	592 sq ft	147,000 sq ft (3.37 ac)

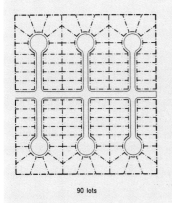

90 lots

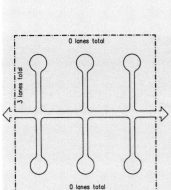

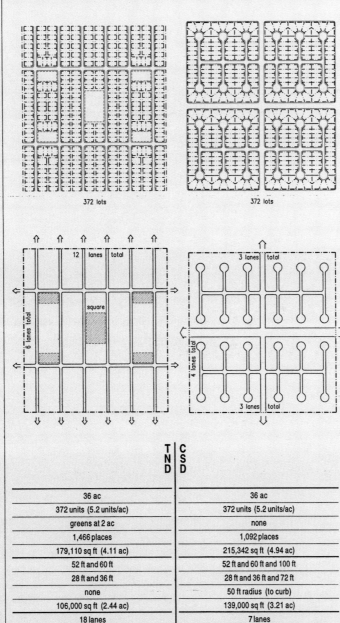

372 lots

372 lots

C S D	**T N D**	**C S D**
17 ac	36 ac	36 ac
90 units (5.2 units/ ac)	372 units (5.2 units/ac)	372 units (5.2 units/ac)
none	greens at 2 ac	none
270 places	1,466 places	1,092 places
53,244 sq ft (1.22 ac)	179,110 sq ft (4.11 ac)	215,342 sq ft (4.94 ac)
52 ft and 60 ft	52 ft and 60 ft	52 ft and 60 ft and 100 ft
28 ft and 36 ft	28 ft and 36 ft	28 ft and 36 ft and 72 ft
50 ft radius (to curb)	none	50 ft radius (to curb)
116,000 sq ft (2.67 ac.)	106,000 sq ft (2.44 ac)	139,000 sq ft (3.21 ac)
3 lanes	18 lanes	7 lanes
170,000 sq ft (3.90 ac)	285,000 sq ft (6.56 ac)	355,000 sq ft (8.16 ac)

Diagram of private
frontages and where
they are applicable
on the Transect.

• **Frontage:** the privately held layer between the facade of a building and the lot line. The variables of frontage are the dimensional depth of the front yard and the combination of architectural elements such as fences, stoops, porches, and colonnades. *See:* **streetscape**

The combination of the private frontage, the public streetscape and the types of thorougfare defines the character of the majority of the public realm. The combination of elements constitutes the layer between the private realm of buildings. It ranges in character from urban to rural as a function of the composition of their elements. These elements influence social behavior.

• **Gallery & Arcade:** a facade of a building or an attached colonnade. The building overlaps the sidewalk above while the ground story remains set back at the lot line. This type is indicated for retail use, but only when the sidewalk is fully absorbed within the arcade so that a pedestrian cannot bypass it. An easement for private use of the right-of-way is usually required. To be useful, the arcade should be no less than 12 ft wide.

• **Shopfront & Awning:** a facade is aligned close to the frontage line with the entrance at sidewalk grade. This type is conventional for retail frontage. It is commonly equipped with cantilevered shed roof or an awning. The absence of a raised ground story precludes residential use on the ground floor, although this use is appropriate above.

• **Stoop:** a facade is aligned close to the frontage line with the ground story elevated from the sidewalk, securing privacy for the windows. This type is suitable for ground-floor residential uses at short setbacks with rowhouses and apartment buildings. An easement may be necessary to accommodate the encroaching stoop. This type may be interspersed with the shopfront.

• **Forecourt:** a facade is aligned close to the frontage line with a portion of it set back. The forecourt created is suitable for gardens, vehicular drop offs, and utility off loading. This type should be used sparingly and in conjunction with the two frontage types above, as a continuous excessive setback is boring and unsafe for pedestrians. Trees within the forecourts should be placed to have their canopies overhanging the sidewalks.

• **Dooryard & Light Court:** a facade is set back from the frontage line with an elevated garden or terrace, or a sunken light court. This type can effectively buffer residential quarters from the sidewalk, while removing the private yard from public encroachment. The terrace is suitable for restaurants and cafes as the eye of the sitter is level with that of the standing passerby. The light court can give light and access to a basement.

• **Porch & Fence:** a facade is set back from the frontage line with an encroaching porch appended. The porch should be within a conversational distance of the sidewalk, while a fence at the frontage line maintains the demarcation of the yard. A great variety of porches is possible, but to be useful, none should be less than 8 ft wide.

• **Common Lawn:** a facade set back substantially from the frontage line. The front yard thus created should remain unfenced and be visually continuous with adjacent yards. The ideal is to simulate buildings sitting in a common rural landscape. A front porch is not warranted, as social interaction from the enfronting throughfare is unlikely at such a distance. Common Lawns are suitable frontages for higher speed thoroughfares, as the large setback provides a buffer from the traffic.

• **Convenience Parking:** A facade no more than 80 ft from the right-of-way. Parking is placed within the first layer. Private sidewalks are provided between the public sidewalk and the building entrances, and between connecting buildings. The parking and private sidewalk system are landscaped to provide shade and shelter and a streetwall buffer. Appropriate transit stops are provided along the frontages, directly linked to the private sidewalk system.

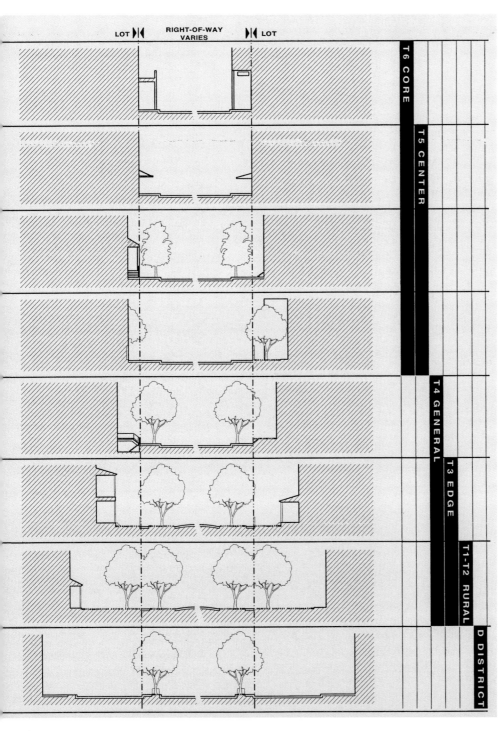

LOT ▶◀   **RIGHT-OF-WAY VARIES**   ▶◀ LOT

T6 CORE

T5 CENTER

T4 GENERAL

T3 EDGE

T1-T2 RURAL

D DISTRICT

165

STREETSCAPE ELEMENTS

	Highway	Rural Road
• **Streetscape:** the publicly held layer between the lot line and the edge of the vehicular lanes. The principal variables of streetscape are the type and dimension of curbs, walks, planters, street trees, and streetlights.		
• **Curb:** the detailing of the edge of the vehicular pavement, usually incorporating drainage.		
Curb Radius	25 ft min	25 ft min
Curb Type	open swale	open swale
Parking Type	none	on grass
• **Sidewalk:** the layer of the streetscape dedicated exclusively to pedestrian activity. There is a choice of sidewalk width, and surface which are important components of the urban to rural character of the Transect.		
Walkway Type	path optional	path
Planter	continuous swale	continuous swale
• **Planter:** the layer of the streetscape which accommodates street trees. Planters may be narrow or wide, continuous or individual, holding **allées** or clusters of trees, all depending on the intended urban to rural character of the location within the Transect.		
Arrangement	clustered	clustered
Tree Type	multiple species	multiple species

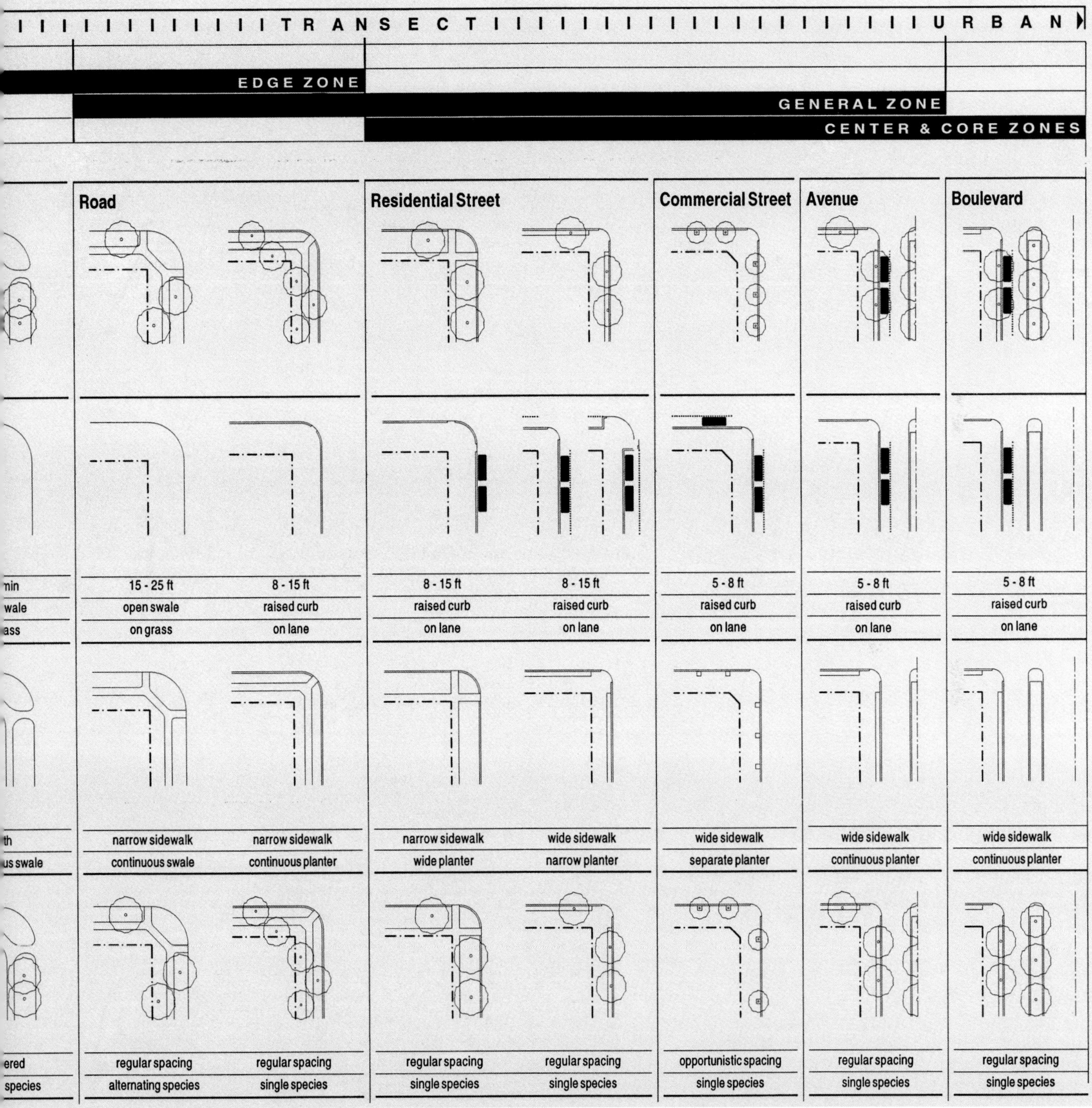

EDGE ZONE

GENERAL ZONE

CENTER & CORE ZONES

	Road		Residential Street		Commercial Street	Avenue	Boulevard
min	15 - 25 ft	8 - 15 ft	8 - 15 ft	8 - 15 ft	5 - 8 ft	5 - 8 ft	5 - 8 ft
swale	open swale	raised curb	raised curb	raised curb	raised curb	raised curb	raised curb
ass	on grass	on lane	on lane	on lane	on lane	on lane	on lane
th	narrow sidewalk	narrow sidewalk	narrow sidewalk	wide sidewalk	wide sidewalk	wide sidewalk	wide sidewalk
us swale	continuous swale	continuous planter	wide planter	narrow planter	separate planter	continuous planter	continuous planter
ered	regular spacing	regular spacing	regular spacing	regular spacing	opportunistic spacing	regular spacing	regular spacing
species	alternating species	single species	single species	single species	single species	single species	single species

167

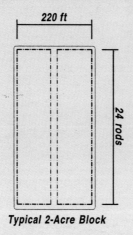

Typical 2-Acre Block

- **Density:** the theoretical capacity of a lot to accommodate quantities of certain building uses. It is a code technique to designate the number of dwellings which may be accommodated within a standard measure of land area. Usually it is expressed in units/acre.

- **Maximum Density:** the capacity of a lot, usually determined by parking capacity, not by lot coverage or floor-area ratio. Thus the size and configuration of a lot is an important determinant of density insofar as it can efficiently accommodate surface parking. The provision of parking in structures or below ground decouples the theoretical density, which is then controlled only by the practical, economic, and aesthetic limits of parking decks.

- **Net Density:** a dependable measure of the efficiency of a building type as it excludes the highly variable areas of thoroughfare and open space included in gross density calculations.

- **Gross Density:** *tbd*

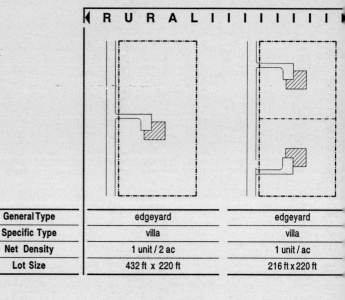

R U R A L I I I I I I I I

General Type	edgeyard	edgeyard
Specific Type	villa	villa
Net Density	1 unit / 2 ac	1 unit / ac
Lot Size	432 ft x 220 ft	216 ft x 220 ft

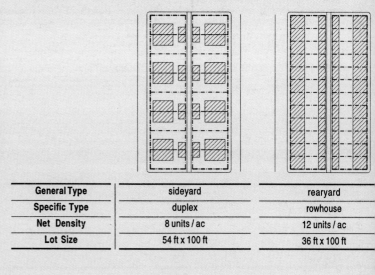

T R A N S E C T I I I I I

General Type	sideyard	rearyard
Specific Type	duplex	rowhouse
Net Density	8 units / ac	12 units / ac
Lot Size	54 ft x 100 ft	36 ft x 100 ft

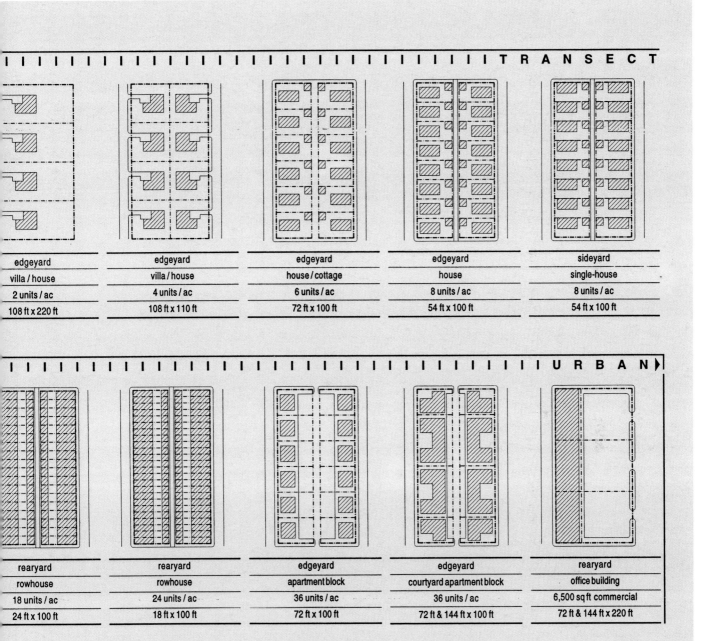

edgeyard	edgeyard	edgeyard	edgeyard	sideyard
villa / house	villa / house	house / cottage	house	single-house
2 units / ac	4 units / ac	6 units / ac	8 units / ac	8 units / ac
108 ft x 220 ft	108 ft x 110 ft	72 ft x 100 ft	54 ft x 100 ft	54 ft x 100 ft

rearyard	rearyard	edgeyard	edgeyard	rearyard
rowhouse	rowhouse	apartment block	courtyard apartment block	office building
18 units / ac	24 units / ac	36 units / ac	36 units / ac	6,500 sq ft commercial
24 ft x 100 ft	18 ft x 100 ft	72 ft x 100 ft	72 ft & 144 ft x 100 ft	72 ft & 144 ft x 220 ft

Diagram showing parts of the Implementation Code.

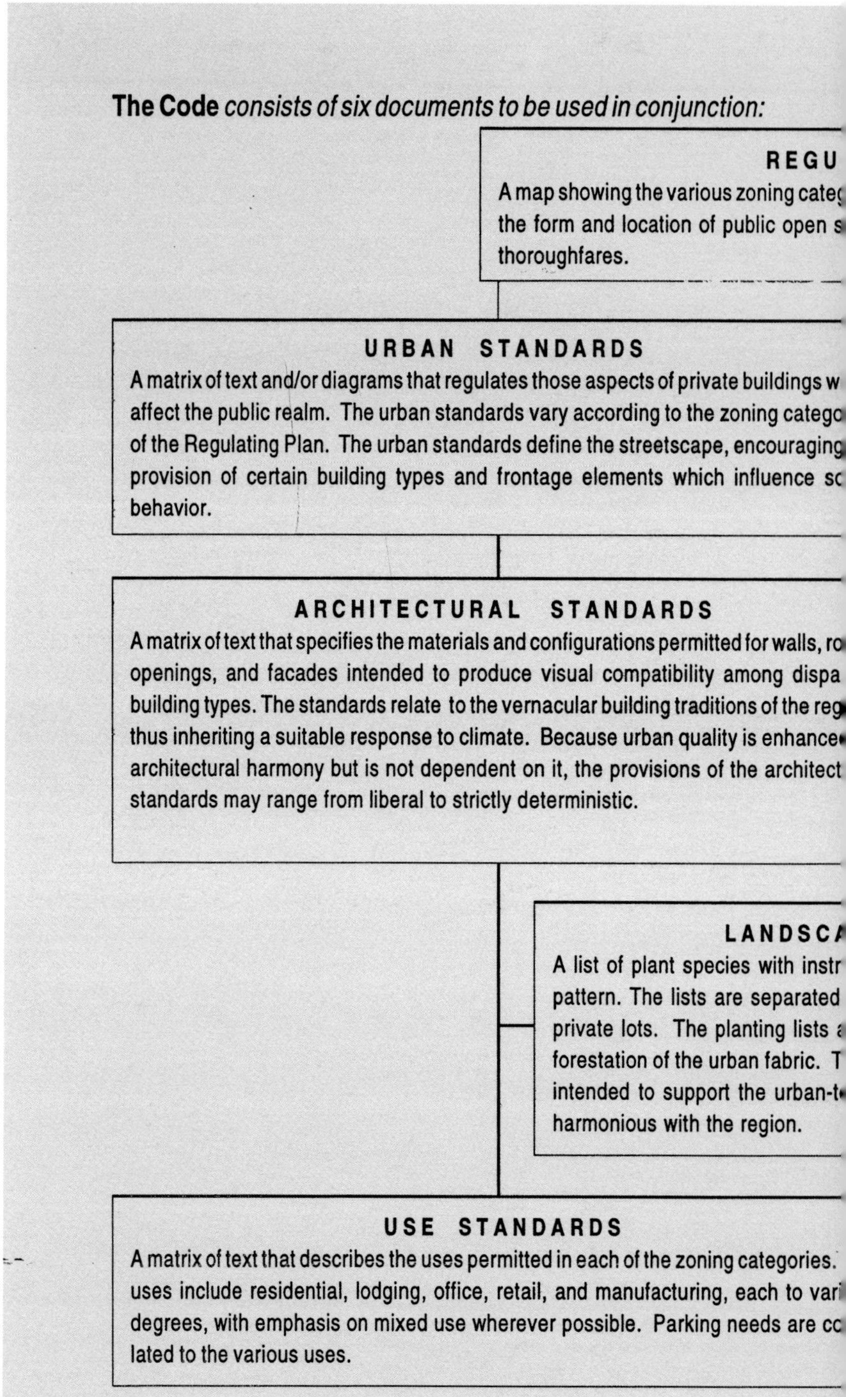

The Code *consists of six documents to be used in conjunction:*

REGU

A map showing the various zoning categ the form and location of public open s thoroughfares.

URBAN STANDARDS

A matrix of text and/or diagrams that regulates those aspects of private buildings w affect the public realm. The urban standards vary according to the zoning catego of the Regulating Plan. The urban standards define the streetscape, encouraging provision of certain building types and frontage elements which influence sc behavior.

ARCHITECTURAL STANDARDS

A matrix of text that specifies the materials and configurations permitted for walls, ro openings, and facades intended to produce visual compatibility among dispa building types. The standards relate to the vernacular building traditions of the reg thus inheriting a suitable response to climate. Because urban quality is enhance architectural harmony but is not dependent on it, the provisions of the architect standards may range from liberal to strictly deterministic.

LANDSCA

A list of plant species with instr pattern. The lists are separated private lots. The planting lists forestation of the urban fabric. T intended to support the urban-t harmonious with the region.

USE STANDARDS

A matrix of text that describes the uses permitted in each of the zoning categories. uses include residential, lodging, office, retail, and manufacturing, each to vari degrees, with emphasis on mixed use wherever possible. Parking needs are cc lated to the various uses.

PLAN

cision. The regulating plan also shows
e type and trajectories of the various

THOROUGHFARE STANDARDS

atrix of drawings, specifications, and dimensions that assembles vehicular and
estrian ways into sets specialized in both capacity and character. These specify
dways, sidewalks, planters, street trees, and street lights. The combinations range
n urban to rural. They are assigned to appropriate locations in the Regulating Plan.

NDARDS

ding their location and planting
rtaining to public areas and to
d toward achieving a coherent
and disposition of the planting is
ct and to create an ecosystem

A Master Plan

is illustrative and
compliance is voluntary

*The illustrations are
formulated as guidelines*

Guidelines

are enforceable
by covenant

*The guidelines are translated to
legal language*

A Code

is instructive and
enforceable by
contract

*The Code is enacted
into law*

An Ordinance

is mandatory and
enforced as
municipal law

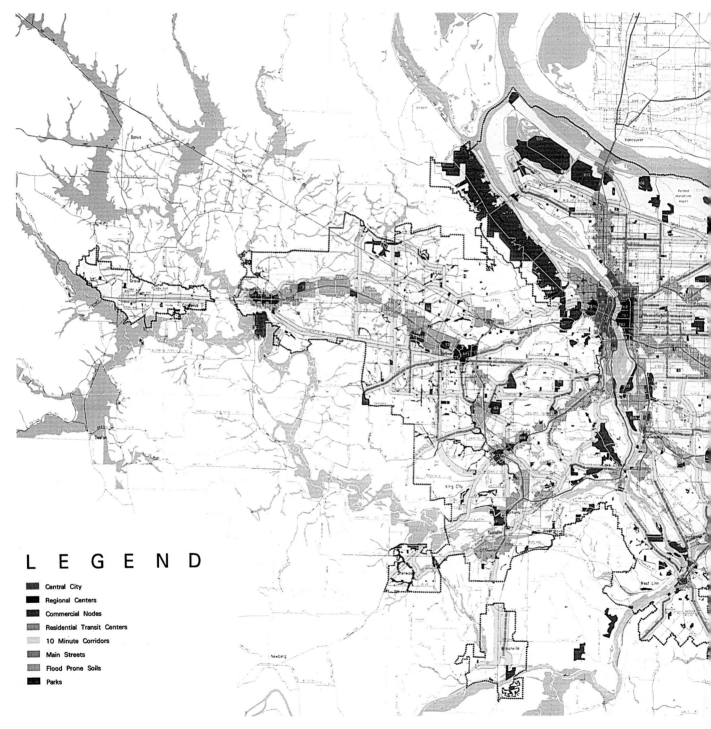

L E G E N D

- Central City
- Regional Centers
- Commercial Nodes
- Residential Transit Centers
- 10 Minute Corridors
- Main Streets
- Flood Prone Soils
- Parks

172

Region 2040, 1994

The Region 2040 Study for Portland Metro, led by Calthorpe and Associates, investigated how to accommodate the expected increase in population of 760,000 over the next fifty years. The study focused on the "interdependence between ... the size of the region as defined by its Urban Growth Boundary (UGB), investments in transit, and the scale of the pedestrian at the neighborhood level." Three conceptual options were depicted: the first allowed the region to grow out by expanding the urban boundary. The second maintained the UGB in place and forced development within, and the third option promoted a series of satellite cities of 20,000 to 30,000 residents each that would contain and minimize the regional expansion.

All three concepts, however, emphasized urban and suburban infill that created transit-oriented districts. Eight sites were explored in more detail: six within the current UGB and two without. Of the sites, Orenco Station has been most successfully developed with a master plan by Fletcher Farr Ayotte.

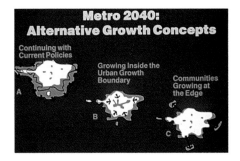

The diagram illustrates the recommended transportation and land use vision for the Portland, Oregon, region. This scheme maintained the current Urban Growth Boundary in place and focused on intensive infill along transportation corridors.

Three conceptual options for the region's urban form that manage anticipated growth.

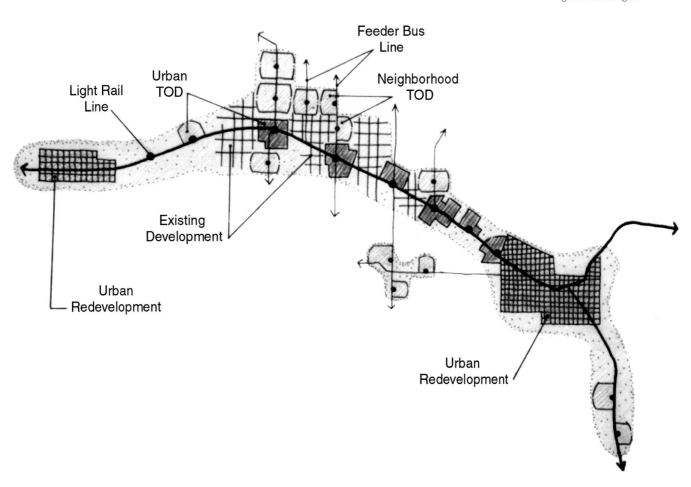

Light-rail in downtown
Portland. (Courtesy:
Calthorpe and Associates)

The diagram shows how
transit lines could define
growth in the region.

Feeder Bus
Line

Urban
TOD

Light Rail
Line

Neighborhood
TOD

Existing
Development

Urban
Redevelopment

Urban
Redevelopment

Photograph showing
the existing malls at
Clackamas Town Center.
(Courtesy: Calthorpe
Associates)

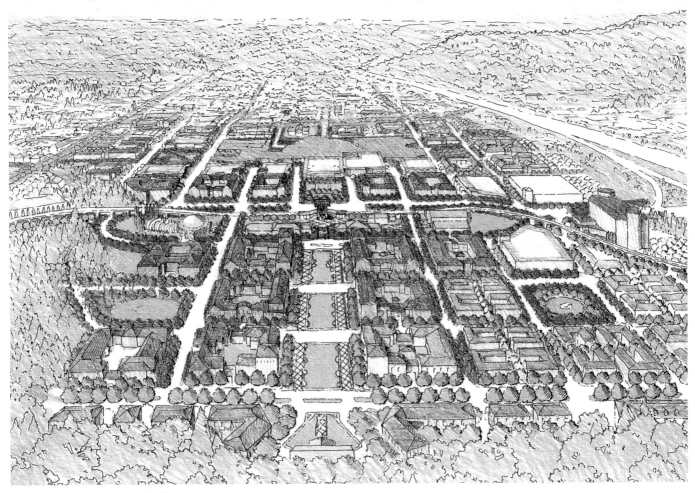

Aerial perspective of the High-Intensity Plan for the Clackamas Town Center looking north. New infill creates a dense mixed-use development around a new transit station.
The former parking lots are carved into streets and blocks that accommodate 29,000 new dwelling units and 4,600 jobs. One of the malls is demolished, and the other is incorporated into the new urban structure.
(See figs. 5.12–5.14)

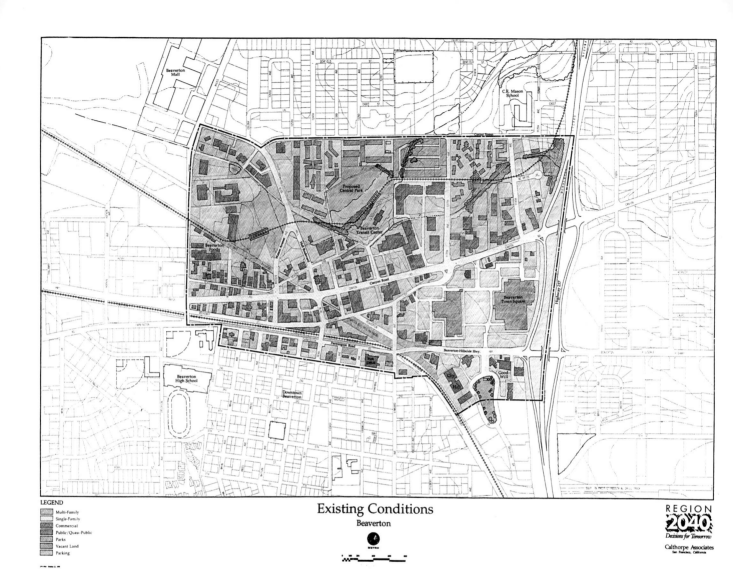

LEGEND

Multi-Family
Single-Family
Commercial
Public/Quasi-Public
Parks
Vacant Land
Parking

Existing Conditions
Beaverton

METRO

REGION
2040
Decisions for Tomorrow

Calthorpe Associates
San Francisco, California

Plan of existing conditions for the city of Beaverton. The study area is just north of the historic downtown, where the confluence of two rail lines and a major roadway have created an irregular pattern of blocks and streets. Commercial uses predominate presently. The proposed rail line and two transit stops are indicated.

The High-Intensity Plan for the city of Beaverton which creates approximately 2,000 new dwelling units and 7,000 new jobs. Where possible, new streets are added. Proposed buildings, many mixed-use containing residential units, line the streets. Parking is kept to the interior of blocks where possible.

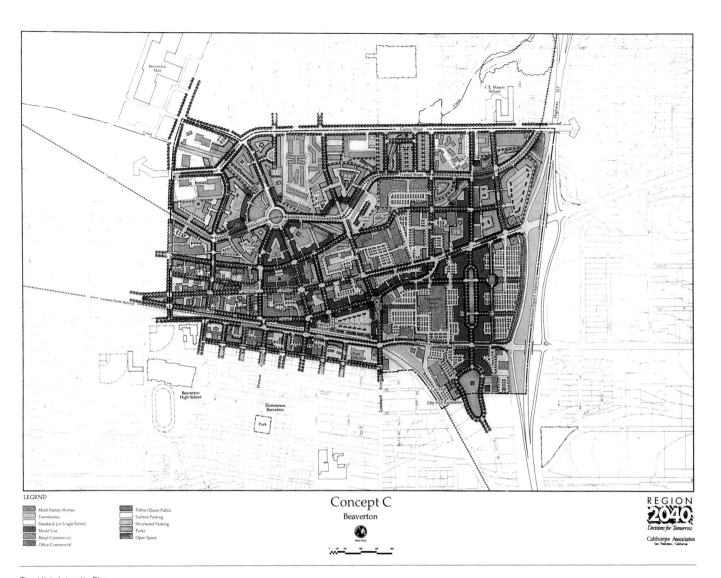

LEGEND

- Multi-Family Homes
- Townhomes
- Standard-Lot Single-Family
- Mixed-Use
- Retail Commercial
- Office Commercial
- Public/Quasi-Public
- Surface Parking
- Structured Parking
- Parks
- Open Space

Concept C

Beaverton

METRO

Calthorpe Associates
San Francisco, California

REGION
2040
Decisions for Tomorrow

The High-Intensity Plan
(Concept C) for the city
of Beaverton.

The existing village
of Orenco.

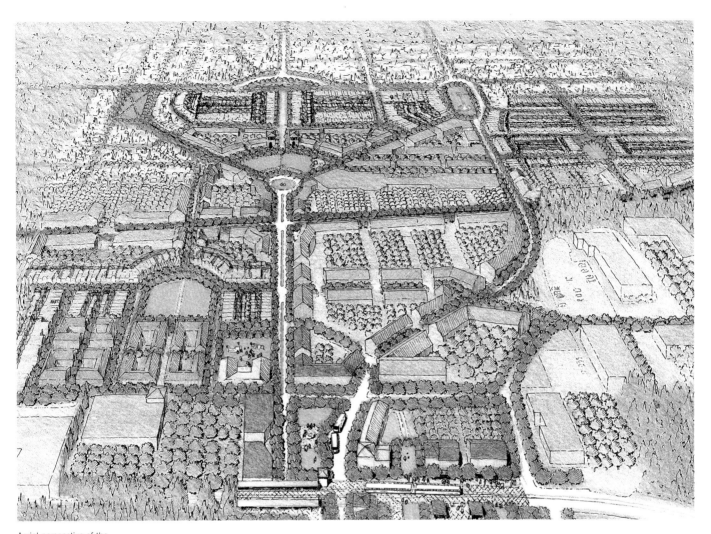

Aerial perspective of the
High-Intensity Plan
for Orenco.

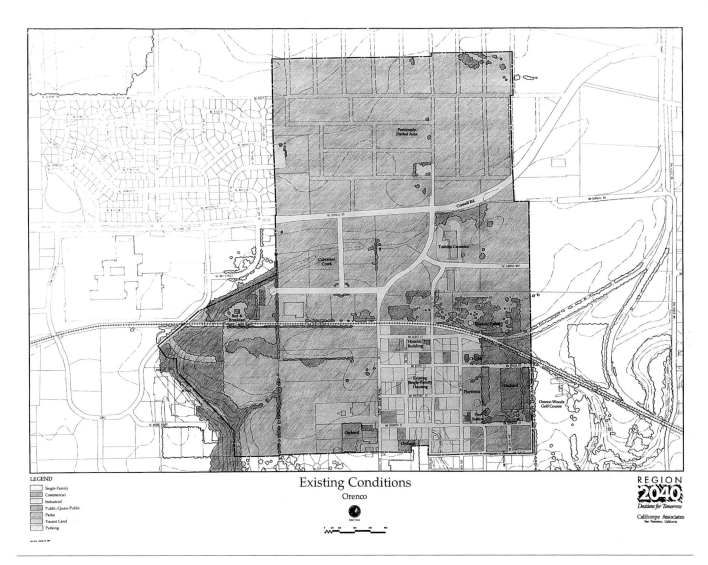

Existing Conditions
Orenco

LEGEND
- Single-Family
- Commercial
- Industrial
- Public/Quasi-Public
- Parks
- Vacant Land
- Parking

REGION
2040
Decisions for Tomorrow

Calthorpe Associates
San Francisco, California

Plan of existing conditions for the village of Orenco. The plan shows the clear grid of the existing village and the newer cul-de-sac sprawl development in the northwest. It also shows the future light-rail line around which the new development will be focused.

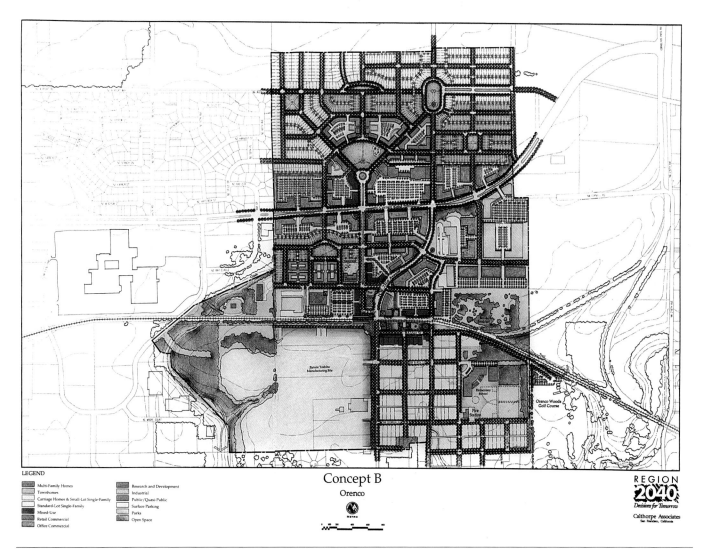

LEGEND

Multi-Family Homes
Townhomes
Carriage Homes & Small-Lot Single-Family
Standard-Lot Single-Family
Mixed-Use
Retail Commercial
Office Commercial

Research and Development
Industrial
Public/Quasi-Public
Surface Parking
Parks
Open Space

Concept B

Orenco

METRO

REGION
2040
Decisions for Tomorrow

Calthorpe Associates
San Francisco, California

The High-Intensity Plan
for Orenco which creates
1,700 new dwelling units
in a mix of types, as well
as substantial amounts
of retail and office space,
industrial uses, civic
buildings, and parks and
open spaces. (Compare to
actual master plan based
on this Study by Fletcher
Farr Ayotte, fig. 26
on page137)

The Charleston
Downtown Plan, 1999

The Charleston Downtown Plan, produced by Ken Greenberg and Andrea Gabor of Urban Strategies, is a strategic plan for the next twenty years. Its subject is one of the most cherished historic American cities. Balancing tourism of the old city with the development of contemporary Charleston has been the largest challenge. The plan establishes parameters to guide future development, anticipating both private and public sector investment. Rather than being a regulatory document, the Downtown Plan provides an interpretative framework within which individual decisions can be made. In this way, the plan intends to foster flexibility and creativity rather than prescribe form. (Collaborating consultants include Development Strategies Inc. and SBF Design)

Transition areas

Redevelopment areas

Stable corridors

Stable neighborhoods

The historic spine of the peninsula, the Upper King/ Meeting corridor will be strengthened with improved transit and infill development.

Cross peninsula trails will connect to Riverwalks.

Upper Lockwood will contain new employment uses such as corporate headquarters and high tech research and development.

Brittlebank Park will be extended south.

MUSC plans to expand its facilities.

Public access to the Ashley River will be improved.

Lower Lockwood contains infill housing opportunities as well as the chance to considerably enhance the public space at the water's edge.

The diagram illustrates the recommended vision for the lower peninsula.

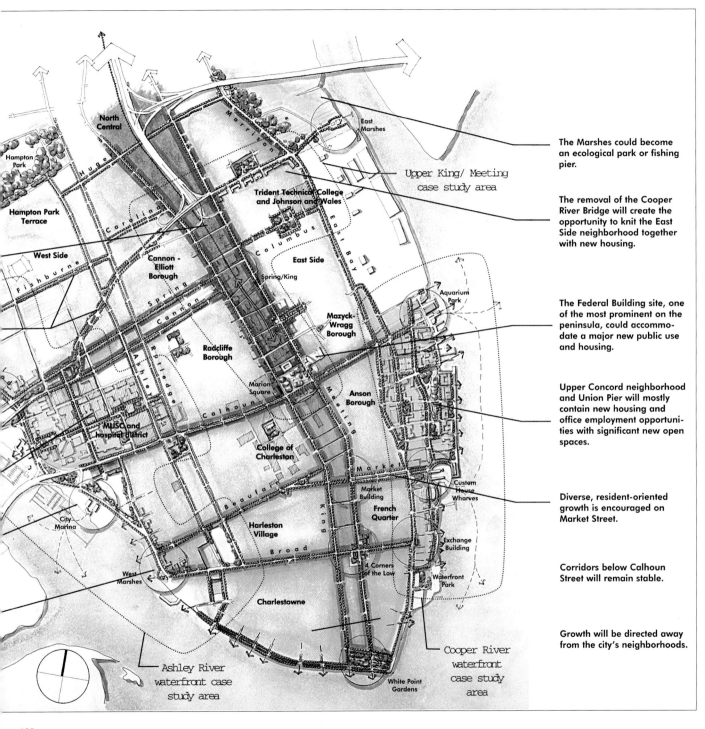

The Marshes could become an ecological park or fishing pier.

The removal of the Cooper River Bridge will create the opportunity to knit the East Side neighborhood together with new housing.

The Federal Building site, one of the most prominent on the peninsula, could accommodate a major new public use and housing.

Upper Concord neighborhood and Union Pier will mostly contain new housing and office employment opportunities with significant new open spaces.

Diverse, resident-oriented growth is encouraged on Market Street.

Corridors below Calhoun Street will remain stable.

Growth will be directed away from the city's neighborhoods.

Upper King/ Meeting case study area

Ashley River waterfront case study area

Cooper River waterfront case study area

North Central

Hampton Park

Hampton Park Terrace

West Side

Cannon - Elliott Borough

Trident Technical College and Johnson and Wales

East Side

Spring/King

East Marshes

Aquarium Park

Mazyck- Wragg Borough

Radcliffe Borough

Marion Square

Anson Borough

MUSC and hospital district

College of Charleston

Custom House Wharves

Market Building

French Quarter

City Marina

Harleston Village

Exchange Building

West Marshes

4 Corners of the Law

Waterfront Park

Charlestowne

White Point Gardens

Aerial photo of Charleston. Although the project focuses on the downtown, or lower peninsula, the entire peninsula and city region were considered in assessing conditions and suggesting recommendations.

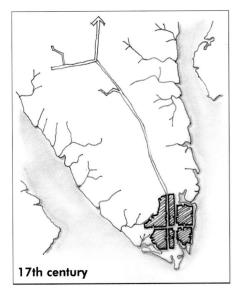

17th century

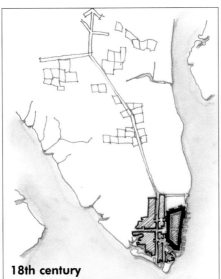

18th century

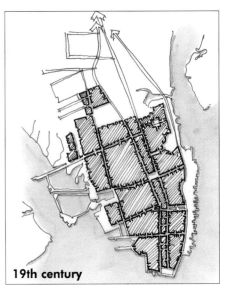

19th century

Illustrations showing the
evolution of the urban
form of the downtown
over four centuries.

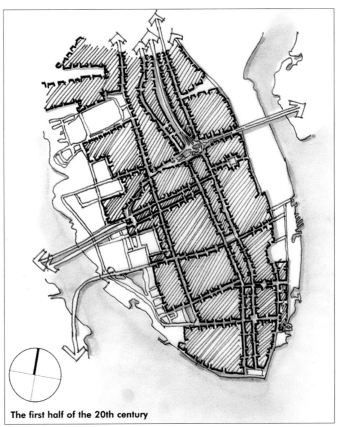

The first half of the 20th century

The Downtown Plan is built upon the understanding that the lower peninsula comprises three distinct place types, categorized under "stable," "transition," and "redevelopment."

The strategy proposes that gaps along the corridors be redeveloped with dense and continuous low to mid-rise structures and supported by transit.

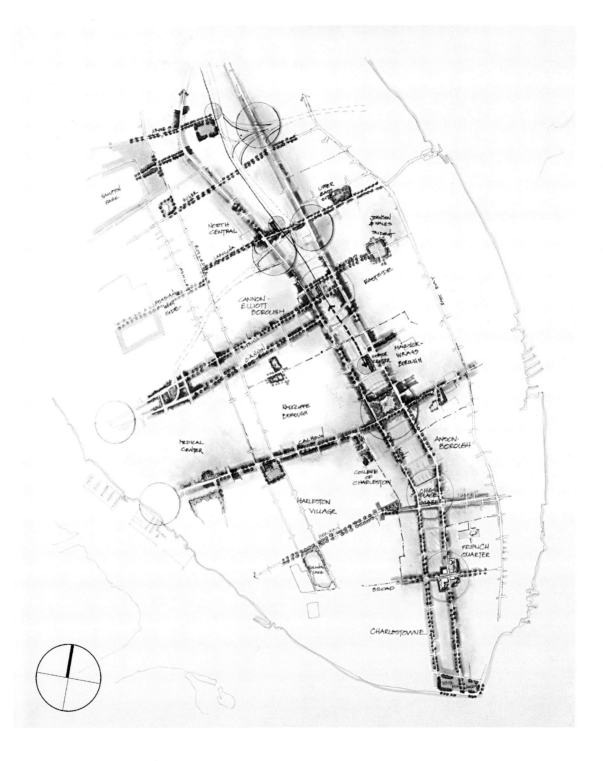

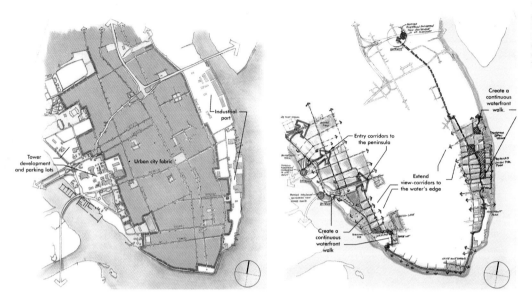

The plan studied the edge conditions outside the historic city fabric, and recommended strategies to extend this fabric, thereby creating linkages to the water's edge.

Tower development and parking lots

Industrial port

Urban city fabric

Entry corridors to the peninsula

Create a continuous waterfront walk.

Extend view-corridors to the water's edge

Create a continuous waterfront walk

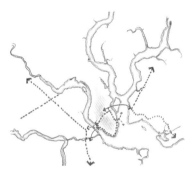

These diagrams illustrate the integration of the existing and proposed open spaces within the downtown, as well as their connection to a regional network.

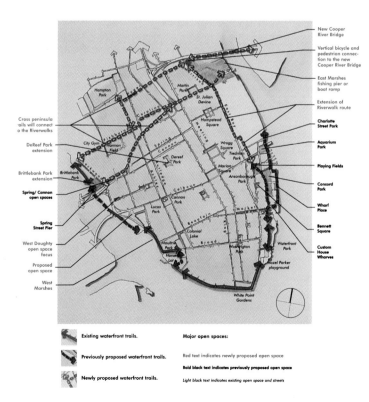

New Cooper River Bridge

Vertical bicycle and pedestrian connection to the new Cooper River Bridge

East Marshes fishing pier or boat ramp

Extension of Riverwalk route

Charlotte Street Park

Aquarium Park

Playing Fields

Concord Park

Wharf Place

Bennett Square

Custom House Wharves

Cross peninsula trails will connect to the Riverwalks

DeReef Park extension

Brittlebank Park extension

Spring/ Cannon open spaces

Spring Street Pier

West Doughty open space focus

Proposed open space

West Marshes

Hampton Park

Martin Park

St. Julian Devine

Hampstead Square

City Gym

Harmon Field

Dereef Park

Wragg Square

Tiedman

Marian Square

Ansonborough Park

Brittlebank Park

Lucas Park

Cannon Park

Calhoun

Colonial Lake

Moultrie Park

Horse Lot

Washington Park

Waterfront Park

Hazel Parker playground

White Point Gardens

Existing waterfront trails.

Previously proposed waterfront trails.

Newly proposed waterfront trails.

Major open spaces:

Red text indicates newly proposed open space

Bold black text indicates previously proposed open space

Light black text indicates existing open space and streets

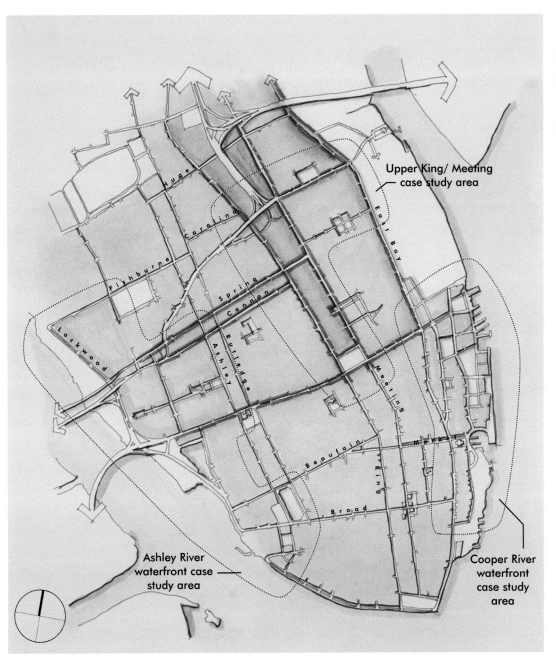

Stable area

Transition area

Redevelopment area

Upper King/ Meeting case study area

Ashley River waterfront case study area

Cooper River waterfront case study area

The diagram illustrates how most proposed growth within the downtown would occur in transition and redevelopment areas, while corridors could accommodate development without impacting the stable, historic neighborhoods.

191

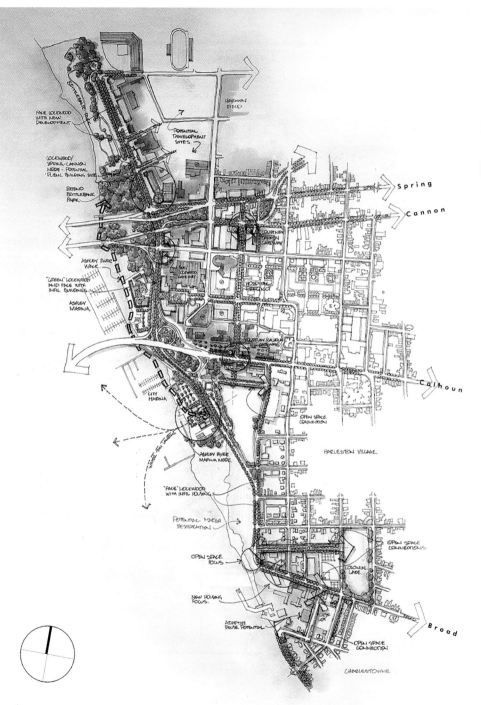

FACE LOCKWOOD WITH NEW DEVELOPMENT

LOCKWOOD/ SPRING-CANNON NODE- POTENTIAL PUBLIC BUILDING SITE

EXTEND BRITTLEBANK PARK

ASHLEY RIVER WALK

"GREEN" LOCKWOOD MID FACE WITH INFILL BUILDINGS

ASHLEY MARINA

CITY MARINA

ASHLEY RIVER MARINA NODE

"FACE" LOCKWOOD WITH INFILL HOUSING

POTENTIAL MIXED DESIGNATION

OPEN SPACE FOCUS

NEW HOUSING FOCUS

ADAPTIVE REUSE POTENTIAL

POTENTIAL DEVELOPMENT SITES.

HAMPTON FIELD

COURTENAY OPEN GREENWAY

NEW LOCKWOOD GATEWAY

HOSPITAL DISTRICT

COURTENAY/CALHOUN GATEWAY

OPEN SPACE CONNECTION

HARLESTON VILLAGE

OPEN SPACE CONNECTIONS

COLONIAL LAKE

OPEN SPACE CONNECTION

CHARLESTOWNE

Spring

Cannon

Calhoun

Broad

Primarily mixed-use commercial

Primarily residential

The Ashley River waterfront redevelopment would create a new western edge to the peninsula. The infill would consist primarily of new mixed-use and residential buildings. Lockwood Drive would be transformed into an attractive riverfront drive through landscape and new pedestrian-friendly development. In this way, a roadway that once separated the city from the river becomes an asset to the adjoining neighborhoods.

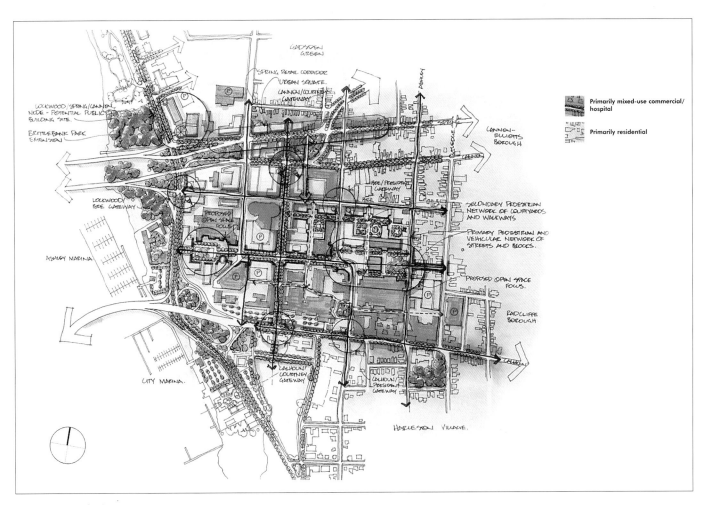

GADSDEN GREEN

SPRING RETAIL CORRIDOR

URBAN SQUARE.

CANNON/COURTENAY GATEWAY

ASHLEY

LOCKWOOD/SPRING/CANNON NODE - POTENTIAL PUBLIC BUILDING SITE.

BRITTLEBANK PARK EXTENSION

CANNON-ELLIOTTS BOROUGH

LOCKWOOD/BEE GATEWAY

BEE/PRESIDENT GATEWAY

SECONDARY PEDESTRIAN NETWORK OF COURTYARDS AND WALKWAYS

PROPOSED OPEN SPACE FOCUS

PRIMARY PEDESTRIAN AND VEHICULAR NETWORK OF STREETS AND BLOCKS.

ASHLEY MARINA

PROPOSED OPEN SPACE FOCUS.

RADCLIFFE BOROUGH

CITY MARINA.

CALHOUN/ COURTENAY GATEWAY

CALHOUN/ PRESIDENT GATEWAY

HARLESTON VILLAGE.

Primarily mixed-use commercial/ hospital

Primarily residential

Recommendations for the
hospital district
on the Ashley riverfront.

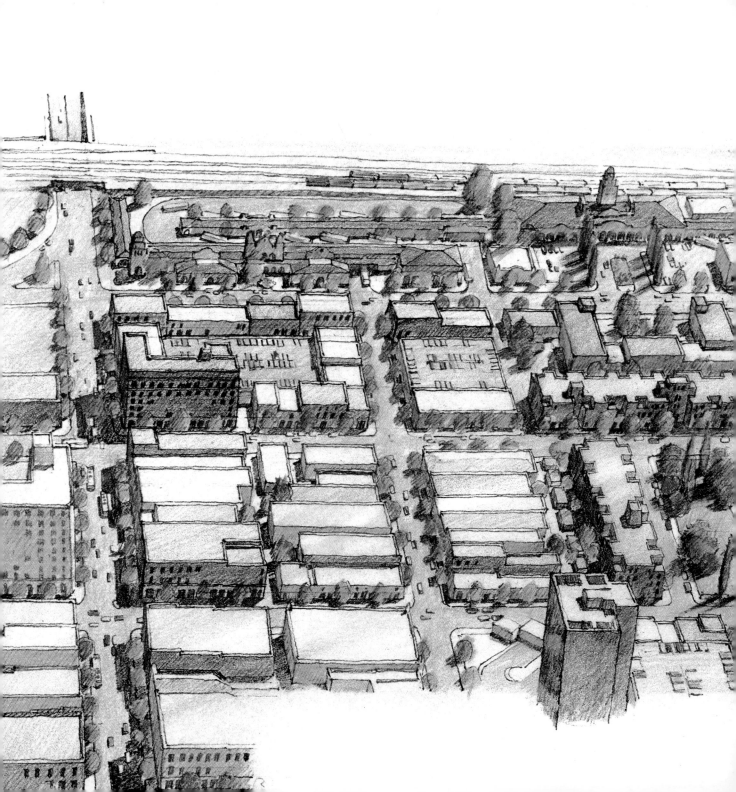

Aerial perspective
of built-out project area
from an early study.

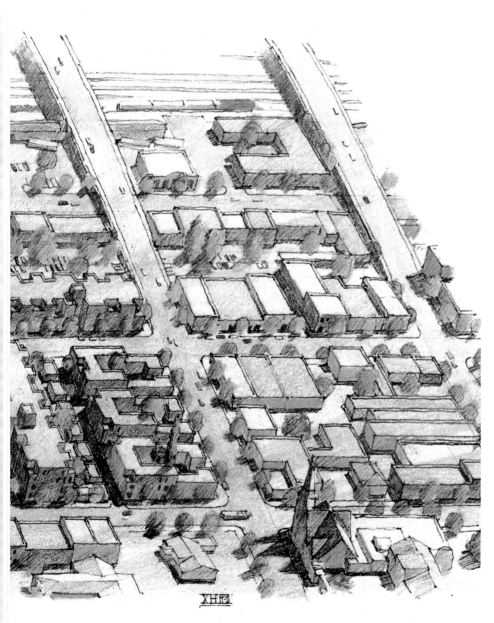

Alvarado Transportation Center, 1999

The Master Plan for the Alvarado Transportation Center Project Area, Albuquerque, New Mexico, by Moule and Polyzoides, Architects and Urbanists, is an urban infill master plan. The strategy builds on the strengths of both existing buildings and activities, and anticipates significant new private and public projects. The plan establishes a regulating plan, which structures the streets and blocks (mainly by restoring the street grid where it had been eroded) and assigns building types to new platting. The plan calls for developing at least two anchors, of civic or commercial nature, and incrementally completing the spaces in-between as market demand allows. Multiple housing types are also introduced as infill building. The strategy draws on the traditional urban and architectural form of the southwest in general, and Albuquerque in particular.

Karow Nord Master Plan, 1998

The Karow Nord Master Plan, by Moore Ruble Yudell, is a major expansion of the town of Karow, northeast of Berlin proper, integrating 5,000 new housing units, schools, recreation, and shopping. The plan drawing from the tradition of Garden Cities, is organized by a network of green spaces which will eventually weave through the town with linear parks extending l to the fields beyond. The plan also incorporates a gradation of building scales, easing the transition from the existing two-story town to new four story housing blocks in the densest areas of the new neighborhood. This is achieved primarily through a variety of housing types, including two-story agrarian row houses, courtyard housing, multifamily urban villas, and dense perimeter-block buildings.

Illustrative plan for the expansion of the town.

View of "Karow Courts."

Illustrative plan for the
expansion of the town.

View of the Karow Nord
Town Center.

The sketch shows part
of an analysis of open
space, building types and
urban linkage for the
town. A diagonal street,
lined with multifamily
"villas," connects a large
public space and market
hall to a prominent public
building.

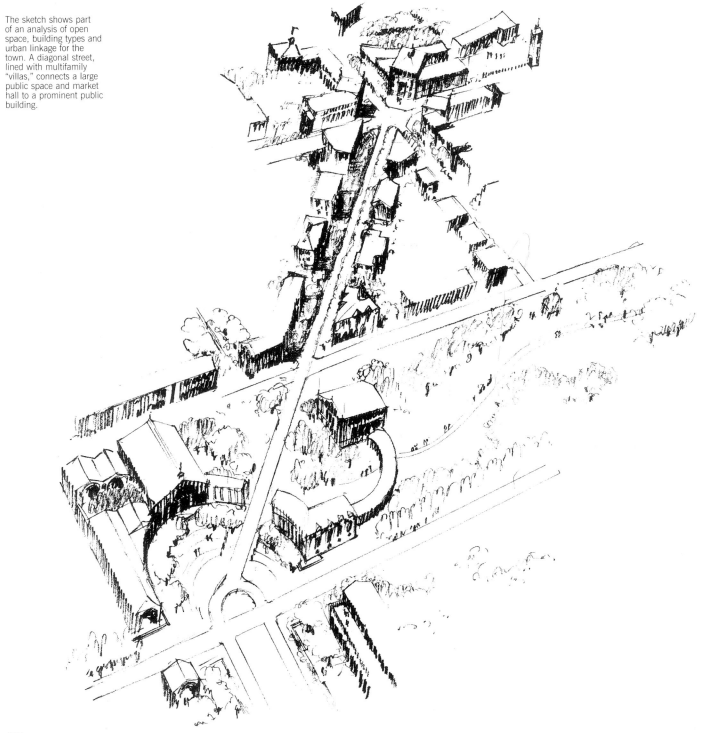

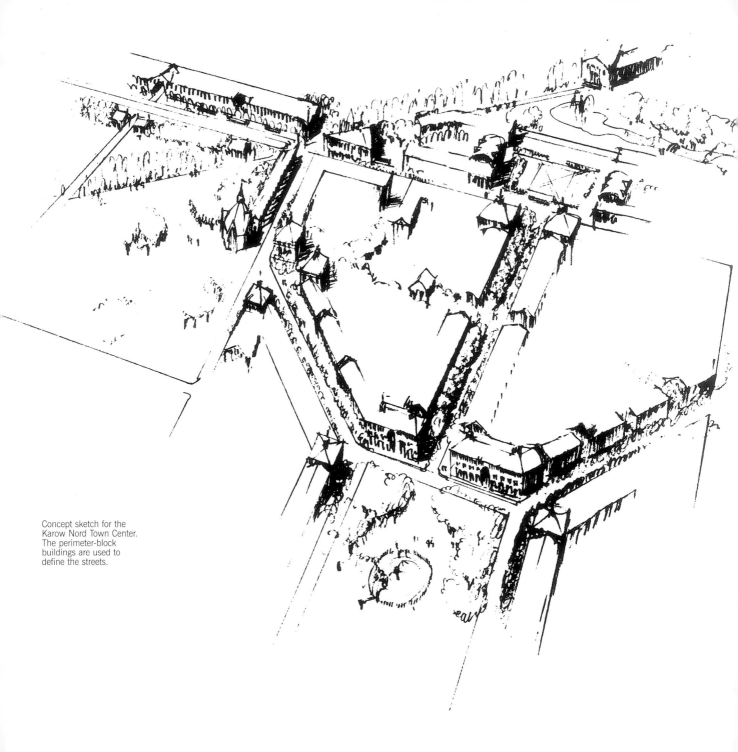

Concept sketch for the
Karow Nord Town Center.
The perimeter-block
buildings are used to
define the streets.

View along a pedestrian
path lined with large
multifamily "villas" on one
side, and four-story
apartment buildings
on the other.

View of "Karow Courts."

View along mid-block
pedestrian path, lined
with medium scale
housing multifamily
housing, and leading to
perimeter-block buildings
in the distance.

Dos Rios Master Plan, 1997

Dos Rios is a 350 acre new town in the Philippines, south of the city of Manila in the district of Laguna. The design is based on the historic type of the compound, in which land was gradually subdivided over generations to house an extended family. Approximately 2 acres in size, a typical compound contains sites for up to thirteen homes. The town is thus comprised of a series of avenues and boulevards of an urban character corresponding to the fronts of the compounds, and a series of roads and lanes of a more rural character corresponding to the interiors of the compounds. The plan is divided loosely into five neighborhoods, each centered on a plaza or green. Two mixed-use town centers, a university satellite site, a church, a hospital, and two schools are also accommodated in the plan. The master plan is by Duany Plater-Zyberk and Co., and the first compounds are being designed by Caruncho, Martinez & Alvarez Architects.

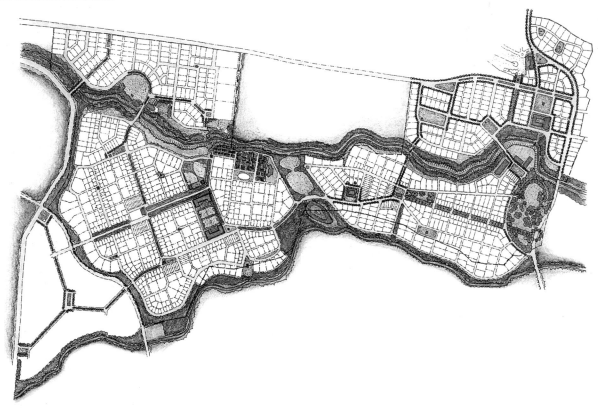

The illustration shows
how multiple increments
of compound house
types combine to define
a town block.

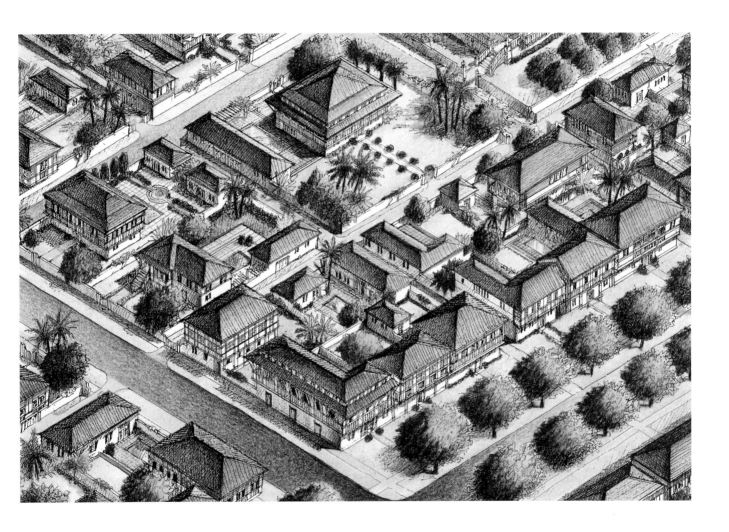

A typical road, with lower
density housing types,
buildings set back
from the street, and street
trees.

A typical street of more urban character, with higher density housing types, buildings set on the street ("zero lot line") to form a more continuous street edge, and minimal landscaping in the right-of-way.

Elevational studies from the charrette of compound wall and fence frontages.

Plans and elevations
of the front layer
of compound housing.
(Caruncho, Martinez
& Alvarez Architects,
1999)

Site/first floor plan of the
first compound in Dos
Rios. (Caruncho, Martinez
& Alvarez Architects,
1999)

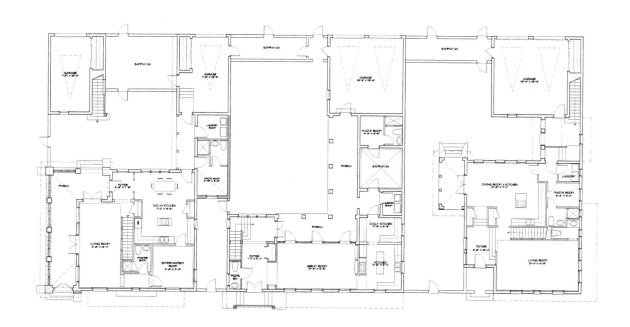

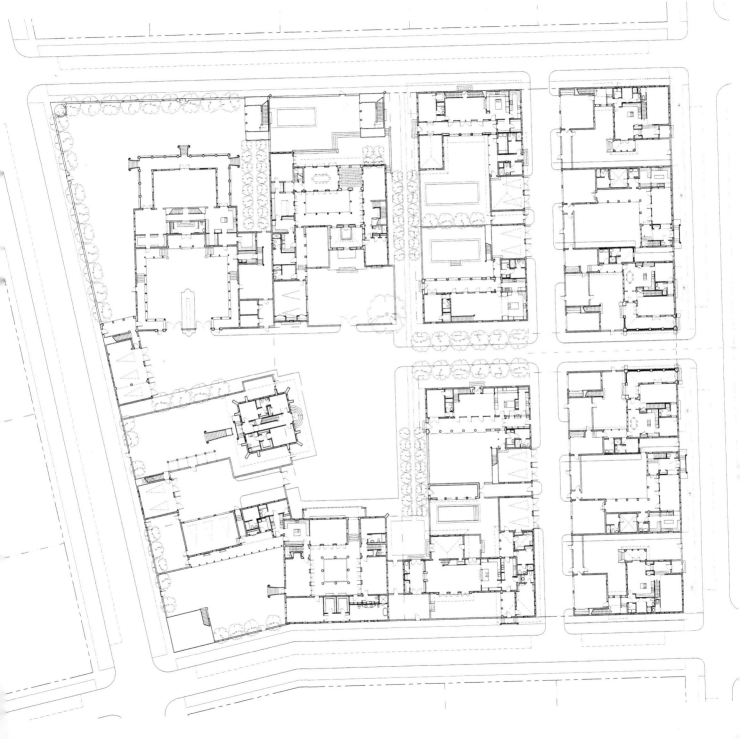

Appendix

Charter of the New Urbanism

The Congress for the New Urbanism views disinvestment in central cities, the spread of placeless sprawl, increasing separation by race and income, environmental deterioration, loss of agricultural lands and wilderness, and the erosion of society's built heritage as one interrelated community-building challenge.

We stand for the restoration of existing urban centers and towns within coherent metropolitan regions, the reconfiguration of sprawling suburbs into communities of real neighborhoods and diverse districts, the conservation of natural environments, and the preservation of our built legacy.

We recognize that physical solutions by themselves will not solve social and economic problems, but neither can economic vitality, community stability, and environmental health be sustained without a coherent and supportive physical framework.

We advocate the restructuring of public policy and development practices to support the following principles: neighborhoods should be diverse in use and population; communities should be designed for the pedestrian and transit as well as the car; cities and towns should be shaped by physically defined and universally accessible public spaces and community institutions; urban places should be framed by architecture and landscape design that celebrate local history, climate, ecology, and building practice.

We represent a broad-based citizenry, composed of public and private sector leaders, community activists, and multidisciplinary professionals. We are committed to reestablishing the relationship between the art of building and the making of community, through citizen-based participatory planning and design.

We dedicate ourselves to reclaiming our homes, blocks, streets, parks, neighborhoods, districts, towns, cities, regions, and environment.

We assert the following principles to guide public policy, development practice, urban planning, and design:

The region: Metropolis, city, and town

1. Metropolitan regions are finite places with geographic boundaries derived from topography, watersheds, coastlines, farmlands, regional parks, and river basins. The metropolis is made of multiple centers that are cities, towns, and villages, each with its own identifiable center and edges.

2. The metropolitan region is a fundamental economic unit of the contemporary world. Governmental cooperation, public policy, physical planning, and economic strategies must reflect this new reality.

3. The metropolis has a necessary and fragile relationship to its agrarian hinterland and natural landscapes. The relationship is environmental, economic, and cultural. Farmland and nature are as important to the metropolis as the garden is to the house.

4. Development patterns should not blur or eradicate the edges of the metropolis. Infill development within existing urban areas conserves environmental resources, economic investment, and social fabric, while reclaiming marginal and abandoned areas. Metropolitan regions should develop strategies to encourage such infill development over peripheral expansion.

5. Where appropriate, new development contiguous to urban boundaries should be organized as neighborhoods and districts, and be integrated with the existing urban pattern. Noncontiguous development should be organized as towns and villages with their own urban edges, and planned for a jobs/housing balance, not as bedroom suburbs.

6. The development and redevelopment of towns and cities should respect historical patterns, precedents, and boundaries.

7. Cities and towns should bring into proximity a broad spectrum of public and private uses to support a regional economy that benefits people of all incomes. Affordable housing should be distributed throughout the region to match job opportunities and to avoid concentrations of poverty.

8. The physical organization of the region should be supported by a framework of transportation alternatives. Transit, pedestrian, and bicycle systems should maximize access and mobility throughout the region while reducing dependence upon the automobile.

9. Revenues and resources can be shared more cooperatively among the municipalities and centers within regions to avoid destructive competition for tax base and to promote rational coordination of transportation, recreation, public services, housing, and community institutions.

The neighborhood, the district, and the corridor

1. The neighborhood, the district, and the corridor are the essential elements of development and redevelopment in the metropolis. They form identifiable areas that encourage citizens to take responsibility for their maintenance and evolution.

2. Neighborhoods should

be compact, pedestrian-friendly, and mixed-use. Districts generally emphasize a special single use, and should follow the principles of neighborhood design when possible. Corridors are regional connectors of neighborhoods and districts; they range from boulevards and rail lines to rivers and parkways.

3. Many activities of daily living should occur within walking distance, allowing independence to those who do not drive, especially the elderly and the young. Interconnected networks of streets should be designed to encourage walking, reduce the number and length of automobile trips, and conserve energy.

4. Within neighborhoods, a broad range of housing types and price levels can bring people of diverse ages, races, and incomes into daily interaction, strengthening the personal and civic bonds essential to an authentic community.

5. Transit corridors, when properly planned and coordinated, can help organize metropolitan structure and revitalize urban centers. In contrast, highway corridors should not displace investment from existing centers.

6. Appropriate building densities and land uses should be within walking distance of transit stops, permitting public transit to become a viable alternative to the automobile.

7. Concentrations of civic, institutional, and commercial activity should be embedded in neighborhoods and districts, not isolated in remote, single-use complexes. Schools should be sized and located to enable children to walk or bicycle to them.

8. The economic health and harmonious evolution of neighborhoods, districts, and corridors can be improved through graphic urban design codes that serve as predictable guides for change.

9. A range of parks, from tot-lots and village greens to ballfields and community gardens, should be distributed within neighborhoods. Conservation areas and open lands should be used to define and connect different neighborhoods and districts.

The block, the street, and the building

1. A primary task of all urban architecture and landscape design is the physical definition of streets and public spaces as places of shared use.

2. Individual architectural projects should be seamlessly linked to their surroundings. This issue transcends style.

3. The revitalization of urban places depends on safety and security. The design of streets and buildings should reinforce safe environments, but not at the expense of accessibility and openness.

4. In the contemporary metropolis, development must adequately accommodate automobiles. It should do so in ways that respect the pedestrian and the form of public space.

5. Streets and squares should be safe, comfortable, and interesting to the pedestrian. Properly configured, they encourage walking and enable neighbors to know each other and protect their communities.

6. Architecture and landscape design should grow from local climate, topography, history, and building practice.

7. Civic buildings and public gathering places require important sites to reinforce community identity and the culture of democracy. They deserve distinctive form, because their role is different from that of other buildings and places that constitute the fabric of the city.

8. All buildings should provide their inhabitants with a clear sense of location, weather and time. Natural methods of heating and cooling can be more resource-efficient than mechanical systems.

9. Preservation and renewal of historic buildings, districts, and landscapes affirm the continuity and evolution of urban society.

Charter published courtesy of the Congress for New Urbanism

Index